About this book

How to Clean (and Care for) Practically Anything comes to you from CONSUMER REPORTS, the testing and consumer-information source best known for product Ratings and buying guidance. We are also a comprehensive source of unbiased advice about services, personal finance, autos, health and nutrition, and other consumer concerns. Since 1936, the mission of Consumers Union has been to test products, inform the public, and protect consumers. Our income is derived solely from the sale of CONSUMER REPORTS magazine and its other publications and services, and from nonrestrictive, noncommercial contributions, grants, and fees. Only CONSUMER REPORTS has 150 secret shoppers who buy all the products we test to be sure that they're the same products you buy. CONSUMER REPORTS accepts no ads from companies, nor do we let any company use our reports or Ratings for commercial purposes.

Other books from Consumer Reports

- Guide to Baby Products
- Best Buys for Your Home
- Consumer Reports Buying Guide
- Travel Well for Less
- New Car Buying Guide
- Used Car Buying Guide
- Home Computer Buying Guide
- Consumer Drug Reference

How to Clean
and Care for
Practically
Anything

How to Clean
and Care for
Practically
Anything

The Editors of Consumer Reports

CONSUMER REPORTS SPECIAL PUBLICATIONS, YONKERS, NEW YORK

A Special Publication from Consumer Reports

Director/Editor, Special Publications Andrea Scott
Managing Editor Bette LaGow
Project Editor Dennis Fitzgerald
Art Director Alison Wilkes
Illustrations Tony Persiani
Special Publications Staff Merideth Mergel, Jay Heath, Joan Daviet

Consumer Reports

Vice President and Editorial Director Julia Kagan
Editor/Senior Director Margot Slade
Executive Editor/Associate Editorial Director Eileen Denver
Design Director, Consumers Union George Arthur
Creative Director, Consumer Reports Tim LaPalme
Director, Production Operations David Fox

Vice President and Technical Director Jeffrey A. Asher
Testing Director, Chemical & Textiles Bert Papenburg
Chemical & Textiles Division Edward Kippel, Edward Miller, Peter Heinlein, Pat Slaven, Joan Muratore, E.A. Lopez, John McAloon, Charles Spatola, Richard Handel, Aminata Ndiaya, Li Wang
Director, Appliances & Home Environment Mark Connelly
Manager, Home Environment James Nanni
Director, Electronics Evon Beckford
Testing Director, Recreation & Home Improvement John Galeotafiore

---

Vice President, Multimedia Publishing John J. Sateja
General Manager, Information Products Paige Amidon
Product Manager, Special Publications Carol Lappin

Consumers Union

President James A. Guest
Executive Vice President Joel Gurin

Senior Vice President, Technical Policy R. David Pittle

Produced by Roundtable Press, Inc.

Directors Julie Merberg, Marsha Melnick, Susan E. Meyer
Editor John Glenn
Editorial Assistant Sara Newberry
Cover and Book Design Charles Kreloff

Banister image (cover) courtesy of Sierra Stair Co., Inc.
Faucet image (cover) courtesy of Moen, Inc.

Contents

Cleaning Appliances and Tools A to Z 191

Brooms, mops, vacuum cleaners, and more, including selected CONSUMER REPORTS test results.

Special Cleaning Advice 223

Index 274

Your Personal Cleaning Adviser

Microwavable meals and wrinkle-free shirts have cut the time Americans must spend on such household chores as cooking and ironing. New household materials, from polyurethane floor varnish to vinyl wallpaper and composite countertops, are easier to care for than the materials they replace. And it's a good thing, too, since Americans have less time than ever to tackle household chores—the time spent on housework (including meal preparation and laundry) fell from almost 32 hours a week in 1965 to 25 hours in 1995. During that period and the years that have followed, the size of the average house has risen, with more space and more things to clean than ever before. So how do you clean more in less time? By using smart strategies and proven time-savers, like the ones found in this book.

Decades of commercials have tried to make people feel guilty about "ring around the collar" and "yellow waxy buildup," but Americans have decided that there is more to life than cleaning and have simply stopped doing certain kinds of chores. According to one study, 35 percent no longer iron their own clothes or hand-wash delicate items, 27 percent say they don't scrub their floors, and 22 percent have sworn off washing windows or woodwork. There's been a certain acceptance of mess and dirt. According to another study, many Americans—nearly one in four—believe their homes are dirtier than the ones they grew up in.

As in the past, a lot of the burden of cleaning still falls on women. They continue to do most of the housework, even though most of them now work outside the home as well. But there are hopeful signs that the workload is becoming more equitable. According to the University of Maryland's Americans' Use of Time Project, while men did only about 15 percent of the housework in the 1960s, they were doing about 33 percent of it by the 1990s. This translates into a significant decrease in the amount of time spent by women on housework—from 27 hours a week in 1965 to 15½ hours a week in 1995. It's not yet parity, but men today share the load more than their fathers did.

To test spot removers in 1977, textile experts at CONSUMER REPORTS stained—and attempted to clean—hundreds of pieces of cloth.

With the right strategies, housework can be manageable and satisfying, if not exactly fun. This book, designed to be your personal cleaning adviser, can help you make the most of your limited housecleaning time. In the pages that follow, you'll find overall strategies, detailed procedures, and tips on preventive maintenance that can save you work in the long run.

Using this book

Housework may be a chore, but everyone enjoys a clean and orderly home. The best way to get the maximum amount of work done in a limited amount of time—and not become overwhelmed in the process —is to go about it in an organized and systematic way. This book is designed to make housework easier for you. It will give you a plan of action, along with the specific information you need to clean and care for every object—from candlestick to carpet—in every nook and cranny of your home.

The chapter **Easy Cleaning Strategies** (page 7) shows you how to simplify your life by creating an efficient cleaning scheme suited to your home and lifestyle. Look here for new ideas on organizing chores, designing your house so it's easier to clean, and planning room-by-room strategies. You'll also find tips on cleaning up after kids—and teaching them how to clean up after themselves—along with safety guidelines for the cleaning products you keep in your house.

Things to Clean A to Z (page 27) lists in alphabetical order various surfaces and items likely to be found in a house. You'll be offered recommendations for routine upkeep as

Vacuum cleaners, which were relatively new when CONSUMER REPORTS first started publishing in 1936, have been tested to see how much of measured "dirt" they removed from a carpet. This test was in 1951.

well as suggestions for dealing with everyday dirt and grime. From acetate to zircon, look here to see how to keep everything around the house clean and in good shape.

Cleaning Agents A to Z (page 153) and **Cleaning Appliances and Tools A to Z** (page 191) take you through the equipment and supplies you'll need and will help you choose the right tool and cleaner for every task you're likely to face. CONSUMER REPORTS has tested equipment and cleaners for more than 65 years and provides a unique perspective on how to choose the best.

The **Special Cleaning Advice** section (page 223) features easy-to-read stain-removal charts that give you fast information for dealing with spots and spills on carpeting, fabric, and floors. You'll also find general advice about doing the laundry, caring for carpets and flooring, and how to deal with fire and flood damage. We include recipes for homemade cleaners that are both inexpensive and often just about as effective as commercial products.

Consumer Reports and the test of time

Consumer Reports has more than 65 years of expertise in advising people on which cleaning products and techniques work best. This expertise is based on years of testing products in the laboratory and in home-use tests, and on side-by-side comparisons to see which work, which clean best, and which are easiest to use.

Over that time, a few key items have made various cleaning tasks much easier. In 1936, when Consumer Reports magazine was launched, vacuum cleaners were relatively unknown and more than half the households in the United States still cleaned with brooms and carpet sweepers. Half the households in the country had no access to a washing machine. Even the most advanced washer on the market was not yet truly automatic: You still had to run wet clothes though a wringer before hanging them up to dry. Soap flakes, no matter how ingeniously pitched by advertising agencies—a relatively new phenomenon at the time—still left gray scum on clothes, especially in hard water.

But expectations of cleanliness were beginning to rise. This was due in part to ads that attributed an astonishing power to soap: "Are you unpopular? Do you have 'Dishpan Hands'? Are your dates spoiled by stocking runs? Are you just too tired to go out on Monday evenings? Then all you need to do is to use Lux to wash your dishes and your stockings, Rinso for the family wash, and all will be well again." So began Consumer Reports' first feature on laundry products.

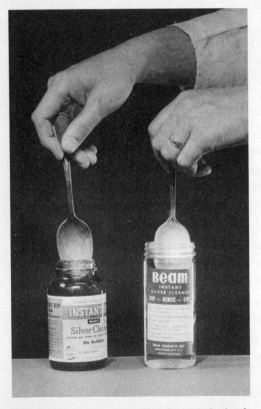

Brand-name cleaners have long been a staple of the Consumer Reports test program. Here, silver cleaner is tested for a 1953 report.

Even the best soap products in those Ratings—including Gondola Floating Soap and Chipso—were soon outshone by detergents, which first reached the consumer market in the late 1930s. Detergents do something soap isn't good at—they emulsify oils and grease and suspend them in the wash water, allowing them to be swept away. By 1955, detergents outsold soap for laundry use. Through the years, Consumer Reports has found that all detergents do a good job of cleaning lightly soiled clothes. Modern technologies, tests show, are getting better at tackling tough stains. Liquid detergents—which make up the bulk of detergent sales—now work as well as powders.

Another key cleaning invention was, of course, the vacuum cleaner. CONSUMER REPORTS first featured vacuum cleaners in 1936, giving top ratings to two General Electric models. Salespeople at the time relied on demonstrations to sell the newfangled machines. CONSUMER REPORTS scoffed at the "tricks" used in the demonstrations: "The cleaner is run with the dust bag off, for you to see the quantity of dirt blown through

Washing machines lined up to be tested in 1957. Testing major appliances involves moving a lot of equipment around.

it—an impressive trick, but a comparatively meaningless one." Instead, CONSUMER REPORTS used laboratory tests to compare machines. Since then, canisters and uprights have mutated to resemble one another in both form and function. CONSUMER REPORTS evaluates these household workhorses regularly, finding, for example, that fancy features don't always make a vacuum cleaner more useful. Recent tests have included some of the same brands featured in that first review—Hoover, Electrolux, and Eureka.

Washing machines were another key invention that helped reduce the housecleaning workload. Electric models dated back to 1911, but the designs weren't worked out very thoroughly, even by 1937, when CONSUMER REPORTS first tested them. After testing ten machines, CONSUMER REPORTS concluded, "At best, this investment will procure a machine that will wash satisfactorily. At worst, it will turn out clothes of doubtful cleanness, involve possible danger of electric shock, and require major repairs every year or so." In fact, sales of automatic models didn't outpace wringer-style machines until 1952. Electric dryers were invented in 1915 but weren't in widespread use until the 1950s. Over the years, CONSUMER REPORTS tests have tracked a huge improvement in the ability of washing machines to clean. Recent tests focus more on differences in how efficiently machines use water and electricity than on evaluating basic cleaning performance.

Easy Cleaning Strategies

Sometimes it seems like housework is an endless series of small crises—first a coffee stain, then mud on the rug, a filthy oven, grime in the tub, chair marks on the floor—that add up to one big, daunting mess. Even once you know how to tackle and vanquish life's stains and messes, creating a workable everyday strategy for keeping your home in order can simplify your life. How much time do you have to devote to cleaning? Is your home too big to clean by yourself? Can family members pitch in? Do you need outside help? Is your home organized in a way that will help you keep it clean? Are your cleaning products and tools stored in places that are safe and convenient? Answering these questions can help you form an overall cleaning strategy.

Get your house in order

You've got better things to do than clean. With smart planning and a few easy-to-establish habits, you can make it a small, simple part of your life. Here are dozens of ideas on how to approach the task.

Divide and conquer. As with any daunting task, housecleaning is easier if you break it into smaller parts. Doing a chore or two a day is easier than letting tasks accumulate and become overwhelming. Cleaning regularly gets rid of dirt before you have to scrub it, saving you elbow grease and the things you clean unnecessary wear and tear. It's easier to remove dust from a side table, sofa, or drapery before it combines with greasy soil, such as body oils or tiny airborne droplets of cooking grease. Frequent vacuuming minimizes the need for professional carpet cleaning and—by removing grit that can grind down fibers—prolongs carpet life as well.

Devise a schedule. Many people find that a schedule lets them take control over housework, rather than the other way around. Start by making a list of cleaning tasks in your home. Then note how often each chore needs to be done—daily, weekly, monthly, or seasonally. (For ideas on seasonal chores, **Cleaning by the Seasons,** on page 22, is a good place to start.) Devise a schedule that spaces your daily chores evenly over the course of a week and your weekly chores evenly over the course of a month. Happily, few chores need to be done on a daily basis.

If it's not dirty... You don't have to clean things that aren't dirty. Sometimes a touch-up is all that's necessary. If there is a handprint on an otherwise perfectly clean mirror, don't clean the whole mirror; just attack the print itself. You don't have to dry-clean a suit that only needs to be aired, brushed, or pressed. Surfaces that you or your visitors can't see—like the top of a cabinet—don't need to be cleaned regularly. Put some paper down, and when it gets dirty, pick the paper up and throw it out.

If you can't clean, straighten up. If you're short on time, getting rid of clutter can make a room feel a lot cleaner. Make it a habit to tidy things up every day or two and there'll be less to do when you do haul out the vacuum cleaner and dust cloth.

Simplify and declutter. If you don't need or like something in your house, give it away, throw it away, or recycle it rather than clean it. The fewer things you have, the less clutter you have. And, of course, the less you have, the less there is to dust, polish, shine, vacuum, and otherwise take care of.

Reevaluate your storage needs. Cleaning is much easier if you have well-thought-out storage space for the possessions you do hang on to. It's difficult to bring order to a room that's filled with clutter. Lots of unorganized little objects or stacks of photos or papers also collect a lot of dust.

Look at each room in your house to see if additional storage can help you solve some of your day-to-day cleaning problems. This needn't always involve elaborate construction or a large amount of space. It just means finding some practical ways to keep things orderly. For example, if you have a crate for shoes and boots near the door, it's less likely that shoes will be scattered around the room. Plastic containers with lids are great for getting such seasonal items as skiwear and beach gear out of the way.

If you need more space for books, try adding shelves in a little-used hallway. If you've run out of room for your sweaters, check out the many forms of under-the-bed storage containers. Look for surprise storage locations. For instance, you can build recessed cupboards into the wall between two-by-fours; they're useful for holding a medicine chest, a spice rack, or an antique-bottle collection.

Keep lists. Everyone knows how making a shopping list before you go to the supermarket helps keep you from making impulse buys. Lists can be handy in organizing your housekeeping, too. List the chores you need to do in a given week. If you notice a problem—a scuff on the wall in the stairs, a wobbly leg on a chair—and you don't have time to fix it now, write it down so you don't forget about it.

Locate supplies conveniently. In the kitchen, you'll probably make frequent use of a few key items: dishwashing liquid, automatic-dishwasher detergent, an all-purpose cleaner, ammonia, glass cleaner, metal cleaner, and white vinegar (a great all-purpose cleaner), along with a mop, cloths, and scrubbers. Store these items close at hand.

Plastic caddies fit conveniently below sinks and can be carried from room to room. Though you probably keep baking soda with your baking supplies, it's such a handy cleaner that you might want to store a box with your cleaning supplies.

In the bathroom, stock the vanity or a nearby linen closet with an all-purpose cleaner, mildew remover, and window cleaner for the mirrors. Store a squeegee or shower-cleaning spray close to the shower, where it's handy for daily use

If you live in a two-level house, having a vacuum cleaner on each floor will eliminate the time and effort you'd otherwise spend lugging these machines up and down the stairs. If one floor has more wall-to-wall carpeting than the other, store the upright vacuum on that floor. (Canisters are better for mixed cleaning, including floors with lots of area rugs.) A stick vacuum or cordless hand vac is a handy addition to the kitchen. A wet/dry vac is useful in the basement or the garage.

On cleaning day, gather all the supplies you'll need in a bucket, caddy, or even a small wagon and carry them with you from room to room. Or use a multipocket carpenter's apron to carry bottles and wipes. If you have to vacuum a very large room, add a 25- to 50-foot extension cord to your portable arsenal—it will help you avoid having to stop and relocate the plug (be sure the cord has the same power rating as the vacuum).

Use cleaning as a way to check on the house. While you're cleaning or doing the laundry, take time to note any item that needs special attention. Do sections of grouting need replacing? Are buttons loose on a shirt? Has the veneer on a table come unglued? Are houseplants draining properly?

The time you take now can save you more time and work later. When crumbling grouting around the bathtub is not repaired, water can leak into the walls. If a dangling button falls off and you can't find a matching one, you may need to replace all the buttons. A loose piece of veneer can catch on a sleeve and break off. If plants aren't draining, they may be staining the furniture on which they've been placed.

In addition to what you notice while making your cleaning rounds, inspect your house regularly. Check the caulking in tubs, showers, and sinks. Check for cracks in the masonry or stucco on the outside of your house. Look at the roof for loose shingles. Keep an eye out for wood decay. Check the attic, basement, garage, under sinks, and dishwasher and laundry areas for stains that indicate leaks. Inspect vacuum cords periodically and replace them if the covers are damaged. When you see a problem, have it taken care of immediately.

Get everyone to help. Make cleaning a family endeavor. Divide up specific tasks between family members. List chores on a calendar so that you all know what your responsibilities are. It might help to set aside a specific time when the whole household does chores. Devise a system of rewards to inspire kids to participate willingly.

Hang up clothes rather than dropping them on the furniture. Put away tools and materials rather than leaving them lying around. Provide baskets at the top and bottom of stairs for items such as laundry, trash, and bathroom supplies that need to be carried up or down. Ask family members never to go up or down stairs empty-handed.

Make low-maintenance choices. Your decorating decisions can directly affect how much time you spend cleaning. Simpler designs require less maintenance. Touch pads on food processors and dishwashers are easier to clean than buttons. Surfaces that have fewer crevices—such as on ranges or boom boxes—attract less dirt. Sofa cushions that have buttons on both sides (or no buttons on either side) can be flipped over when one side gets dirty. If you put washable curtains in a kitchen, you can just throw them in the washer; louvered blinds have to be washed by hand.

Doormats strategically placed at each entrance to your home will collect dirt that would otherwise be tracked in from the outside onto carpets and floors. Encourage friends and family to wipe their feet before entering the house.

Built-ins—for example, bookcases or cupboards—eliminate the need to vacuum under or behind a piece of furniture.

Select easy-care materials, such as fabrics that don't require ironing, nonstick surfaces that don't need scouring, and glass items that can be machine-washed rather than metals that need polishing. Polyurethane wood floors need far less attention than those with wax finishes. Glossy paint holds up better when washed than flat paint does.

Your color choices also have an effect on how much work you'll have to do. Obviously, white carpets can be problematic because they show every speck of dark soil. So can very dark ones, which show every speck of lint. Medium tones and busy patterns hide dirt best. If you have pets that shed and sit on the couch, select upholstery that is the same color as their hair (or better yet, keep a towel or blanket on your pet's favorite chair and remove it when company comes and for regular cleaning). White floors show every hair in bathrooms and every spill in the kitchen. Dark grout disguises mildew better than white grout.

Basic Cleaning Kit

- All-purpose cleaner
- Ammonia
- Baking soda
- Bleach
- Broom and dustpan
- Bucket
- Cloths or sponges
- Dishwashing liquid
- Feather duster
- Metal cleaner
- Mop
- Paper towels
- Rubbing alcohol
- Scrubbers
- Vacuum cleaner
- White vinegar

Making your strategies work

Figuring out a cleaning routine makes the task easier because you don't have to figure out how to do it again and again. Whatever routine you devise must be one you and your family can follow. If it doesn't work, alter it.

Sometimes changing the timing of your housework can help you get it done. If you find that you're not spending an hour and a half a day after work on chores as you planned to, try another approach. Do laundry or vacuuming in the morning for 45 minutes, then devote another 45 minutes in the evening to other housework. Become conscious of how long household chores take, and when you have a few spare minutes, devote them to one of the tasks on your list. Multitask when you can. Throw a load in the wash when you take the newspapers to the recycling bin or while you're waiting for the iron to heat up.

Plan the most demanding work at a time when you have the most energy. If you discover that you're not getting around to mopping the kitchen at the end of the day, try dealing with it first thing in the morning. If you're not getting everything done, try alloting a certain amount of time to a task and move to another when the time is up.

Break a big job down into smaller parts. If one of your spring-cleaning goals is to wash the windows in your home, the job might seem more manageable if you do one room of windows each week until they're all done instead of trying to wash all the windows in one day.

Strategies for specific rooms

In general, start at one end of the house, completing chores in each room before you tackle another one. Here's an efficient technique for routine cleanups in rooms other than the kitchen or bath: Close the windows before you start, and work around the room, moving from left to right or right to left. Clean from top to bottom, since gravity carries dust down onto lower surfaces. Dust windowsills, open shelving, blinds, furniture, mirrors, picture frames, and TV screens. Use a feather duster or cloth on hard surfaces, and knock the dust to the floor. Use a hair dryer to blow off dust from fabric items, like drapes, lampshades, and silk or paper flowers. If you stop to clean or remove a stain, make sure you have sufficient light so you can attend to every drop and splatter, however small. Finish by vacuuming.

The kitchen. Of all the rooms in the house, the kitchen needs the most attention, but small amounts of effort go a long way. If you're actively using the kitchen, try to wipe all surfaces—cooktop, oven, backsplash, countertops, microwave, sink—once or more a day, so that dirt won't become encrusted and pests won't be attracted. Try to sweep or vacuum every day or so, and damp-mop every week or so.

Using your space more efficiently in the kitchen can save you time and effort when cleaning and putting away utensils. Store picnic gear and other seldom-used items on higher cabinet shelves and in the back of cupboards. Use a wide-mouthed crock to store often-used cooking utensils like wooden spoons, kitchen shears, and salad servers, and keep it next to the stove for convenience. Put dishes, flatware, and glasses in cabinets and drawers near the dishwasher so you spend the least amount of time unloading.

The kitchen tends to be the communications center of the household, and sometimes the refrigerator door becomes a clutter of papers and magnets. Instead of hanging every item separately, place a pocket holder with a magnetic back on the refrigerator to hold train schedules, take-out menus, and other frequently consulted papers. You can create extra room for notes and keep some of the clutter out of sight by mounting a corkboard inside a cabinet door to hold coupons, recipes, and notes.

The bathroom. Though it's usually the smallest room in the house, the bathroom needs a lot of maintenance. The easiest way to keep it in good shape is to do a light cleaning after every use. If everyone who takes a shower wipes down the walls when done, soap scum and minerals won't build up. Make it a house rule to wipe the sink after each use, and keep a sponge or cloth nearby for that purpose.

Towels are easier to hang on hooks than on bars, where they have to be folded to look neat. Fold and roll extra towels and store them in a cubicle, the way spas and hotels do. Hotel-style chrome wall units can hold stacks of guest towels. Keep toilet paper stacked and handy. A cordless vacuum can make quick work of stray hairs and help keep the bathroom looking tidy (but be sure it is stored well away from the bathroom's water sources). A roll of paper towels under the sink or mounted inside the bathroom door will encourage family members to wipe up spills.

Nothing makes a bathroom look as messy as clusters of bottles on the toilet tank, tub edge, and around the sink do. Think about adding shower caddies, shelves that hang from existing towel racks, and other space savers.

Laundry room. Put open hampers in the laundry room—one for lights, one for darks—and ask family members to place dirty clothes in the appropriate one. Assign each person a color-coded laundry basket to hold clean, folded laundry, and make all family members responsible for collecting their baskets, emptying them, and returning them to the laundry room. Put up a bulletin board in the laundry room with cleaning instructions for any special garments. And keep needles, thread, and spare buttons nearby so you can make repairs as necessary.

Foyers and mudrooms. Clutter tends to accumulate in the entranceway to a house. Keep things organized by mounting a key holder near the door, along with hooks to hold coats, mittens, and hats. Place a basket in a convenient spot to collect the mail, with a wastebasket nearby for tossing junk mail immediately. Use a similar setup near the back door: an "in" basket to collect items that need to be taken to the proper room indoors and an "out" basket for clothes to be taken to the dry cleaner, books to be returned to the library, and other items to be put in the car. If you visit several destinations regularly, have a basket for each.

Stairs. Use baskets to carry things when going up and down, and ask everyone to carry something when making a trip. To vacuum stairs, use the nozzle attachment of a canister vacuum. For quick touch-ups, use a damp cloth to pick up any dust or hair. To make the carpeting on your stairs last longer, at the time the carpeting is laid, fold an extra foot of length under and against one or two risers at the top of the staircase. From time to time, you can lift the entire length of the stair carpeting and move it downward an inch or two. The extra carpet that is moved to the foot of the stairs can be trimmed off or folded under or against the bottom riser.

Bedroom. A bed acquires a fair amount of moisture during a night's sleep. Keep it fresh longer by letting it air out while you're taking your morning shower or getting dressed. If bed-making is a chore you or a family member can't seem to master, try a duvet system: a fitted bottom sheet and a washable cover for the duvet (comforter). To make the bed, just shake out the duvet and pull it into place.

Storage for clothes and shoes is a common problem in the bedroom. You can have your closets rebuilt by a professional, or you can do it yourself with closet-organizing modules. Other storage tips: Use shoebags not just for shoes but also for gloves and stockings. Hang a couple of four-towel kitchen racks on the back of the closet door to hold pants. Use a kitchen mug rack mounted vertically or horizontally on a closet or wall to hang jewelry, scarves, or small purses.

Other rooms you live in a lot. Try to vacuum high-traffic areas at least once a week. You should also vacuum the upholstered furniture in these rooms on a regular basis—try to hit every piece of furniture at least once a month. Protect floors by using glides on the legs of furniture. (Be sure floors are clean before you slide furniture on them to avoid scratching.) Wood floors and furniture with a polyurethane finish are easier to maintain than those that are waxed or untreated. Choose area rugs, which are easier to clean and cheaper to replace than wall-to-wall carpeting.

Add shelves to hold videos, CDs, and books. Use baskets to hold magazines—and clear out magazines periodically. Items on display will need less frequent dusting if you store them in glass-fronted cabinets. When you sweep out the fireplace, collect the ashes on dampened newspaper so they won't fly around the room.

Rooms you don't use much. With guest rooms, formal living rooms, or other spaces that don't get much use, vacuum and dust on an as-needed basis. Keep guest beds made up and ready so when unexpected company comes, you can concentrate on them, not the bedding.

Utility area, garage, and basement. Set up a shelf or cupboard near the washer and dryer to hold laundry supplies. Include a pair of scissors to deal with loose threads as you load the washer. A spray bottle filled with water is handy for dampening stubborn wrinkles before ironing. Keep a wastebasket near the laundry equipment for easy disposal of dryer lint. Keep another by the workbench, along with a whisk broom for cleanup after each project. The classic peg board still works—paint the outline of the tool on the board so you know at a glance where it belongs. Tools and equipment in the basement should be hung on walls or otherwise raised off the floor in case of flooding.

Patio, deck, and yard. If you keep your gas grill and outdoor furniture protected you'll have less cleaning and maintenance work. In summer, store furniture in a shady place when not in use, and cover outdoor furniture in winter with plastic covers or tarps. To prevent water from standing in metal chairs, drill two or three holes in the middle or lowest spot of each seat; apply a thin layer of clear nail polish around the holes to prevent rust. Stow garden equipment in a small wagon or attach a rope to a plastic basket so you can pull tools with you as you work in the garden.

Develop a routine

Whenever you have a moment, walk around the house with a basket and gather up items that are out of place. Redistribute them where they belong, either en route through the house or when you have time. If this is all you have time to do, at least the rooms will look cleaner. Periodically open windows and air out the rooms.

Every day. Make beds. Pick up clothes and throw dirty ones in the laundry. Clean the sink and shower after each use. Straighten up newspapers and magazines and other papers. The kitchen is the one room that really needs daily attention. Keep on top of the dishes. Some people prefer to wash and dry them after each meal; others prefer to take care of a day's worth in the evening. Depending on your preference, load dishes into the dishwasher after each meal or rinse them off and put them in the sink. Wipe kitchen counters after each meal. Clean the kitchen sink and wipe the range surfaces (including the microwave oven) after each use and at least once a day. Empty the garbage.

Every week or so. Dust furniture, shelves, radiators, woodwork, pictures, and mirrors. Vacuum rugs and floors. Vacuum or brush upholstered furniture. Empty the wastebaskets. Wash bathroom basins, fixtures, and floors. Sweep or mop the kitchen floor. Clean kitchen-range burners. Wipe the refrigerator and the fronts of kitchen cabinets. Do laundry. (With a large family, you may need to do laundry more than once a week.)

Safe Storage of Cleaning Supplies

Many cleaning products are poisonous. In households where there are babies or young children, do not leave such products in a place where children could find them and eat or drink them. Never decant cleaning products into containers that a child might recognize as a favorite food or drink. If you have a poisoning emergency, call the National Capital Poison Center at 1-800-222-1222. If the victim has collapsed or is not breathing, call 911. Affiliated with Georgetown University, the Poison Center is staffed by nurses and pharmacists specializing in toxicology and is open 24 hours a day, seven days a week. For more information, visit *www.poison.org*.

You should also keep ipecac syrup—one bottle per child—in your home. This medicine causes vomiting and may be needed to treat a poisoning. It is the only safe and effective way to induce vomiting. It can be bought from a pharmacy without a prescription. However, never use ipecac syrup before calling the Poison Center. And beware: Statistics show that a child who swallows poison once is likely to do it again within a year.

Every month or so. Vacuum or brush curtains and draperies. Clean under and around furniture and appliances. Wipe woodwork, windowsills, and walls where needed, especially around doorknobs. Dust or brush lampshades and blinds. Wax floors and furniture, if needed. Vacuum books and bookshelves. Organize or store books, CDs, videos, photographs, and other loose paraphernalia. Vacuum upholstered furniture, paying special attention to cleaning under cushions and in crevices around the cushions. Clean the oven, if needed.

Seasonally. Window-washing and many other housekeeping chores need be done just once or twice a year, often when the weather changes in spring or fall. See the table on page 22.

Cleaning around kids

When you have small children, keeping them safe is the priority. By educating yourself about the real risks your child may face in the home—and how to minimize them—you can safely enjoy playtime, bedtime, mealtime, and every other time with your child. There are plenty of sources of expert advice. In addition to books and web sites that address child-safety issues, hospitals, birthing centers, and community groups offer classes on administering CPR to infants and toddlers and ways to childproof your home.

How clean do you need to be? You don't need to be excessively concerned about germs, even if your household includes babies. Although you should obviously take care in sterilizing bottles and washing hands and work surfaces before preparing food, there is no need to provide a clinical environment. In fact, bacteria commonly found in dust helps kids build resistance by stimulating an immune response. And young children who have been exposed to common household germs and infections are less likely to develop asthma and wheezing by the time they turn six.

Childproofing. Think about creating a safe environment before your baby comes home from the hospital. Though in the first months there's not a lot a baby can get into, that will change rapidly. Before you know it, your child will be highly mobile. Your goal should be to finish the babyproofing before your child has begun to crawl or grab.

You can handle installation yourself or hire a safety consultant who specializes in in-home babyproofing. Such childproofing services usually charge $60 to $75 per hour to make recommendations and do installation, plus the cost of such products as cabinet locks, outlet covers, and safety gates. For a list of companies, visit the International Association for Child Safety's web site (*www.iafcs.org*).

You'll want to keep childproofing measures in place until they're no longer needed or effective. For instance, a safety gate's useful life ends at about age 2, or when a child is big enough to climb over it. Other measures can be relaxed as your child begins to show some judgment—perhaps by age 4.

Special kid strategies. Children and clutter go hand in hand. First come the toys (and all their tiny pieces), then the rock collection, the shell collection, the penny collection, the baseball card collection, and so on, not to mention the doll clothes and shoes, the art supplies, and the sports equipment. The solution: bins, baskets, hooks, and shelves.

Get plenty of storage bins, plastic shoe boxes, and other organizers that keep everything from being in one big jumble. However, don't impose grown-up standards of neatness: Your child will probably not care if the tiny kitchen equipment is mixed together with the tiny pirate coins.

Make sure that items in the room are placed at the right height for little occupants. If toys and books are on shelves low enough for children to reach, they can take down what they want all by themselves—and, more important, put it back. Hang kid-high hooks or peg boards for hats, jackets, and gloves so children can hang up their own clothes. You can teach children to use small baskets in their own rooms as hampers if adult-sized hampers are too tall. For large or unusually shaped items, consider unusual storage solutions. For example, hockey sticks, toy swords, and some kites can be stowed in a tall wastebasket. Attach pretty, painted clothespins to a strip of painted wood, hang it on the wall, and clip stuffed toys to it, or store stuffed toys in large baskets.

Cleaning strategies for people with disabilities

While cleaning may be more difficult and time-consuming if you are physically disabled, there are aids to make tasks easier.

Such items include holders for brushes, cloths, and scouring pads; dishcloth wringers; and window-cleaning gadgets. There are also telescopic handles for brooms, brushes, and mops. You can fit special trigger handles to aerosol sprays to make them easier to use. For laundry, using an elevated cart on wheels saves you from having to bend. If your eyesight is poor, you can have the knobs on your washing machine converted to braille.

Many of these items can be found at a discount store, a kitchenware outlet, or a specialty store for people with disabilities. Also check with occupational or physical therapists for local sources of specialty equipment.

You or any sick or disabled person in your household may be entitled to special services that give practical help with cleaning the home. In some cases, you may get information about these services through local agencies that coordinate services for seniors. In New York, for example, there are services that provide household management and personal care for aged or handicapped adults. A home-management program in New Mexico provides assistance with daily chores for people age 60 or over that includes light housekeeping services.

Such services may also be provided by agencies charged with taking care of families and children. In Oregon, for example, the State Office for Services to Children and Families sometimes provides housekeeping services.

Hiring housekeeping help

Depending upon the particular demands of your work and family, it may make more sense to hire housekeeping help than to clean your home yourself. How much such assistance lightens your load depends mostly on the quality of the work, but your own planning and expectations are also factors.

Your first consideration is the amount of help you need. If your home is small and your cleaning needs modest, someone can probably do the job in a half-day per week or every other week. If your family has small children, your home is large, or your household tends to be messy, you can expect housekeeping to take longer and cost more. For occasional large-scale jobs, such as washing the walls or cleaning out the garage, or for getting the house really sparkling before you do some major entertaining, hiring a cleaning service might be the way to go.

Finding a cleaner. As always, your best bet is to get a personal recommendation. Otherwise, check local want ads or go to an agency specializing in supplying domestic help. You'll want someone whom you can trust with access to everything in your home and who is a competent cleaner as well.

Be sure to check references. If you have any doubts, look elsewhere. Using an agency will save you the bother of checking references, because the agency will have done it for you. Either the agency will charge you a fee and you will pay the cleaner directly, or the agency will pay the help and bill you. Some people prefer the latter arrangement, even though it's probably slightly more expensive, because the agency will handle any problems—including firing a worker who isn't doing a satisfactory job and finding a replacement. (Check with your financial adviser regarding your tax obligations and the need for workers compensation insurance for a domestic worker.)

During the interview, show your potential employee around your home and be very clear about your expectations—and try to determine if your cleaner-to-be is agreeable to them. Some cleaners are unwilling to do certain jobs—such as cleaning ovens or inside windows—and if these chores are priorities for you, you need someone who is prepared to do them. Discuss the hourly rate and method of payment, how many paid holidays you will provide, your policy regarding sick days, and what happens if your cleaning day falls on a public holiday.

Finding a cleaning service. If you can't get a recommendation from a friend and must resort to using the yellow pages, the first question you should ask is how long the firm has been in business. Longevity can be a clue to reliability. You should also check with the local Better Business Bureau to see if there have been any complaints lodged against the firm.

Before service begins, make sure that you and the firm agree on what it's providing. Get a contract that spells out terms and conditions, and check that the company is insured in case of breakage or theft. Find out if the firm you have engaged will be doing the work or is planning to subcontract the job.

Having your expectations met. Be realistic about the amount of work that can be done. Don't expect hired help to accomplish more than you could in the equivalent period of time. Prioritize the jobs to make sure the ones you value most will get done. Try to pick up around the house before the cleaner comes. This will make it easier to clean thoroughly and allow the cleaner to work faster, too. So, if you're paying by the hour, you may save yourself some money.

The first time or two, discuss what kinds of cleaning equipment and tools the cleaning person is accustomed to using and which ones you would prefer. Make sure everything needed is on hand before your employee begins work. Make a point of being at home so you can demonstrate how you might want specific tasks to be handled—for example, how you want sheets folded or a special lamp cleaned.

For later visits, it's a good idea to provide a checklist that includes both the routine chores and anything special you want done.

Decide whether or not to give your cleaning person a key for access when you are not home. (You may be required to inform your insurance company if someone other than a family member has access to your home.) Otherwise, you or another family member will have to be home when your cleaner arrives.

Cleaning products basics

Finding the time to clean—and sticking to a cleaning schedule—can be a difficult task all by itself. But your cleaning will go more smoothly and you'll save time and unnecessary aggravation if you also think ahead about the storage and safety of your cleaning products and equipment.

"Green" Cleaning Products

"Green" products, which are supposed to have a minimal impact on the environment, make up a small share of the household-cleaners market. Total sales for all "green" household cleaners are a mere $21 million—a tiny fraction of the $4.6 billion spent annually on just laundry detergents alone. Not all "green" cleaners are widely available, and some are more costly, thanks in part to expensive ingredients but also to their small market share.

Some manufacturers claim that their products do not contain toxic chemicals, such as chlorine, phosphates, or synthetic, petroleum-based compounds. Hydrogen peroxide might be substituted for chlorine, and ingredients such as citrus, vinegar, and coconut oil might replace synthetic cleaning chemicals. CONSUMER REPORTS has tested various "green" products over the years. For the most part, they were OK, but less effective than mainstream products. That's not necessarily bad if the mess isn't severe. "Green" household cleaners were found to be less harmful to the surfaces being cleaned than most traditional cleaners.

Don't assume "green" claims mean a lot. Products that claim to have an "environmentally sensitive formula" or to be "environmentally certified" might indeed be kinder to the earth. But claims like these are too vague to be meaningful, verifiable, or useful when you buy.

Storage. Keep your cleaning equipment well organized and in a convenient location. It will be easier for you to work, and you won't waste time looking for something when you need it. If you keep only truly necessary items on hand, it will be easier to find what you need. All-purpose cleaners, as their names claim, should be fine for use in a variety of tough cleaning tasks around the house. But task-specific products often outclean multipurpose ones. Because they streak the least, glass cleaners are generally (but not always) the best choices for cleaning glass, and bathroom cleaners are generally the most effective on bathroom grime.

Avoid cluttering your collection of cleaning paraphernalia with rarely used supplies and equipment. Use a marking pen to date new purchases (keep the pen with the supplies), and if you haven't used a bottle of cleaning solution in several years, get rid of it. You probably don't need it, and it may no longer even be effective—chemicals in some products become destabilized and impotent over time.

Clean your cleaning equipment before you put it away. This way, it will be ready for the next use. Remove fluff and hairs from vacuum cleaner attachments, brooms, and brushes. Wash dirt and grit out of buckets. Wash or discard dusters and polishing cloths that have become too dirty to use. Hang brooms and brushes so they don't rest on their bristles, which can deform them and make them useless.

Cleaning by the Seasons

The cleaning and maintenance needs of every household are different and, in many cases, will be defined by the climate of the region in which you live. No matter where you live, though, there are some things that just don't need to be done more than once or twice a year. Use this table as you start thinking about the seasonal chores particular to your home.

Spring

- Go through closets and discard unwanted clothes; get winter coats cleaned.
- Pack away winter clothes (or have them stored for free at a dry cleaner).
- Turn mattresses and wash mattress pads and blankets.
- Hang blankets on clothesline to air out before putting away.
- Wash curtains and draperies or have them dry-cleaned.
- Clean the oven if necessary.
- Dust coils behind or underneath the refrigerator.
- Clean blades of ceiling fans.
- Shampoo rugs and upholstery.
- Have central air conditioners serviced; clean or replace filters in room air conditioners, vacuum and reinstall units.
- Oil snow-removal equipment before storing.
- Change the engine oil and sharpen blades of lawn tractors and gas or riding mowers.
- Check that garden tools are in working condition.
- Open attic louvers.
- Secure any loose shingles or siding.
- Touch up the paint on outside of house.
- Clean gutters and downspouts; clear debris from roof.
- Remove storm windows.
- Patch screens.

Summer

- Clean the oven if necessary.
- Dust coils behind or underneath the refrigerator.
- Have the furnace cleaned and tuned.
- Clean or change the furnace filters.
- Clean out the garage.

Autumn

- Go through closets and discard unwanted clothes.
- Pack away summer clothes (or have them stored for free at a dry cleaner).
- Turn mattresses and wash mattress pads and blankets.
- Wash curtains and draperies or have them dry-cleaned.
- Clean the oven if necessary.
- Dust coils behind or underneath the refrigerator.
- Clean filters and reservoirs of humidifiers.
- Clean blades of ceiling fans.
- Store or cover and seal window air conditioners; cover central air-conditioning units and schedule a cleaning every few years.
- Check that snow-removal equipment is in working condition.
- Clean or replace air filters and spark plugs of lawn tractors and gas or riding mowers and add a preservative to the fuel at the end of mowing season.
- Close attic louvers.
- Check seals on windows and doors; weather-strip if needed.
- Change smoke alarm and carbon monoxide detector batteries (say, on the weekend in October when standard time resumes).
- Have the chimney or furnace flue cleaned.
- Touch up the paint on outside of the house.
- Clean gutters and downspouts; clear debris from roof.
- Put up storm windows.

Winter

- Clean the oven if necessary.
- Dust coils behind or underneath the refrigerator.
- Trickle-charge battery of lawn tractors and gas or riding mowers.
- Clean out the basement.
- Wax floors and furniture if necessary.

Safe use of cleaning products. Store all household cleaning products in their original containers, with original labels intact so you'll have at hand the directions for use, suggested precautions, and possible antidotes. Don't decant cleaning products into other containers without labeling them clearly and in a way that can't be erased. Since cleaning products are often hazardous, make sure to store them in locked cabinets or on shelves that are high enough to be out of reach of young children.

Before using any new cleaning product, read the label carefully and note any cautions. Spot-test it on an inconspicuous part of the item for possible damage. Pretesting for possible damage is important (you'll see this precaution mentioned throughout this book). Product formulations can change, so you might want to compare the labels of new and used-up products.

If you plan to have your carpets or furniture cleaned professionally, remove pets and plants that might be affected by cleaning chemicals. Keep family members and pets away until everything is dry and you are given the "all clear" to enter the area.

Disposal of household cleaning materials

Usually, the best way to dispose of a cleaning product is to use it up. If you can't use it, try to give it to someone who can. If neither of these options is feasible check the label for recommendations regarding disposal. Follow instructions carefully.

Water-soluble products. Water-soluble cleaning products are formulated to be treated in municipal sewage treatment plants or household septic systems. Accordingly, products that do not recommend special handling may be poured down the drain. These include all-purpose cleaners, bleaches, dishwashing and laundry products, toilet-bowl cleaners, and water-based metal cleaners and polishes. Be sure to run copious amounts of water while discarding, and never mix cleaning products—certain combinations, especially ammonia and bleach, can release dangerous fumes.

Solid cleaning products. Solid cleaning products—such as soap bars, rinse agents, soap pads, and towelettes—should be disposed of in the trash.

Solvent-based cleaning products. This category includes such cleaning materials as turpentine, mineral spirits, and other products used to clean paintbrushes; spot removers; some metal and furniture cleaners; and any cleaning product labeled flammable. Solvent-based products should be disposed of in the same manner as household hazardous waste. Contact your municipality for local procedures, or call the manufacturer's telephone number—found on some product labels.

Don't flush solvent-based wastes down the toilet; don't pour them down a storm drain; don't dump them in a ditch, your back yard, or a vacant lot; and don't throw them out with the trash. If you store hazardous cleaning materials, keep them in the original container—tightly sealed and kept dry—on well-ventilated racks that are safely out of the reach of children and animals. If a container begins to leak, place it in a larger container made of a similar material.

Hazardous-waste collection centers. Many municipalities have some type of household hazardous waste drop-off center. These services may be permanent, or they may open periodically—say, several days per week or one or two days a year. Each center should list the specific types of waste it will and won't accept. Commonly, centers accept such items as drain cleaners, solvent-based cleaning products, paints, paint strippers, pesticides, batteries, gasoline, motor oil, charcoal-lighter fluid, and solvents. Most do not accept such banned chemicals as PCBs, chlordane, and radioactive waste. Call your local sanitation authority for center locations and collection schedules.

Some communities may not accept empty containers from such products as bleach, toilet-bowl cleaners, and oven cleaners, either for recycling or regular trash collection. You may be required to take these containers to the collection site for household hazardous waste as well.

A to Z
Things to Clean

Acetate

This material, used in inexpensive satin and the lining of clothing and draperies, usually requires dry cleaning. If the garment's label specifically permits washing, launder it in cold water with mild suds. Don't wring or twist the garment and don't soak colored items. Once it is clean, do not dry the garment in a dryer. Instead, air-dry by carefully spreading the garment out on terry-cloth bath towels on a horizontal surface or by draping it over a clothesline. Press the garment while it is still damp on the wrong side with a cool iron. If pressing on the right side, be sure to use a pressing cloth. Do not use nail-polish remover or other cleaners that contain acetone for stain removal. Acetone will dissolve acetate. Acetate may also be adversely affected by perfumes containing organic solvents.

Acrylic

Acrylic fabrics resemble wool and are often blended with wool. Modacrylic is an acrylic fiber that is flame-retardant, lightweight, bulky, and warm. It is commonly used in fake fur, curtains, and wigs and for stuffing toys. Most acrylic garments are hand- or machine-washable, and dry cleaning is OK. Delicate items should be washed by hand in warm water. For machine-washable items, use warm water and your machine's Gentle cycle. Acrylic may pill, so turn your garments inside out before washing. Use fabric softener every third or fourth washing to reduce static electricity. After laundering, gently squeeze excess water from the garment. Then smooth or shake it out. Acrylic sweaters should be pulled into shape and left to dry flat on a horizontal surface. Dry other garments on rust-free hangers. If the care label permits machine drying, use a low temperature setting and remove the garment from the machine as soon as it is dry. Acrylic tends not to wrinkle, but if ironing is needed, set the iron to medium.

Acrylic paintings

Acrylic paints sometimes fleck and chip. If you notice this happening to a valued acrylic painting, consider having a professional clean and restore it. For a painting in good condition, simply dust occasionally with a feather duster or a soft watercolor brush.

Air

The U.S. Environmental Protection Agency estimates that indoor air is two to five times as polluted as air on the other side of the window. The American Lung Association claims even higher levels and calls indoor pollution a health hazard for millions of Americans with asthma or allergies. Indoor pollutants range from visible particles of dust, pollen, and smoke to invisible combustion byproducts, such as carbon monoxide and nitrous oxide, and to other gaseous invaders such as fumes from carpet adhesives and upholstery.

There are two commonsense approaches: ventilation and controlling the pollutant at the source. If dust is a problem, you might want to leave floors bare or use area rugs instead of wall-to-wall carpeting. Frequent vacuuming may help, though some vacuum cleaners stir up dust. If pet dander is a problem, designate pet-free rooms, particularly bedrooms. A ducted range hood can rid kitchen air of smoke and odor. An exhaust fan in a bathroom can squelch mold, mildew, and odor.

When those measures don't address the problem, there is another alternative to consider. If your house has forced-air heating and cooling, choose an appropriate whole-house filter for your system. (A room air cleaner's work would be quickly undone by the central system's continual circulation of unfiltered air from other rooms.) If your home lacks forced-air heating and cooling, your only option is a room air cleaner, which uses a fan and generally a filter to clean a single room.

See **Air cleaners,** page 192, and **Carbon monoxide detectors,** page 47.

Air conditioners

Clean window units once a month when you are using them regularly. Turn off the power, remove the unit's front panel, and vacuum any visible dirt from the interior coils. Remove the filter (with newer models you slide it out) and wash it at the kitchen sink, using a mild solution of dishwashing liquid and warm water. After the filter dries, put it back in the unit. Brush leaves, dust, and dirt off the outside of the unit.

If you have a central unit, you should also clean air filters once a month during heavy use; if the filters can't be cleaned, follow the manufacturer's instructions about replacing them

Keep your central air-conditioning unit clean to maintain its operating performance. Make sure that leaks in ducts are sealed and that ducts in uncooled spaces are insulated. Check that the weather stripping around windows and doors is air-tight and that vents and grilles inside the house aren't blocked.

regularly. Keep the outside condenser unit clear of leaves, grass clippings, lint from the clothes dryer, dirt, and shrubs. Follow the manufacturer's instructions for keeping the condenser coils clean. If there's a pipe for draining condensed water from the unit, check it regularly for blockages.

You might consider buying a service plan for your central unit. Many plans cover both cooling and heating systems. At the beginning of each cooling season, make sure your service contractor changes the filters; cleans and flushes the coils, drain pan, and drainage system; and vacuums dust and dirt from inside the blower compartments.

Alabaster

Since water leaches into this porous material and leaves rings and spots, never let an alabaster vase or ornament become saturated. Instead, clean the vase with a cloth dampened with soapy water and remove any stains with a cotton ball dipped in lemon juice or turpentine. If you want to use an alabaster vase for fresh-cut flowers, place a jar or glass filled with water inside it.

Animal skins

If an animal-skin rug is at all worn, delicate, or of great value, take it to a professional cleaner. Otherwise, gently dust it with a soft brush, or take it outside and shake it. Depending on the color, you can also rub an absorbent powder—such as fuller's earth or cornmeal—into the skin and leave it for several hours. Then take the rug outside and brush it with a soft brush, or hang it on a clothesline and gently beat it with a tennis racket. Repeat several times if necessary. Or wipe the rug with a damp sponge dipped in a mild detergent-and-water solution, then wipe it with clean water. Brush fur with a clean brush and allow it to dry, or vacuum it with an attachment nozzle covered with an old nylon stocking.

Answering machines

An answering machine requires only an occasional dusting. If the housing is grimy, wipe the machine with a soft, lint-free cloth dampened with rubbing alcohol. Dust around the keys or buttons and inside the machine, if necessary, with a soft synthetic artist's paintbrush, or use compressed air to dislodge dust caught in nooks or crannies.

Artificial flowers

Dusting frequently with a hair dryer set on low prevents buildup that can become hard to remove. To clean safely (and this means without using water), pour some salt into a plastic bag, put the flower heads down into the bag, and shake. Place a nylon stocking over a vacuum nozzle and gently remove the salt, which will have absorbed the dirt from the flowers.

Audio equipment

Frequently wipe audio equipment—CD players, audiocassette players, and record players—with an anti-static dust cloth. Use a cloth dampened with rubbing alcohol to remove fingerprints. Keep audiotape and CD-player compartments and record-player lids closed to prevent dust from collecting. Follow manufacturers' instructions to remove dust that might accumulate. For audiocassette players, use a head-cleaning cassette as directed. To clean a phonograph stylus, flick off dust or dirt with a soft watercolor brush dipped in rubbing alcohol, wiping from back to front.

Automobiles

Cleaning the exterior. Wash your car regularly. Avoid abrasive substances or brushes. Warm water will help dissolve hard deposits. Never wash a car in direct sunlight or when the finish is hot to the touch. That is when the finish is softer and more vulnerable to scratching.

Start by cleaning the wheels or hubcaps, using a specially formulated spray detergent. Most wheel cleaners work best when applied to a dry surface. For alloy wheels, be sure the

....
Cleaning Caveat
Failure to properly care for an answering machine may invalidate the warranty. Read the manufacturer's instructions carefully.

cleaner you choose can be used on their protective clear coat. Apply the cleaning spray, then wipe with a clean, soft cotton towel or special mitt or use a brush. Rinse if so directed. Dry and polish with a soft, clean, dry cloth. Next do the tires with a solution of dishwashing liquid and warm water. Apply with a wet rag and rinse off.

Wash the body of the car using a special detergent made for cars to avoid damaging the finish. Wash one section at a time, starting at the top. First squirt with a hose set for a low-pressure flow, then apply a detergent solution with a clean, soft cotton towel or a special mitt. Rinse with the hose before the dirty water can dry. To reduce the chance of scratching, dunk the towel or mitt frequently and change to a fresh one periodically. (Don't use the same towel or mitt that you used for the wheels or hubcaps.) Rub gently, and use a soft brush for stubborn stains.

Dry the sections of the car in the order that you washed them. Lay a clean, dry all-cotton towel or synthetic chamois (the acids in natural chamois can strip wax) on the surface to blot the water, then wring it out. Use a second clean, dry towel to remove remaining moisture. Alternate towels as you complete the process.

Wipe chrome trim with a soft cloth dipped in a mixture of warm water and dishwashing liquid to which you've added a few drops of ammonia. Dry and polish with a soft, clean, dry cloth. Clean rusted chrome with steel wool or a commercial rust remover. If you use a rust remover, you'll need to wash the surface with a neutralizing solution, then dry it and seal with a thin coat of polyurethane.

For windows, use a window cleaner.

Adding a protective layer. The terms "wax" and "polish" are used interchangeably. Both usually refer to a liquid, paste, or spray that adds luster to a finish and sometimes can remove oxidation and embedded grime. Spray polishes are easiest to use but are not effective on a very dirty or oxidized finish.

The paint on older automobiles is usually covered with a thick coat of colored enamel, while newer cars have a thinner layer of colored enamel under a thin layer of clear enamel. Before you buy an auto polish, be sure that you need it. If the beads of rainwater on your car's finish are the size of a quarter or smaller, you don't need to wax it. Simply wash the car regularly. The abrasive ingredients in some polishing products (for deep cleaning and polishing in one step) can do more harm than good to new or nearly new paint by leaving behind fine scratches or a residue that is hard to remove.

If your car's finish is weathered, the cleaning ability of the wax or polish is especially important because ordinary washing removes only loose surface dirt. For a badly oxidized finish you may need to start with a dedicated paint cleaner or a special, highly abrasive polishing compound.

Polishes are advertised to last up to a year, but CONSUMER REPORTS has found that even the most durable tend to last only two months, with liquids and pastes outlasting sprays. Your experience will depend on such factors as the climate and whether you garage your car.

On dark-colored cars, test the polish in an inconspicuous spot, such as the doorjamb, to be sure it will not scratch, then follow instructions. Scratching is less obvious on light-colored cars. A warning on the label not to get polish on plastic or vinyl trim indicates that the polish is likely to stain or mar the surface.

You can protect the car's chrome trim with a light coating of car silicone wax polish. Buff it with a soft, dry cloth. If you use a chrome polish, be sure to rub it in well.

Special brands of glass protector provide an outer, water-resistant layer for windows. These products can also keep a car's windows cleaner in muddy or dusty conditions.

Cleaning the interior. Clear out any accumulated trash or debris. Then use an attachment of a canister vacuum or wet/dry vac to remove superficial dirt from the upholstery and dashboard and to clean nooks and crannies, such as cup holders and map pockets. Shake out and vacuum the floor mats. Vacuum the bottoms and backs of the seats before you vacuum the carpeting and beneath the seats.

Vigorous vacuuming may be required to get out sand, dust, and dirt embedded in the floor carpeting. Use the vacuum cleaner's nozzle attachment to knock on the carpeting or scrape its surface to loosen ground-in particles.

Before cleaning interior vinyl and plastic, read the instructions on a car-interior cleaner, vinyl protector, or all-purpose cleaner. Spray the product on a towel, and pass it over the hard surfaces, including door handles and vinyl upholstery.

To remove stains from fabric upholstery, apply a small amount of carpet shampoo or upholstery cleaner to a damp towel. Gently rub the stain, working inward from its outside edge to avoid staining the surrounding fabric. Use a damp sponge to remove the shampoo or cleaner.

Two or three times a year (more often for light-colored interiors) apply a commercial leather cleaner to leather upholstery. Using an upholstery brush (sold at automotive supply stores), work the cleaner into a lather one section at a time. Remove any residue and wipe several times with a damp cloth, then dry with a fresh towel. In arid regions, use a leather conditioner as often as once a month. Follow the manufacturer's instructions, applying it one section at a time. With most conditioners, you let the product soak in for a few minutes, then buff off the excess. To keep the leather looking nice, occasionally wipe with a damp towel to remove grime

Autos: Special Cleaning Situations

Bird droppings. Remove these promptly because they contain acid that can destroy the finish. Pour seltzer water on the affected area, allow it to bubble up, then wipe clean.

Bugs, tree sap, or tar. Remove these sticky items by applying a pre-wash spray. Allow it to work briefly, then rinse it off. Or use car detergent, a commercial product created for this purpose, or pine oil: Apply it full-strength to the mitt or towel, then to the car.

Rust spots. Treat spots with a rust inhibitor and primer, then touch up with the correct color of auto paint.

that might spoil the surface. When driving, put a towel under your bare legs if you have used lotion or sunscreen products. They can damage the leather.

For the interiors of windows, use a window-cleaning spray and a soft cloth.

Awnings

Clean awnings two or three times a year to prevent hard-to-remove buildup. Since the acid content of bird droppings can fade colors, clean them off as soon as possible. You can use a pressure sprayer to clean away debris, apply cleaner, and rinse the awning, but it may tear fabric or dent vinyl. Take care to point the nozzle away from the awning when you first pull the trigger so you can adjust the spray to the desired level.

Remember that bleach can cause materials to change colors, while other cleaning products can strip protective plastic coating and inflict other damage. Follow the manufacturer's instructions for the best cleaners to use and do your own safety test by first applying the cleaning agent you're using in an area of the awning that is hidden from view.

Sweep dust or debris off the awning and, using a stiff brush, scrub it with warm water and a mild detergent solution. To remove most stubborn stains, sprinkle the affected areas with baking soda and let it sit for five minutes before rinsing; apply a solution of one part bleach and three parts water to mildew stains. Let the awning dry thoroughly before rolling it up or storing it to discourage the growth of mold.

Bakeware

Be sure to follow the care instructions that come with most bakeware. As a rule of thumb, avoid steel wool and abrasive cleaners. It's usually best simply to rinse bakeware with a damp sponge. Soak in a solution of water and a little baking soda to loosen stubborn deposits; if they remain, remove them with a plastic-edged scraper, not a knife.

Season uncoated metal bakeware to prevent rusting. Brush with unflavored vegetable oil and heat in the oven at a low temperature for an hour. Remove, let cool, and wipe away any excess oil with a paper towel. Spread a little vegetable oil onto the sides and bottom with a paper towel after each use.

For information on cleaning **Cookware**, see page 54.

Bamboo furniture

Vacuum with an upholstery attachment or dust thoroughly with a soft brush. If the piece is still dirty, use a brush to scrub it with a solution of ¼ cup of borax and 1 tablespoon of liquid detergent mixed in 1 quart of warm water. Rinse, wipe lightly, and allow to air-dry. To prevent bamboo furniture from drying out and cracking, apply lemon oil or a little furniture cream once a year.

For bamboo blinds, see **Blinds,** page 40.

Bamboo steamers

Don't clean with a detergent because the bamboo will absorb it and transfer the taste to the food. Instead, simply rinse a bamboo steamer with water after use. Occasionally oil it with a neutral-tasting vegetable oil to keep the bamboo resilient and prevent splintering.

Barbecue grills

Keep the grill covered when you're not using it. For routine cleaning, get the grill very hot and stroke a long-handled metal brush dipped in water over the grates. Once the grates cool, use a paper towel to wipe them clean with hot water. Brush away powdered charcoal and other debris that has gathered beneath the grates. Remove any rust spots from the grates with the wire wheel attachment of an electric drill (wear gloves and goggles while doing this). To make future cleanups easier, spray the grates with one of the special "no-stick" grill products available in most grocery stores.

Baskets

Vacuum with an upholstery attachment or dust thoroughly with a soft brush. If necessary, use a brush dipped in warm water and dishwashing liquid to scrub the basket, and rinse with warm water. If the basket is painted, test the detergent solution on an inconspicuous spot before cleaning. Air-dry in a warm spot.

Bath and shower mats

It is safe to launder most fabric bath and shower mats; check the care label. Air-dry mats with rubber backing. Rubber bath and shower mats collect dirt in their indentations. Use a scrub brush to clean these with warm water and dishwashing liquid. To remove mildew, submerge the mat in a solution of one part chlorine bleach and three parts water. Rinse well and air-dry.

Bathtubs and sinks

Encourage everyone in the family to wipe down tubs and sinks with a soft cloth after every use to prevent dirt and soap deposits from building up. If the sink is stainless steel, go over it a second time with a dry cloth. Standing water will cause spots to form.

The material of a tub and sink determines how you clean it. Check the manufacturer's guidelines. As a rule, never use abrasive cleaners, such as scouring powders or steel wool, on acrylic, fiberglass, stainless-steel, or sealed-marble tubs and basins. Instead, use a sponge to clean them with hot water and liquid detergent. Use a little extra detergent on stubborn dirt and grime. It's safe to clean tubs made of vitreous or porcelain enamel with scouring powder and warm water. Because cleaning solutions can stain an unglazed enamel surface, test them first in an inconspicuous spot.

Reglazing Bathtubs and Sinks

When tubs and sinks are stained, chipped, or so porous that they trap dirt and aren't easily cleaned, reglazing may be the solution. A professional service can repair any chipped or damaged areas, prepare the surface, apply and cure an adhesive coating, and apply a finish (usually an epoxy-based paint). Select a company that has been in business a long time and offers a good warranty. Be sure to ask how much experience the installer has, if the products to be used are toxic, and what precautions you should take against fumes while the work is being done. Also ask for the names and numbers of previous customers you can call to check on the company's work.

The material of the tub and sink also determines how you treat stains and scratches. Remove small scratches from acrylic with a plastic polish that's sold for this purpose; buff with a clean cloth and rinse. Use ultrafine sandpaper or a paper grocery bag to remove stubborn stains from solid-surface synthetic tubs and sinks, and buff with a clean cloth. For stains in a stainless-steel sink, use a special stainless-steel cleaner. Regularly apply a sealer to marble and other stone surfaces to prevent staining.

For stains on vitreous or porcelain enamel, apply a solution of 1 cup of chlorine bleach and 1 quart of water. Leave for only 15 seconds, then rinse. Clean heavy mineral deposits with warm water and vinegar or a special product such as CLR. For stubborn stains on glazed enamel surfaces, add ammonia to calcium carbonate to make a paste, apply, leave for an hour, and rinse. If the surface is unglazed, sponge uncolored household scouring powder and water onto the area and leave for five minutes. Scrub with a stiff-bristled brush and rinse.

Blue-green stains on enamel surfaces are a telltale sign of a continually dripping faucet. After repairing the faucet, rub a paste of borax and lemon juice onto the stain. Leave it on for several minutes, scrub with a plastic scrub pad, rinse with warm water, and buff dry. Or use products such as CLR or Lime Away.

Beds

Vacuum the bases and headboards of beds as needed, or at least once every six months when you flip the mattress. Use a soft dusting brush for upholstery and a crevice tool for wood slats. If castors aren't running smoothly, use an aerosol lubricant such as WD-40.

Wipe down brass, iron, and wood bed frames with a damp cloth. To remove hair-oil stains from wooden headboards, moisten a cloth with lemon oil or another furniture polish and rub in the direction of the grain. Buff to a shine. Use a commercial stain remover to remove hair oil and other stains from a fabric-covered headboard. Begin at the outside edge of the stain, working inward so you avoid subjecting fabric around the stain to unnecessary cleaning, which can leave a noticeable ring.

If the lacquer on a brass bed is peeling, you may want to strip it with a lacquer remover, clean the brass with a special brass cleaner sold in hardware stores, and apply a new coat of lacquer. Clean rust spots on an iron-frame bed with steel wool or a wire brush, then apply a rust-inhibiting primer. Be sure to follow the manufacturer's instructions carefully when changing or treating the water in a water bed and when cleaning the mattress and base.

Bedspreads

Read the care label to see whether you should launder or dry-clean a bed spread. If you have a spread dry-cleaned, be sure to air it thoroughly before using to make sure all the fumes have dissipated.

For information on cleaning **Mattresses**, see page 99.

Bicycles

Remove debris from the spokes and other components. Hose down the bike while it is upright. Spray gently around the crank bearings and wheel hubs. Sponge off dirt and grease with warm water and a mild detergent, using a plastic scourer if necessary on the wheel rims. You can clean the components that tend to get greasy with a mild degreaser. Use steel wool or chrome polish to remove any rust from chrome parts. Rinse the bike off and then turn it upside down to wash the underside of the frame. Turn the bike upright and towel dry.

Lubricate the chain with specially formulated oil. After a few minutes, remove excess oil with a clean, dry cloth. Lubricate the derailers and any suspension components according to the manufacturer's instructions. Wipe down the seat with a damp cloth; use saddle soap on a leather seat as needed. Between cleanings, wipe down the bike with a dry, clean cloth after each ride, and lubricate moving parts every few weeks or after riding on a wet surface.

Binoculars

Wipe the casing with a soft cloth after use. Frequently dust the lenses with a clean, lint-free cloth and then clean with a lens-cleaning fluid. You can buy these products at most photography-supply shops.

Blankets

Read the care instructions on the label before laundering any blanket. You can machine-wash most acrylic and cotton blankets, while it's usually recommended that you dry-clean those made of wool. You can wash many types of electric blankets, though you should do so infrequently and follow instructions carefully.

    If your machine can't accommodate a blanket, use one of the large machines at a coin laundry. Use the Gentle cycle, mild detergent, and warm water. Tumble-dry if the label recommends, or hang over two or more parallel clotheslines. To prevent colors from running, hang striped blankets so the stripes run vertically.

    If you are storing a blanket, launder it first. To ward off dust, wrap it in sheets or put it in a plastic bag, a pillowcase, or a blanket bag that you can purchase at most department stores. Add mothballs if the blanket is wool. Never fold an electric blanket when storing it because you can damage the heating elements. Instead, lay it flat on a spare bed if you can.

Blinds

Be sure to follow the manufacturer's instructions carefully. Incorrect cleaning can shrink and discolor blinds and damage protective finishes that inhibit mold, mildew, and staining. A convenient way to dust aluminum, PVC, and wood blinds is to

Helpful Hint

Read instructions to see how often you should return an electric blanket to the manufacturer for a safety check and servicing. Many manufacturers recommend that you do so every two to three years.

put on a pair of soft cotton cleaning gloves and do the job with your hands. You can also use a soft dust cloth or the dusting attachment of a vacuum cleaner. To dust both sides of the blinds, dust horizontal blinds with the slats turned up, then with the slats turned down; for vertical blinds, dust with the vanes turned in one direction, then in the reverse direction. Or use a two- or three-pronged brush, available in hardware stores, that dusts both sides of several slats or vanes at a time. Use the dusting attachment of the vacuum cleaner or a soft brush to dust bamboo and fabric blinds.

To clean aluminum and PVC blinds, wipe with a cloth or sponge dampened in a solution of warm water and dishwashing liquid. Or stuff pieces of cotton rags into the fingers of cotton gloves for extra absorbency, dip them into a detergent solution, and run them over the slats. Wipe the blinds with a dry cloth or dry pair of cotton gloves. If the blinds are greasy, wash them in warm soapy water in the bathtub and rinse, taking care to keep the roller mechanism dry and to protect the surface of the tub bottom with a towel. Rehang the blinds and let them air-dry, leaving them at full length to ensure that the tapes dry thoroughly without shrinking. When the blinds are dry, wipe them with an anti-static polish, available in grocery stores, so they will attract less dust.

To clean wood blinds, use a nonwax furniture polish. Don't use water. To clean bamboo blinds, lay them flat and wipe with a cloth that's barely dampened in a solution of water and dishwashing liquid. Rinse with a clean, lightly moistened cloth and air-dry away from heat. For fabric blinds, spot-clean with an upholstery cleaner. Test the cleaner on an out-of-sight spot first to make sure it doesn't cause colors to fade.

Bone

Knife handles are often made of bone, which is porous and will stain and discolor if it's immersed in water. Just wipe the bone surface with a cloth dipped in water and then buff with a dry, soft cloth.

Books

Consult a professional about caring for rare and antique books. Most other books require only annual cleaning. Remove them

Book Emergencies

Depending on the problem, you can usually rescue treasured books with one of these methods:

Damp or wet books. Dry in an oven at the lowest heat. To dry individual pages, place toilet paper between each page and let the book dry flat with a light weight placed on top.

Insects. Place the book in a plastic bag and leave the bag in the freezer for a couple of days. Deter insects from making their homes in your books by placing bags of cloves or bay leaves on the shelves behind them.

Mildew. Use a baby wipe or a damp cloth dipped in white vinegar to carefully remove mildew. Or vacuum it off. Then set the book in direct sunlight for no more than 30 minutes. The pages will start to yellow if the book is exposed to sunlight any longer.

from the shelves and wipe each book and the shelves with a magnetic cleaning cloth that attracts and holds dust. (An ordinary cloth or feather duster will just spread the dust around.) Use an art-gum eraser to remove marks and dirt from cloth-covered books, and clean leather bindings with a leather-cleaning solution and restorer. Wipe plastic or imitation leather bindings with a cloth that's only very slightly damp. When you return books to their shelves, leave space behind them so air can circulate; this will help prevent a musty odor and possibly even mildew from developing. Regularly vacuum a room where you keep books to prevent dust from getting on them.

Bookshelves

Remove the books and use a wiping cloth that is chemically treated to attract and hold dust. If you don't have the time and energy to clean shelves thoroughly, vacuum the front of the shelves with the crevice tool. Vacuum floors around the shelves regularly to prevent dust from collecting on books.

Brass

Brass is often coated with a thin layer of lacquer to prevent tarnishing. The safest way to clean brass objects treated this way is simply to wipe them with a damp cloth. More extensive cleaning can cause the lacquer to peel.

Clean brass objects that haven't been lacquered the same way. Allow to air-dry, then use a soft cloth to polish the brass to the desired shine. You will occasionally need to remove tarnish from unlacquered brass objects with a commercial brass cleaner. To prevent future tarnishing, shine the object to the degree of luster you prefer and spray or brush on two coats of a transparent metal lacquer.

Scrub engraved brass, whether it's lacquered or not, with a soft toothbrush dipped in household detergent. If old polish has built up on patterned brass, rub the affected area gently with a solution of mild detergent and water. Use a soft toothbrush to get polish out of crevices in the detailing.

If you are cleaning brass that is attached to another surface, such as the handles on a chest of drawers, make a template by cutting the shape of the brass object out of a piece of cardboard. Hold the template over the brass area so you can clean or lacquer it without damaging the surrounding surfaces.

Brocade

Care instructions on the labels of clothing and accessories made from this heavy material usually call for dry cleaning. If wrinkled, iron gently so you don't the flatten the weave.

Bronze

Clean with a soft brush. If you notice the surface is still dirty, sponge lightly with soapy water, wipe dry, and polish with a chamois cloth. Remove stubborn marks with a little paint thinner on a soft cloth, and polish with a chamois cloth.

Butcher block

This type of countertop dents, scratches, burns, and stains easily. It's also vulnerable to fluctuations in humidity, so it's a poor choice for use over a dishwasher. Cleanups will be much easier if you seal a butcher-block counter with at least two coats of polyurethane; be sure to use a type that is suitable for use on surfaces where food is prepared.

Clean the countertop with water and a little dishwashing liquid after each use. If you've been preparing raw chicken, fish, or meat on the countertop, clean and then apply unscented chlorine bleach diluted in water to the surface and let it sit for about two minutes. You can also use an all-purpose spray cleaner that contains chlorine bleach. Rinse thoroughly and let air-dry.

Helpful Hint

Save yourself some elbow grease: There's no need to keep outdoor ornaments made of bronze squeaky clean and shiny. Bronze is intended to have a dull patina and usually doesn't look as attractive when it's polished to a high shine.

For light stains, scrub the surface using a nylon pad. If the stains remain, apply a diluted solution of chlorine bleach directly to them and let it sit for a couple of minutes before rinsing. To remove deep stains, as well as scratches and burns, sand the affected area with very-fine-grade sandpaper. It may be necessary to apply another coat of polyurethane to the places you've sanded. If the countertop is severely stained, scratched, or burned, you may want to hire a professional to refinish the surface.

See also **Countertops,** page 58.

Cabinets

Greasy fingerprint marks seem to appear like magic on kitchen cabinets. Fortunately, it's easy to remove them. For painted wood, metal, laminated-plastic, and wood-grain-vinyl surfaces, use a solution of dishwashing liquid and warm water. You can also use an all-purpose cleaner, but read the label carefully and test it first on the inside of a door or another inconspicuous spot to make sure it doesn't cause colors to fade or run. Rinse with a second cloth dipped in warm water, and dry with a third cloth.

If there's a heavy buildup of grease and grime, use a commercial cleaner designed especially for wood. Be sure to read labels carefully and observe all cautions since some cleaners are flammable. Apply a no-buff liquid-solvent polish from time to time to restore shine.

Clean out the interior of cupboards every few months or so, or more frequently if necessary. Remove shelf lining before cleaning a cupboard because dirt and insects can become trapped beneath it. If you want to remove soiled or ripped contact paper, switch a hair dryer to high and direct the hot air onto the paper until you can loosen it from shelf. Remove any adhesive with a cleaner such as Citra-Solv or Goo Gone.

Wash shelves with hot water and detergent, paying special attention to spills and greasy spots. Rinse with a clean, damp cloth and wipe dry with another cloth. Sponge clean dusty cans or bottles with warm water and dishwashing liquid, and throw out items that have passed their expiration dates. Allow the cupboards to air out for at least a couple of hours before replacing contents.

Camcorders

Keep the lens covered when you're not using the camcorder. Put a clear filter on the lens if your camcorder will accept one. A scratched or broken filter is a much smaller problem than a scratched or broken lens. Any dust or smearing on the lens will show up on the tape if you shoot into the light, so clean the lens regularly, under a bright light. Blow off dust with a blower brush, then use special lens cleaner and tissue. Buy these products from a photography-supply shop. A "noisy" picture may be the result of incorrectly set tracking control.

Helpful Hint

There's no need to use shelf lining in cupboards unless the shelves are made of bare, untreated wood. You'll find that it's easier to keep shelves clean when they're not lined.

For VHS-type models, it may also happen because the video heads are clogged by oxide buildup, which can be corrected by using a wet or dry cassette-cleaning tape as the manufacturer instructs. Don't overdo it or you'll wear down the heads. If a few tries don't help, get professional advice; there may be another problem, such as a bent mechanism or circuit failure.

Cameras

Always store a camera in a dust-free case when it's not in use. Clear the lens of dust as necessary with a blower brush. If there are smudges or fingerprints, wipe with lens-cleaning paper or a lint-free cloth to which you've applied a drop or two of commercial lens-cleaning fluid. You can buy the cleaning products at a photography-supply shop. Clean in a spiral motion from the center outward. You can also use the blower brush to remove accumulated dust particles from the film chamber. If you think your camera requires further cleaning, take it to an authorized service center.

Candlesticks

An easy way to remove wax from candlesticks made of silver or other metals is to place them in the freezer until the wax is hardened. Then, using a plastic spatula so you don't mar the surface, carefully scrape off the wax. Melt away any remaining wax by pouring boiling water over the candlestick or immersing it in a pot of boiling water. If the base is covered with felt, be sure to hold the candlestick upside down in the water so the bottom remains dry. To remove wax from a candlestick made of wood, glass, or plastic, point a hair dryer at the wax and blot with paper toweling as it melts. Be careful not to overheat wood because it can crack.

Cane

Dust regularly with a feather duster or the upholstery attachment of the vacuum cleaner, making sure you reach into cracks and crevices. If the cane has been varnished, you should be able to remove any dirt simply by wiping it with a damp cloth. Wash unvarnished cane with a scrub brush dipped in warm water to which you've added ¼ cup of borax and 1 tablespoon of liquid detergent. Towel dry, then apply lemon oil to prevent the cane from cracking. Don't leave cane furniture outdoors for long periods of time because when exposed to rain, harsh sunlight, and temperature extremes, cane will split and crack.

Carafes and decanters

Since these are often used for fine wines, it's important to keep them clear of unwanted tastes and odors. Don't let the dregs of wine, port, or other spirits stand too long because they can leave a hard-to-remove residue. As soon as possible after use, fill a carafe or decanter with a mixture of warm water and laundry detergent and let soak for several hours. Shake occasionally, or agitate the solution from time to time with a bottle brush. Rinse thoroughly with warm water until the smell of the detergent solution and alcohol have disappeared. Stand the glassware upside down in a bowl to drain. A decanter with a very wide base can tip over when you set it on its neck, so you should pad the bowl with towels to support it.

Carbon monoxide detectors

Carbon monoxide (CO) detectors can be battery-powered, plug-in, or built-in. Battery-powered CO detectors are usually mounted on a wall. Plug-in models go where there's an outlet. A CO detector with a display tells you how high the concentration of CO is. Whichever type of CO detector you have, press the Test button at least monthly to make sure the unit works. If your CO detector runs on batteries, replace them once a year on an easy-to-remember date, such as the weekend in October when clocks return to standard time.

Regularly vacuum a CO detector with an attachment; insects, dust, or cobwebs may reduce a unit's effectiveness or cause false alarms. Remove grime from the exterior by wiping with a paper towel sprayed with an all-purpose cleaner. Replace a CO detector every five years. New models have a date stamp to help you keep track.

Cashmere

Turn a sweater made of cashmere inside out and machine-wash in cold water. Lay the garment inside out and flat to air-dry. Press with a cool iron.

Cast-iron garden furniture

Durable and easy to maintain as cast-iron pieces are, they tend to rust easily. Remove rust spots regularly with a commercial rust remover, then paint with a metal primer, followed by a coat of rust-inhibiting, exterior-quality paint. Oil the hinges of the furniture frequently in order to keep them from rusting.

Ceilings

If you use a stepladder when cleaning your ceilings, make sure it is sturdy and that you can stand on it safely while reaching above your head. Dust the surface and clear away cobwebs with a long-handled brush or dust mop or the floor-dusting attachment of your vacuum cleaner. You can also tie a clean towel over a broom, securing it with a rubber band.

It's very difficult to clean a painted ceiling without streaking it or leaving dirty patches. If needed, use an all-purpose cleaner or a solution of 2 tablespoons of TSP (trisodium phosphate) and 1 gallon of water. Use a sponge to gently wipe the dirty area with the cleaner or cleaning solution, and another one to rinse with warm water. Work carefully to avoid damaging the paint.

You can't remove the yellow stains that water leaks leave. Instead, apply a special primer sealer, which will cover the stain thoroughly and prevent it from bleeding through. Once the sealer dries, paint the area to match the rest of the ceiling.

Ceramic tile

Mop floors with a solution of mild detergent and water. Buffing with a chamois cloth will restore shine to the tiles. Use a commercial tile cleaner for heavy-duty cleaning, but make sure it's safe to use on ceramic surfaces. Be careful when walking on wet ceramic tiles because they can be extremely slippery. A wipe- down with a sponge soaked in soapy water is usually sufficient to clean walls. If soap scum and mineral deposits remain on the tiles, spray with a commercial cleaner designed

Removing Stains and Mildew from Ceramic Tiles

First try to remove stains from ceramic tiles with liquid detergent and water. If this doesn't work, try the following: baking soda and water for greasy stains; ammonia for iodine; hydrogen peroxide for blood; a mild bleach solution for inks and dyes; hydrogen peroxide or a mild bleach solution for coffee, tea, food, and fruit juices.

Act at the first signs of mildew. Wipe tiles and grout with a solution of one part bleach and four parts water or stronger. When working with bleach, make sure the area is well ventilated and wear gloves and old clothes. If you're sensitive to the fumes, wear a mask and eye protection. Never use bleach in combination with ammonia or cleaners containing ammonia.

for use on ceramic tiles, allow to stand five minutes, and then rinse it off. A shower will be easier to clean if everyone in the family wipes the walls down with a cloth after every use. As necessary, clean grouting with a solution of one part bleach and six parts water or with a special grout cleaner.

Glazed ceramic tiles are suitable for countertops because they resist staining and are easy to clean. Usually, you just need to wipe them down with a sponge dipped in warm water and detergent. Don't use abrasive cleaners on ceramic countertops because they will wear down the surface. Instead, rub stubborn spots with half a lemon onto which you've shaken a little salt.

Grouting between tiles can stain easily. Scrub it with a toothbrush dipped in a solution of one part bleach and six parts water, or use a special grout cleaner. As a labor-saving measure, apply a sealer to grout so it will be more resistant to dirt and stains. Or replace existing grout with acrylic or epoxy grout, which is stain-resistant and impermeable to water and other liquids. You can also tint grout in a darker shade that is less likely to show dirt and stains.

See also **Countertops,** page 58; **Flooring,** page 260.

Chandeliers

If you want to simplify the task, leave the chandelier in place, spread plastic sheeting on the table or floor beneath it, and set a sturdy stepladder so you can reach the chandelier easily and safely. Put on a pair of gloves and then climb up the stepladder, making sure you feel steady. Dip one hand into a bowl of window cleaner and clean each piece of the chandelier. Dry each piece with the other hand.

Another approach is to take the chandelier out of the ceiling and dismantle it for cleaning. First, make a diagram or take a photo of how the pieces fit together so you can reassemble the chandelier correctly. Then switch off the circuit that provides electricity to the chandelier. (Since fixtures are sometimes miswired and stay "hot" even when switched off, make absolutely sure electricity is no longer going to the chandelier.) Take the chandelier apart and clean as above. Rinse each piece in clear warm water and set it on a lint-free cloth to dry.

If you feel daunted by this task, call in a professional who specializes in cleaning chandeliers.

Chiffon

If garments, curtains, or other items made of this material are elaborate or especially valuable, you should have them dry-cleaned. Otherwise, hand-wash chiffon in cool water and mild detergent and iron it while still damp on a low setting.

Chimneys

If you use a wood-burning fireplace regularly, have the chimney cleaned professionally at least once a year to remove built-up soot and creosote—a flammable tar-like substance. The flues of wood-burning and solid-fuel stoves should be cleaned yearly as well.

China and porcelain

It's best to wash fine china and porcelain pieces by hand, using mild dishwashing detergent and placing an old towel in the sink to prevent chipping. In the dishwasher, forceful water jets and the jostling of pots and pans can cause delicate items to chip and break. Also, dishwasher detergent and extremes of heat may damage glaze and fine decoration and cause patterns to fade.

To make cleanups easier, choose china for everyday use that can safely be machine-washed; look for a manufacturer's label that says "dishwasher safe."

Antimicrobial Cutting Boards

Enterprising manufacturers have incorporated the antibacterial chemical triclosan, usually known by the trade name Microban, in dozens of durable products—cutting boards, shower curtains, knife handles, socks, pillows, mattress pads, underwear. But triclosan offers minimal protection for cutting board users, say experts consulted by CONSUMER REPORTS. Triclosan does help prevent bad odors because it inhibits the growth of bacteria and mildew. Even so, there's not enough Microban on the surface of a cutting board to stop the accumulation of bacteria there. Even if your cutting board is impregnated with Microban, you still have to clean it properly if you want it to be free of disease-causing germs.

Chopping and cutting boards

Chopping boards can be breeding grounds for bacteria, so you must take care when using them. One way to cut the risk of contamination is to use different boards for raw meats, cooked meats, and vegetables. Whether you use a wood board or a plastic board, wash it as soon as possible after use in the dishwasher or use a brush to scrub it with dishwashing liquid and hot water. Never let a wooden board sit in water, which can cause it to warp. Disinfect boards frequently by wiping them down with a solution of one part bleach and 10 parts water and then rinsing.

Wood boards tend to trap odors. You can help alleviate these by storing a board on its side so both surfaces can air. If odors persist, rub the board with half a lemon dipped in salt. With normal use, water will cause the joints of a wooden board to open, creating a trap for bacteria. "Swell" the board by laying it flat and covering it with a damp cloth for a few hours. Let air-dry and then wipe with vegetable oil.

Chrome

Gentle is a key word when cleaning chrome because chrome plating can be so thin it wears off easily. In general, remove marks and smears from a chrome surface by wiping it with a soft cloth or a sponge dipped in warm water and dishwashing detergent. Dry with a soft, clean cloth to restore the shine. You can keep chrome shiny and clean longer

by applying a light coat of the silicone wax polish used on cars and buffing it.

Gently remove any rust spots with steel wool or a commercial rust remover, but make sure the cleaning product isn't too abrasive. Then wash the surface with mild detergent and warm water, and apply a neutralizing solution if you have used a commercial rust remover. Dry with a soft cloth and apply a thin coat of solvent-based polyurethane to protect the chrome from moisture that might cause further rusting.

Lime deposits often build up on chrome bathroom fittings. Clean first with detergent and warm water, then wrap the chrome fitting with a cloth soaked in white vinegar or a commercial descaler such as CLR. The deposits should soon dissolve. If they don't, chip them off gently with a plastic scraper.

Clocks

Dust the exterior regularly. For wood or metal, use polish only once or twice a year. As needed, clean the glass with rubbing alcohol. To keep the inner workings of an old and valuable clock in good condition, they should be oiled by a professional once every three years and cleaned once every 8 to 10 years.

Cloisonné

Vases and jewel boxes made with this type of decorative enamel finish should be regularly dusted without polish. If you need a little extra cleaning power, rub gently with a polishing cloth sold for cleaning silver. Don't use water, which can damage the enamel.

Coffeemakers

Dried coffee oils can ruin the taste of even the best blend. After every use, wash the carafe and brew basket in detergent and water, rinse, and dry. Once the hotplate cools, wipe any coffee that may have spilled onto it and remove burned-on stains by using a little baking soda on a damp sponge. To avoid accumulation of minerals in tanks and tubes, especially if you live in a region where the water is hard, occasionally run equal parts of water and white vinegar through the machine. Then run water through it a couple of times. Or use a solution made with a special detergent for coffee-making equipment.

Coffeepots

After every use, wash the brew basket and other inner workings in detergent and water, rinse, and let air-dry. From time to time, remove coffee oils from the pot by "brewing" a solution of one part vinegar and four parts water and then just water. To remove stains, use a little baking soda on a damp sponge, or fill the pot with one part baking solution and two parts hot water and let stand overnight. You can also use a special detergent for coffee-making equipment.

Comforters

See **Duvets,** page 70.

Compact discs (CDs)

While CDs are quite sturdy, large amounts of dirt and oil can affect sound quality or tracking. Handle carefully, touching nothing but the edge or center of a disc, and return to the case after each use. As needed, dust with a soft, clean cloth. If you notice fingerprints or dirt on the surface, wipe them off with a cloth dampened in mild detergent and dry with a lint-free cloth. You can also use special cleaning products sold in music stores. When cleaning or dusting CDs, work in straight lines from the center, never in a circular motion.

Computers

Check your owner's manual for instructions. Dust all components regularly. Remove visible grime from the CPU housing and monitor (but not the screen) with a cloth moistened with rubbing alcohol.

See also **Inkjet printers**, page 88; **Keyboards (computer)**, page 91; **Laptop computers**, page 93; **Monitors**, page 100; and **Mouse (computer)**, page 100.

Concrete

For easiest maintenance, have concrete sealed. Sweep it regularly. As needed, wash it with TSP (trisodium phosphate) or

TSP phosphate-free detergent (available at hardware or paint stores and home centers).

Protect the concrete floor of a garage from the grease and oil that might drip from a car by placing a shallow metal tray filled with an absorbent powder such as kitty litter (the non-clumping type), fuller's earth, cornmeal, or sawdust under the car's engine. Replace the material when it's saturated. If there's an oil or grease spill, sprinkle an absorbent powder to soak up as much of the spill as possible. Leave for a couple of days, then sweep. For a rust stain, use a solution of one part citric acid crystals and six parts water and enough fuller's earth to make a paste. Apply, let dry, and scrape off. The rust stain should be gone.

To remove a grease or oil stain that has set, dissolve 3 to 4 ounces of TSP or TSP phosphate-free detergent in 1 gallon of hot water. Pour on the solution, leave for 15 to 20 minutes, then scrub with a stiff brush or broom, working from the outside of the stain to the middle. Rinse thoroughly with a hose. Repeat if necessary. Or try a commercial product made for this purpose. Note that these powerful chemicals are not meant for asphalt. When working with them, wear goggles and gloves.

Because concrete is porous, the oil or grease may have penetrated to a considerable degree and the stain may reappear over time. You may want to paint the concrete with garage-floor paint and seal it, but you'll first need to clean the surface and then etch it with a wash of diluted hydrochloric acid. This job requires gloves and goggles, in addition to extremely good ventilation.

Cookware

With proper cleaning, cookware should last for years. It's important, though, to keep the material from which it is made in mind and clean accordingly.

Wash aluminum cookware by hand or machine as soon as possible after use, and dry thoroughly to avoid pitting. Aluminum dulls easily, so occasionally shine up the surfaces with a soapy scouring pad or steel-wool pad. When the interior of a pot or pan becomes discolored, fill it with 1 quart of water, add 2 teaspoons of cream of tartar or some lemon or apple peel, bring the mixture to a boil, then rinse and dry.

You must season cast-iron cookware before using it. Brush the sides of a pot, pan, or saucepan with unflavored vegetable oil, then pour in enough oil to cover the bottom. Heat over a low flame or in the oven at low temperature for an hour. Remove, let cool, pour out the oil, and wipe away any residue with a paper towel. After each use, wash with hot water and dishwashing liquid, and dry thoroughly to prevent rusting. If you notice rust spots, scour with steel wool and a little cooking vegetable oil. To keep the cookware properly seasoned, spread a little vegetable oil onto the sides and bottom with a paper towel after each use.

Acids in food react with copper to create a toxin, so copper cookware is lined with a thin layer of tin. Instead of scouring, which can destroy the lining, wash pots and pans with warm water and dishwashing liquid and soak in the same solution, if necessary, to remove baked-on food. Clean the copper exterior of the cookware with a solution of white vinegar and salt, then rinse and polish. Or use a commercial copper cleaner, which can reduce the need for elbow grease considerably.

Machine- or hand-wash stainless-steel pots and pans with detergent and water as soon as possible after use to reduce the chance of staining. Don't use scouring powder or steel wool, which may scratch surfaces and leave them prone to staining, and don't leave stainless-steel pans to soak for long periods, because mineral salts in the water may cause them to pit. Use a stainless-steel cleaner to remove stains on the outside of a pot or pan. Excessive heat causes bluish stains to appear on stainless steel. You can't remove these, so take preventive measures by never turning the heat beneath a stainless-steel pot or pan too high and making sure that a pot or pan you are using covers a gas burner completely so flames can't crawl up the side.

Copper

Copper objects and fixtures are often plated only with a very thin layer of copper and are often lacquered so they maintain a shine. As a result, you'll want to use the gentlest cleaning method possible so you don't rub through the plating or peel away the lacquer. Just go over lacquered copper with a cloth or sponge that's been dampened in a solution of mild detergent and warm water, then rinse and buff dry with a clean cloth.

Copper that hasn't been lacquered tends to tarnish and require more cleaning. You can use a commercial copper cleaner; a brand of cleaner that you simply rub off rather than wash off is handy for handles, locks, and other copper pieces that can't readily be rinsed or submersed. You can also use a paste made of equal parts salt and flour moistened with white vinegar (leave it on until it dries) or lemon juice. Rinse with cold water, then polish with a soft cloth. If copper is unlacquered, you may want to spray or brush on two coats of a transparent metal lacquer to prevent tarnishing and make cleaning easier.

Coral

The safe way to clean jewelry and other objects made from this porous material is to wipe it occasionally with a damp chamois cloth. You can harm coral by cleaning it with any kind of chemical solution or even immersing it in water.

Corduroy

To protect corduroy's distinctive pile, wash a garment or anything else made of this fabric inside out, following instructions on the care label carefully. Iron inside out while still damp, then smooth the pile in the correct direction with a soft cloth.

Cork

Cork floors and walls are almost always sealed, waxed, or coated with a vinyl finish to prevent water and dirt from penetrating their porous surfaces. As a result, they're quite easy to clean. Mop or sponge sealed cork regularly with only hot water, and clean it once a month with a solution of one part rubbing alcohol and 10 parts water. Buff occasionally with a dry mop or cloth. Go over vinyl-finished cork with a damp mop or sponge as needed, and occasionally apply emulsion polish. Simply sweep or dust waxed cork, and treat with a solvent-based cleaning wax as needed. When waxing and polishing a cork floor, try to avoid leaving a buildup around the edges of the room that can become sticky and attract dirt. Use the back of a knife blade to remove it.

Scrub a fishing-rod handle made of cork with a washcloth dipped in soapy water, rinse, and dry with a towel.

Correction fluid spills

Let the fluid dry before attempting to clean it up. Then use your fingernails, a credit card, or a blunt knife edge to remove it. Any stain that remains on clothing should come out in the wash or during dry cleaning. You may, however, need to shampoo carpeting or upholstery or have it professionally cleaned to remove the fluid stain. Use rubbing alcohol to remove correction fluid that is smudged onto the flatbed of a copying machine; never scrape it because you can scratch the glass, which in turn will distort the appearance of copies.

Cotton

A "natural" product of the cotton plant, cotton is absorbent and comfortable, and helps keep you cool when it's hot. The wide range of cotton fabrics includes canvas, chintz, corduroy, denim, gabardine, jersey, lace, muslin, organdy, percale, poplin, seersucker, ticking, and voile.

Cotton wrinkles easily and may shrink, but cotton fabrics are usually washable, iron well, and are not vulnerable to moths.

Cotton-polyester fabric combines qualities of both cotton and polyester in different proportions according to purpose and manufacturer. It's more wrinkle-resistant than cotton and breathes better than polyester, so it's more comfortable. But it can pill and is more likely to stain than cotton alone.

Cotton fabrics are usually washable and can be dry-cleaned, but read care instructions on labels carefully. Unless a garment or other item made from cotton is "pre-shrunk," it may emerge from the wash several sizes smaller if you use anything but cool water. Cotton-polyester should be washed on the Permanent Press cycle. Wash similar colors together, especially reds and other darks, because cotton tends to lose its color in water. Chlorine bleach is safe for white cottons, but use color-safe bleach on dyed cottons. To maintain shape, it's best to air-dry cotton on a line, but if you must use a clothes dryer, set the machine for air-drying or very low heat. Use the Permanent Press setting for cotton- polyester, and turn garments inside out to reduce pilling. Since 100 percent cotton is not easily scorched, you can press it with an iron set to high. Sometimes 100 percent cotton fabric is treated with a wrinkle-resistant finish.

Countertops

Sponges, dishcloths, and cleaning rags are havens for germs and bacteria, so using them to clean countertops can leave more bacteria behind than were originally there. Using paper towels to clean countertops can help to avoid this. Thaw food in the refrigerator rather than on the countertop to keep from breeding food-borne bacteria. Specific care, cleaning, and disinfection directions will vary according to the material from which the countertop is made. For individual materials, see **Butcher block**, page 43; **Ceramic tile**, page 48; **Granite countertops**, page 85; **Laminated countertops**, page 92; **Marble**, page 98; **Slate**, page 126, **Solid-surface synthetic countertops**, page 128; **Stainless-steel countertops**, page 129.

Curtains

Dust curtains and drapes regularly with your vacuum cleaner's soft brush attachment or with a soft, long-handled brush with synthetic fibers (they're much better than natural fibers at collecting dust). If you use a vacuum cleaner, set it for reduced suction so you don't draw the fabric into the nozzle. You might want to place a stiff piece of plastic screen between the nozzle and the fabric to prevent this from happening. If you can take curtains and drapes down and rehang them with relative ease, occasionally air them outdoors on a clothesline or put them in a clothes dryer set to the No-Heat or Delicate cycle.

Before cleaning your curtains and draperies, read care instructions carefully to determine whether you can wash them or if you should have them dry-cleaned. Even if they are made of washable fabric, the linings and the threads used in sewing may shrink in water. Play it safe and opt for dry cleaning if you are in doubt. Definitely dry-clean curtains and drapes with stitched-in pleats, swags, or other elaborate ornamentation that may not withstand a washing. You can freshen up vel-vet draperies without washing them or dry cleaning them; just brush them from time to  time with a chamois cloth dipped in hot water and wrung out thoroughly.

Constant exposure to sunlight can render even sturdy fabrics fragile. So when machine-washing curtains and draperies, use the Gentle cycle, cool or lukewarm water, and mild detergent. If possible, hang on a clothesline to dry, or put them in a dryer on a No-Heat or Delicate setting. If instructions call for hand washing, as is often the case with silk fabrics, do so in lukewarm or cool water and use mild dishwashing detergent. Swish gently and never twist or wring.

Wash so-called sheers on a regular basis even if they don't appear to be soiled because by the time dirt appears they can be permanently discolored. Clean these fragile fabrics gently. Make sure they fill no more than half the machine, and let them soak for five minutes in cold water. Use a mild detergent and, if you wish, a whitening agent. Turn the dial to Rinse to drain the water, then run the machine on a Gentle wash setting for just two to three minutes. (To restore stiffness to sheer curtains, you can also soak them in a solution of 1 teaspoon starch to 1 quart of water.) Put the sheers and a couple of terry-cloth towels in a dryer set to no heat for another two to three minutes. Rehang while still slightly damp, and pull into shape. If necessary, move an ironing board next to the window and iron the hems while the curtains or draperies are hanging.

Be careful when washing fiberglass curtains or draperies because fiberglass fragments can break off. Wear rubber gloves to protect your hands, and try not to twist or wring the fabric if you are washing the curtains or draperies by hand. If you use a washing machine, clean it out afterward by running it through a full cycle with detergent while empty.

Curtain and drapery cords and rods

When laundering curtains and draperies, take the opportunity to clean cords and rods, too. You should usually be able to clean these while they are still in place.

Tips for Washing Curtains

Here are some ways to make the task easier and to ensure the results reward your efforts:

- Measure curtains before washing in case you need to stretch them back into shape. Be sure to remove hooks and any weights, and loosen the tapes so they lie flat.

- Before washing, dust curtains by running them through a dryer set to the No-heat cycle. Or shake them out, lay them on a bed, and dust them off with the vacuum brush attachment.

- Don't overload the washing machine, and remember that curtains will become much heavier when wet.

- If hand washing, don't rub or wring the fabric; just agitate it gently.

- Try to dry curtains over two parallel lines so wet surfaces don't touch. Don't let the curtains rest on wood, which may stain them.

- Iron while damp along the vertical length on the side that doesn't show. If parts of the fabric have already dried, dampen the entire curtain again to avoid water marks.

- Stretch seams gently while ironing to avoid puckering, then spread the curtains out on a clean surface, such as a bed, and pull them to the correct size.

- When curtains are dry, insert hooks and weights, and pull the tape to the correct width.

- Before rehanging the curtains, clean valances fixed to the wall. Vacuum an upholstery valance with the upholstery attachment and a wooden valance with the crevice tool; clean a plastic valance with a sponge dipped in a solution of liquid detergent and water.

- Rehanging is easiest when one person stands on a ladder to insert the hooks and another stands below to make sure the curtains don't drag on the floor.

Don't dampen cords because they can shrink. Just run a dust cloth over them instead. Dust surfaces around and behind the rods with the crevice-tool attachment of the vacuum cleaner or with a long, soft brush.

Since brass rods are almost always treated with a protective coating of lacquer, you only need to dust them with a clean cloth. Do the same for wooden rods, then apply a light coat of furniture polish, making sure you rub it in well so fabric that comes in contact with it doesn't absorb residue.

Place a plastic sheet on the floor beneath plastic rods, then use a sponge or clean cloth to wash them with liquid detergent and warm water and rinse with cold water. (If the rods are quite dirty, you may want to take them down and soak them in soapy water before washing them.) Remove gliders and soak them in soap and water, then rinse. Once the rods are clean and dry, spray the channel of the tracks with WD-40 or another general-purpose lubricant and allow it to dry before re-hanging the curtains.

Cushions

To give loose cushions a fresh look, frequently remove the covers, if possible, and launder them; make sure you follow the care instructions for the type of fabric. You should also clean the cushions themselves regularly, washing them or having them dry-cleaned, depending on the material from which they are made.

Washing removes natural oils from feathers and down, so you should always have cushions made from these materials dry-cleaned. Hang them outdoors on a clothesline at least once a year to air.

It's generally safe to machine wash polyester-filled cushions; read the care instructions on the label. Use the Delicate cycle, lukewarm water, and mild detergent. Dry the cushions thoroughly to prevent mildew by setting them out to air-dry for a couple of days or machine-drying for two or three hours on a medium setting.

Decks

Lumber, like skin, doesn't fare well unprotected. The sun's ultraviolet rays are always on the attack, breaking down lignin, the polymer in wood that gives it rigidity. Rain and sun alternately swell and dry wood, eventually causing it to crack and split. Moisture promotes the growth of mold and mildew. And dirt lodges between wood fibers and sticks to treatments (coatings) you may apply.

Before applying a treatment to a new deck, be sure that its moisture level is stabilized (usually about a month after installation). Older decks must be cleaned of mildew and dirt before being treated. Clean and treat older decks at least once every three years—more often if you are using a clear product. To determine if small black spots are mildew, drop full-strength household bleach on one; if it disappears after a minute or two, it's mildew. To eliminate mildew on a larger area, use 2 to 3 ounces of TSP (trisodium phosphate) household liquid bleach or a phosphate-free substitute mixed with a gallon of water. Use a stiff brush to scrub the area, and rinse it after 15 minutes.

For routine cleaning of decks to remove dirt and mildew (or on new decks, to remove mill residue), wash with oxygen-based bleach from the paint store, applied with a pump sprayer. For redwood and cedar, use oxalic acid deck cleaner rather than bleach to remove graying and stains. Follow the instructions and cautions on the label. After cleaning, allow the deck to dry for 72 hours, then treat it.

Removing Stains and Discolorations From a Deck

Scrub immediately with a detergent that contains a degreasing agent. Set-in stains may require light hand-sanding with very fine sandpaper. The sanded area will stand out at first but will weather to match the surrounding wood. Commercial deck-cleaning agents—powders or liquid concentrates—from a home center or hardware store have a base of chlorine bleach, nonchlorine bleach, or oxalic acid and may include detergent. Bleach-based products eliminate mildew and graying. Acid-based products eliminate graying and some stains. Some products may darken such woods as redwood and cedar, so be sure to test any material in an inconspicuous place.

Deck-treatment products may be solvent- or water-based, and some are applied in a two-step process: a base coat followed by a top coat within a year. There are several main categories of deck-treatment products.

• Clear finishes are generally water-repellent, but they usually don't protect from ultraviolet and visible light. They let the wood's natural grain show through and allow the wood to turn gray. Few clear finishes resist mildew effectively. Expect to clean the wood and reapply the finish annually.

• Toned finishes contain color pigments that help block ultraviolet light. They enhance the wood's color but may allow the wood to turn gray. Semitransparent finishes are more opaque and contain pigments that help block ultraviolet and visible light. The wood grain is somewhat masked. For both toned and semitransparent finishes, expect to clean the wood and reapply the finish every two to three years.

• The longest-lived products are opaque finishes, which contain pigments that help block ultraviolet and visible light. Opaque finishes mask the wood grain entirely. Expect to clean the wood and reapply the finish every three to four years.

CONSUMER REPORTS tests have found that semitransparent and opaque products perform the best overall, clear finishes the worst by far, and toned products somewhere in the middle. Over time, solvent-based products lose their initial advantage over water-based finishes.

Consider the deck appearance you want and how often you intend to renew the finish. But be sure the treatment claims to kill mildew and inhibit ultraviolet light.

Denim

Most denim is pre-shrunk; if not, it is vulnerable to shrinkage. Before you launder denim, check the label for the appropriate temperature. Wash the item separately until you are sure the color no longer bleeds. Wash jeans inside out to avoid streaky lines. Iron while very damp.

Dentures

Clean dentures twice daily, using a commercial denture cleaner or soap and warm water. Do not use toothpaste, which scratches the pink plastic, removes the high gloss of the "teeth," and makes future cleaning more difficult. Dentures are fragile when not held in place by the jaw. Grasp one side at a time rather than holding them in the palm of your hand, which makes it possible to squeeze them and snap the "horseshoe" shape. Also, the dentures will become slippery as you clean them, so work over a basin filled with water; if you drop them, they'll be cushioned by the water rather than hit a hard surface. Use a toothbrush that you reserve for this purpose. Scrub the dentures up and down, taking special care with areas that touch the cheek, palate, and gums.

Diamonds

Swish around in a solution of 1 tablespoon of ammonia and 1 cup of hot water. Then dip in rubbing alcohol and pat dry with tissue paper. Or use a commercial jewelry cleaner, following the instructions on the bottle.

See also **Jewelry,** page 89.

Dishes

With hand washing, you can complete the entire operation in one period of time, with less potential damage to your tableware (unless you drop something, of course). Machine washing provides a sense of convenience and gets dishes out of the way quickly, but later you have to unload the machine and put dishes away. And fine tableware and glassware can suffer subtle or more obvious harm in an automatic dishwasher.

Hand washing. Start by filling the sink with very hot water and adding a squirt of dishwashing liquid. Using a sponge or a dishcloth, wash the least-soiled items (usually glasses and flatware) first, followed by plates and bowls, then serving dishes, and finally pots and pans. Avoid using scrub pads that are very abrasive, except when washing pots and pans, which may need them; for newer non-stick materials, consult the manufacturer's instructions, which may advise cleaning with a nonabrasive sponge and sometimes even without detergent. Then rinse. Air drying is the most sanitary method, but wiping with a towel prevents spotting. Flatware and dishes with stuck-on foods—such as flour-based mixtures, eggs, milk, rice, pasta, or corn—may need a longer soaking.

Machine washing. If you don't rinse before you load—which is usually unnecessary—a dishwasher uses no more water than hand washing with a double sink and less than you would use washing dishes under a running faucet.

Over time, dishes may chip, the pattern may fade, or the glaze may develop tiny cracks on the surface. You can prolong the life of tableware by washing the following by hand: delicate, heat-sensitive items; wooden items; glass or china with a metal trim; cut glass; lacquered items; and antique china. Don't put

Dishwasher Tips

- The Rinse and Hold option can be useful for small households. Rather than stack dirty dishes in the dishwasher, gradually accumulate a full load, rinsing as you go.

- A Pots and Pans cycle won't clean as well as abrasive cleaners and elbow grease.

- Think twice before subjecting good crystal or china—especially china with gold trim—to your dishwasher's China/Crystal setting. Harsh detergents and jostling can etch or otherwise damage fine items.

- No-heat air drying uses retained heat and evaporation and produces reasonably dry dishes, but it takes a few hours. To speed drying, try propping the door open.

- Load flatware with the points down to avoid cutting yourself on a knife or a fork as you reach into the dish rack.

- The heating element can inflict a serious burn. Be sure it has cooled before you reach into the bottom of the tub to clean a filter or retrieve an item.

- Keep children away while the dishwasher is running. Door vents, often at a toddler's eye level, can emit steam. Some electronic models have a hidden touch pad that locks the controls so children can't play with them.

stainless-steel and silver items in the same basket or let them touch each other. A chemical reaction may cause the silver to become pitted.

Load the dishes so the sprayers can get to the soil: Don't crowd items; don't let large pieces block smaller ones; and don't overload. Consult your manual for specifics. Also check the manual to see if it's necessary to rinse or scrape dishes. The water should be at least 120° F. (If you'd like, check the temperature with a food thermometer placed in a glass of water from the dishwasher. Just let the dishwasher run for a minute or so before you do this.)

Use only detergent made for dishwashers. If you have a problem with spotting, ask your water utility if the water in your area is hard. If so, increase the amount of dishwasher detergent, or use a rinse agent (such as Jet-Dry).

Fancy controls don't necessarily mean better cleaning. Most machines, electronic or not, work quite well overall. Most use their water-heating element to dry the dishes; some have a blower or separate, duct-mounted heater. Whatever the method, your machine should do at least a good job of washing and drying china and dishes; some machines don't do a very good job of drying flatware.

To get the most out of your machine, make sure you understand all of its settings:

- The Normal or Regular cycle of a dishwasher typically includes two washes interspersed with two or three rinses.
- A Heavy cycle can entail longer wash periods, a third wash, hotter water, or both of the above.
- A Light cycle usually means just one wash.

Although additional options are available, these three are probably all that are needed. A final "sanitizer" cycle with extra-hot water doesn't serve much purpose; once you put "sanitized" dishes into the cupboard, household microbes quickly settle onto them.

Dishwashers

Don't use abrasives or scouring powders on the interior or exterior of a dishwasher.

Clean the exterior with a clean sponge dampened in plain water or water with a bit of dishwashing liquid; then use a clean, damp sponge to rinse it off. To remove built-up dirt, spray glass cleaner onto a sponge and then apply the sponge to the exterior dishwasher. (Spraying it on directly may damage the controls.)

If there is discoloration in the interior or around the door as a result of hard water or too much dishwasher detergent, use a product made for cleaning dishwashers. Or put a clean bowl filled with 2 cups of white vinegar in a central location inside the dishwasher and run it on a regular cycle without detergent or a heated dry cycle. Repeat if necessary.

Dolls

Many cloth dolls or stuffed animals can be washed in a washing machine. Some dolls that can't be machine-washed can be cleaned with upholstery shampoo or dry-cleaning fluid. But don't use those products to clean a soft doll that a young child might put in his or her mouth.

If a doll's hair is integral and not glued on, you can wash it with shampoo. Do not use conditioner, which can leave residue. Never wash a doll's hair if it is gauze-mounted with glue.

Test doll clothes for colorfastness. Hand-wash them in a mild solution of 2 tablespoons of laundry detergent and 1 gallon of water. Rinse the clothes thoroughly, and lay them on a towel to air-dry.

A valuable antique doll or any doll with a "fabric" body should be cleaned by a professional. Repair of damage to the hair, body, or eyes of any doll also requires professional help.

You can clean a bisque-porcelain doll face with a cotton ball dipped in a mild detergent solution. Be gentle, and don't get water on the cloth part of the doll.

Rub a wax doll with a cosmetic cold cream, wipe it off with a clean cloth, and polish with a soft cloth. To clean a vinyl doll (one with rubbery skin), remove the clothing, put a small amount of nonabrasive, nonbleach cleaner on a cloth, rub it on the doll, then wipe it off with a clean, damp cloth. Don't scrub too hard or you may rub off the doll's features.

Clean a rag doll according to the label. Many can be machine-washed, but put it in a mesh bag if it has hair.

Door mats

For indoor door mats, use an upright vacuum cleaner or canister vacuum's power nozzle with a beater bar to get deep-down grit. You can hose off exterior door mats that are made to be exposed to the elements.

Drains

The best option for do-it-yourself drain care is prevention. However, if you're confronted with a clogged drain, try using a plunger. Fill the sink or toilet with water and try to get as little air under the plunger as possible. Plungers work fine on soft, fatty kitchen clogs but not so reliably on bathroom blockages, which may be composed of facial tissue, soap, toothpaste, human hair, and toilet tissue.

Or try using a plumber's auger, known as a "snake." This device is more versatile than a plunger, since it can both break up a greasy clog in the kitchen and snag clumps of hair in a bathroom blockage. Plus the snake alone can remove all or part of a blockage, so the clog won't be worked loose only to cause trouble farther down the drain.

You may need help turning a snake while feeding it into the pipe, and the openings it must thread through may be too small to accommodate it. Also, it may not fit through the trap

Maintaining Free-flowing Drains

Take some simple measures to keep drains throughout your house flowing freely.

• Use strainers in all your sinks.

• Kitchen clogs are generally a buildup of vegetable scraps and congealed fats. Avoid pouring grease down a kitchen sink.

• Bathroom drains tend to clog with soap scum and hair. Use a hair trap (available in hardware stores) in bathtub and sink drains. These simple devices also capture soap, skin oils, and other residues that can contribute to buildup in a drain.

• Periodically clean or replace the drain-plug mechanism in your bathtub and sinks.

• Once a week, pour a gallon of boiling water down the kitchen drain—half a kettle at a time—to break up the grease.

below the sink, though it can fit in the open pipe once the trap is removed. Don't use a snake with a garbage disposal.

If the drain is still clogged, call a plumber. CONSUMER REPORTS is reluctant to recommend a chemical cleaner for tackling a clot or preventing blockages. The powerful ingredients in such cleaners can cause serious harm if they are inhaled or touch the skin or eyes, and if the cleaner doesn't dislodge the clog, you'll have a corrosive mess to clean up.

Biological treatments are mainly useful as preventive measures and must be applied regularly.

See also **Drain cleaners,** page 168.

Dried flowers

Frequently blow dust off with a hair dryer set on low. If the flowers are still dusty, place them in a bag with salt and cornmeal. Gently shake the bag, then remove the flowers and dust them with a hair dryer. Apply a little hair spray to protect them.

See also **Artificial flowers**, page 31.

Dryers, clothes

Wash the exterior, usually made of baked enamel, with a solution of mild detergent and water, then wipe with a damp sponge; or use any all-purpose cleaner without abrasives.

When lint collects in the filter, it causes the machine to operate inefficiently, and accumulated lint is a fire hazard; so clean the lint filter every time you run the machine. Use a vacuum-cleaner crevice tool to occasionally clean lint from the area around the filter and to clean the dryer's hot-air hose. Wipe the inside of the dryer from time to time with a cloth lightly dampened with a solution of mild detergent and water. Check your dryer's maintenance manual for specific instructions. Periodically check dryer ducts and remove any buildup of lint. Replace the filter as advised by the manufacturer.

Duvets

Use a duvet cover to protect the casing from body moisture and spills. When you use a cover, you will need to clean a duvet only infrequently—say, once every two to four years. Occasionally air a duvet outside in the sun. If that's not practical, drape it over the footboard of the bed or over the backs of two chairs.

To avoid staining, immediately blot up spills that fall on the casing. Shake the feathers or synthetic filling out of the stained area, tie it off with a string, and treat it with the stain-removal method suitable for the fabric. See page 246.

For cleaning a down duvet, first check the care label; some recommend dry cleaning only, while others strongly advise against it. For machine washing, use a gentle soap and a gentle wash cycle.

For duvets filled with synthetic material, follow the care instructions. Most can be washed in a washing machine. If the duvet is too large for your machine, take it to a coin laundry or have it dry-cleaned. Or you can hand wash it in the bathtub, using a mild soap-and-water solution. Rinse it thoroughly, then hang it outside to dry over two or three parallel clotheslines. Dry it in a clothes dryer if the instructions permit.

Duvet covers

Duvet covers—removable outer coverings that protect the duvet casing and keep it clean—should be washed according to the care label. Wash dark-colored ones separately a few times or until you are sure they are colorfast. A blended fiber cover (such as cotton-polyester) won't need ironing if it is folded promptly. Others should be ironed when slightly damp, then aired thoroughly before being put back on the duvet.

DVD players

Wipe off dust with an anti-static dusting cloth. Use a cloth dampened with rubbing alcohol to remove fingerprints. Keep disc compartments closed to prevent dust from collecting inside these devices. Follow the manufacturer's instructions to remove dust that might accumulate.

DVDs (Digital video disks)

While DVDs are quite sturdy, large amounts of dirt and oil can affect sound quality or tracking. Handle carefully, touching nothing but the edge or center of a disc, and return to the case after each use. As needed, dust with a soft, clean cloth. If you notice fingertips or dirt on the surface, wipe them off with a cloth dampened in mild detergent and dry with a lint-free cloth. You can also use special cleaning products sold in electronics stores. When cleaning or dusting DVDs, work in straight lines from the center, never in a circular motion.

Earthenware

Wash glazed earthenware with hot water and a squirt of dish-washing liquid. To remove difficult stains, soak the item in hot water, then use a plastic scrub pad.

Season unglazed earthenware pots before use by soaking them in water, which prevents food juices from being absorbed. Wash in hot water. Never use detergent. Soak in hot water if the food is difficult to remove. Never scour an unglazed surface.

Ebony

Water may damage ebony. Regularly dust it and then rub it well to retain its shine. Very occasionally, apply a little cream furniture polish.

Enamel

Aluminum, cast-iron, or pressed-steel pans and baking dishes covered with enamel can be washed by hand or in the dish-washer. Avoid abrasive cleaners and scrub pads because enamel scratches easily. When washing enamel-coated pans, always do so in a plastic pan in the sink, since the enamel may chip. If the inside of the pan becomes stained, soak it in water with a tablespoon of chlorine bleach for a few hours, then wash normally. This should only be done occasionally, since the bleach may remove the protective glaze from the enamel.

To clean enamel-covered teapots, fill with a solution of 1 quart of water and ¼ cup of bleach, and let soak overnight. Rinse thoroughly with hot water.

See also **Cloisonné**, page 52.

Eyeglasses

For a quick cleaning, use cold water to rinse dust off lenses and wipe dry with a facial tissue. Never try to rub dirt off the lenses when they are dry, since this can scratch them. For a thorough cleaning, dip the glasses in a small bowl containing cold water and a drop of dishwashing liquid. Wipe dry with a facial tissue.

Fans

Clean fan housings with a damp cloth and an all-purpose cleaner, or a cloth dampened with a solution of water and mild detergent. Don't let liquid get into the motor.

Dirty fan blades don't move air efficiently. When cleaning the blades, be careful not to bend them; bent blades may vibrate when the fan is operating.

Attic (whole-house) fans. Brush and vacuum the louvers and screening at least once a season for maximum airflow.

Ceiling fans. Clean these difficult-to-reach fans at least once a season. A special tool—a long-handled, U-shaped brush—is available from hardware stores and home centers. The blade fits in the inner part of the U, so both sides can be cleaned at the same time. Two or three times a year, wash the blades and housing with a damp cloth and an all-purpose cleaner or a mild solution of water and mild detergent. Dry thoroughly because damp blades attract dust.

Exhaust fans. Dust these with a vacuum-cleaner brush or a damp cloth. If the fan covers can be removed, twice a year wipe down the blades and other nonelectric parts with a cloth sprayed with or dipped in an all-purpose cleaner and clean or replace the filter.

Floor and window fans. Dust regularly on both sides of the grille using a vacuum-cleaner brush attachment, or a lamb's wool duster. Clean blades and inner workings with a hair dryer or a can of compressed air. If the grilles can be removed, hose them down or put them under the shower two or three times a year; scrub with a brush to remove dirt. Clean blades and other plastic parts with a cloth sprayed with or dipped in an all-purpose cleaner. The blade shaft may need lubricant.

Fax machines

Check the manual. For most machines, it's recommended that you dust the housing with a dry cloth and remove visible grime with a cloth moistened with rubbing alcohol. Use rubbing alcohol to clean the scanning glass and document rollers.

Use adhesive cellophane tape to pick up any debris. Fax machines use various printing technologies that require different cleaning procedures for the printing mechanism. For an inkjet fax machine, see **Inkjet printers,** page 88. For fax machines that use toner, the cleaning procedure varies from model to model. The printheads on fax machines that use thermal paper can be cleaned with swabs moistened with rubbing alcohol.

Feathers

Frequently blow dust off of feathers with a hair dryer set on low. If the feathers are still dusty, place them in a bag with a mixture of salt and cornmeal. Gently shake the bag, then remove the feathers and dust them with a hair dryer. Some feathers can be washed in warm water, rinsed, then gently blown dry with a hair dryer.

Fireplace irons

When the irons have cooled down after a fire, wipe off any wood ash or coal dust and soot with a damp cloth. To prevent rust, rub the tips of the irons with mineral oil. Wipe brass implements with a damp cloth and let them air-dry. Scrub engraved brass with a soft toothbrush dipped in an all-purpose cleaner. Use a soft cloth to polish. Remove tarnish with a commercial brass cleaner.

Fireplaces

For general maintenance, sweep out built-up ashes and debris. Use a brush to get dust off the brick- or stonework surrounding a hearth.

To clean a brick fireplace, scrub with a hard brush and clean, warm water. If that is not enough, scrub with white vinegar and wipe with a sponge dipped in warm water. Don't use soap or detergent, which may seep into the bricks. For stained bricks, scrub with a strong ammonia solution and rinse with warm water. Or clean them with a commercial preparation made for this purpose.

Wipe ceramic tile, when cool, with mild liquid detergent and water. Remove scorch marks with a nonabrasive all-purpose cleaner applied with a cloth—a brush might damage the glaze.

Rub stubborn marks off marble with mild detergent and water and a soft scrubbing brush. Rinse with warm, clean water. Wipe with a soft cloth and buff until dry.

Sponge a stone fireplace with clean warm water. Where soiling is heavy, use a scrub brush and mild detergent. Don't use soap or scouring powder, which may change the color of the stone. Scrub a soiled stone fireplace with a bleach solution (1 cup to a bucket of water); be sure to cover and protect the surrounding surfaces. Or rub a paste of powdered stone over the stains and leave for about an hour. Scrub off with a soft brush and hot water.

Flatware

Stainless-steel flatware is so easy to clean and maintain that it's often the choice for everyday use. To prevent acids and salts in foods from pitting stainless steel, rinse as soon as possible after use, then machine- or hand-wash with detergent and hot water. Occasionally buff stainless steel when dry with a clean cloth to restore its shine.

Stainless steel is somewhat vulnerable to scratching, which in turn diminishes its stain resistance. Don't use scouring powder or steel wool on stainless steel. Use a commercial stainless-steel cleanser and polish as needed to remove scratches and stains and restore shine.

You can safely hand-wash sterling-silver flatware, but do so with care. Don't wash sterling and stainless steel together; a chemical reaction can cause the sterling to become pitted. Avoid lemon-scented cleaning products and detergents with chlorides, which can damage silver, and don't let detergent powder come in contact with it. The powder may cause pitting. When hand-washing, use mild detergent, rinse thoroughly, and dry immediately to prevent streaking.

Machine washing is generally not recommended for silver, but should you do so, rinse the silver first, and add less detergent than you normally would. Be sure to use a nonchlorine detergent, and, to avoid pitting, make sure the silver pieces don't touch any other metal.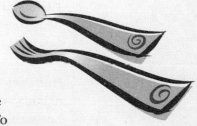

Remove the silver from the machine before the Dry cycle starts and hand-dry it with a soft cloth. To prevent tarnishing, store sterling silver immediately in a dry, airtight container lined with anti-tarnishing flannel. Remove tarnish regularly. It's easiest to use a polishing mitt or glove, but a silver paste does a better job with medium to heavy tarnish. Apply it with a damp sponge, and use a toothbrush to polish pieces that are deeply patterned. Buff with a dry cloth.

See **Silver**, page 124.

Foam-backed carpets

Use a steam-cleaning machine or a dry shampoo; do not get the backing wet. Use a double dry stroke. If you have central heating beneath the floor, don't buy a foam-backed carpet.

For more information about caring for your rugs, see **Carpeting**, page 239.

Freezers

For manual defrosting, empty the freezer. Follow the manufacturer's instructions. Turn the controls to Off and unplug the appliance. Leave the freezer door open, and place old towels on the freezer floor if it is a chest freezer or in front of the freezer if it is an upright model, replacing them as necessary. Use wood or plastic spatulas or a windshield ice scraper to scrape off ice that has thawed, but do not use sharp tools, which might damage the freezer. When defrosting is finished, empty any drip trays, dry the interior with a clean towel, then rinse with ¼ cup baking soda in 1 quart of water and dry again. Clean removable parts with detergent and water, then wipe dry. Apply a coating of nonstick spray inside your freezer to make future defrosting easier.

Wipe the freezer exterior with soapy water, then dry it with a cloth. An open container of baking soda keeps odors down in the freezer.

Furniture

While regular dusting will keep furniture relatively clean, different types of furniture require specialized care.

Iron furniture. An iron piece must be properly sealed by the manufacturer. To clean the piece without removing the seal, occasionally wipe it with a damp cloth or a mild solution of dishwashing liquid and water, and spray WD-40 on moving parts only. (Touch-up paint won't adhere to surfaces covered by WD-40.) Check with the manufacturer about removing stains and scratches. Remove any rust stains immediately with a wire brush and apply touch-up paint from the manufacturer. In winter, cover iron furniture and, ideally, store it inside.

Lacquered or polyurethane-sealed furniture. Dust as needed. Clean using a sponge dipped in warm soapy water. Rinse and wipe dry. If lacquer is peeling, the item will need stripping and relacquering. Avoid solvents and highly caustic products.

Leather furniture. Color may be applied to leather upholstery with a pigmented coating, which resists water based spills, or with an aniline dye, which is more vulnerable, meaning that stains should be treated immediately. The manufacturer's guidelines should specify how color has been applied and provide care instructions. If you're not sure, place a drop of water on a hidden location. If the drop doesn't soak in, the coating is pigmented; otherwise, it is aniline-dyed. For aniline-dyed leather, simply vacuum regularly, especially in crevices and along seams where dirt can gather. Pigmented leather should be vacuumed and wiped periodically with a soft, white cloth dampened with water. For both pigmented and aniline-dyed leather, once a year use saddle soap or other cleaner or a pol-

Leather Stains

Wipe up any spills on leather as quickly as possible. Typically, when water-based stains (ketchup, cola, coffee, grape juice, milk, and red wine) are blotted with a damp washcloth a minute or so after a spill, they disappear. But oil-based stains (crayon, ballpoint-pen ink, lipstick, Italian salad dressing, and cream shoe polish) do not come off. When applied in an effort to remove these stubborn stains, commercial leather cleaners are likely to remove some color. Since color is essentially painted onto pigmented leather, cleaning solvents, ink removers, and paint removers may remove it. To find a professional who can help, ask at the store where you bought the furniture, check the yellow pages, or ask a local dry cleaner. The cleaning will probably be costly, and the furniture will have to be removed from your home. Since removing dirt and stains can remove dyes, clean the entire piece to avoid mismatching colors.

ish made specifically for leather, following product directions and allowing it to dry. If the leather starts to crack, apply neat's-foot oil.

Painted wood furniture. Regularly dust a delicate decoupage or faux-painted piece, or one made of distressed wood, and wipe it occasionally with a barely damp cloth. If the wood has been sealed, dampen it with a sponge, and wipe dry. Apply furniture polish if desired, then buff.

Plastic laminated furniture. Furniture with a laminated plastic finish should be dusted regularly and occasionally wiped with a damp, soft cloth.

Redwood furniture. To clean, scrub with detergent and water, rinse with a damp sponge, and dry. Redwood should be sealed occasionally—after cleaning and possibly sanding—to keep out moisture and prevent cracking. If it has grayed, a wood-rejuvenation sealer can restore color. Remove grease and soot stains with a mixture of 1 cup of TSP (trisodium phosphate) in 1 gallon of water, then rinse. Cover and store for the winter.

Suede furniture. Suede is a vulnerable surface, not only because of the dyeing process but also because the material is

Choosing the Right Furniture Polish

Wood oil is recommended for wood furniture without a laminated plastic finish. But if you use furniture polish, it is important to understand that not all polishes are alike:

Aerosol. Typically silicone, best on hard surfaces, not for fine furniture.

Silicone cream. Similar to aerosol, meant especially for high-gloss furniture.

Cream. Often made up of wax, water, and oil emulsion.

Liquid wax. Contains natural and synthetic wax as well as a cleaning solvent.

Paste wax. Similar to liquid wax; may contain silicones. Apply sparingly, in small circles, and rub in the direction of the wood grain.

porous and quick to absorb stains. For routine care, gently brush suede furniture with a soft brush or a textured cloth, such as a towel, to remove dirt. Vacuum regularly, especially in crevices and along seams where dirt can be trapped. To clean a greasy stain, rub it with ground oatmeal, leave the oatmeal in place to absorb the grease, then brush it off and vacuum it. To raise the nap on a section of suede, brush it with a terry-cloth towel. If suede has been flattened by spills or wear and tear, only a professional leather refinisher can restore it.

Teak furniture. An oil-finished product, teak should be dusted regularly and cleaned with mild detergent. Oil occasionally with teak oil—annually for outdoor furniture, every two or three years for indoor furniture. Rub the oil on with a clean, soft cloth, leave overnight, and buff with another clean, soft cloth to remove excess.

Other wood furniture. You can use an appropriate wood oil every six months, although some of these can make surfaces sticky and more prone to fingerprints and dust. Do not use furniture polish, which may muddy the finish. Wax won't create, increase, or even protect the mirrorlike luster of a highly finished wood surface, like a piano top. Wax buildup can darken and mask the grain.

CONSUMER REPORTS tests have shown that a supermarket furniture cleaner isn't likely to protect a wood finish against common stains or even to remove new ones. But occasionally you do need a cleaner to remove smudges, fingerprints, and grease left from cooking (for homemade alternatives, see **Homemade cleaning products**, page 271). Whichever you choose, test on an inconspicuous area first, making sure it does not leave a film behind. Read the label carefully.

Dust antique wood furniture regularly with a soft cotton cloth. Wax (if appropriate) once or twice a year. Some dealers recommend waxing at the beginning and end of the heating season. Wax unfinished surfaces (under tables and inside highboys and other such pieces) so that the raw wood can absorb the wax and minimize the chance that it will crack or the veneer will lift. Don't use silicone polishes on antique furniture.

Helpful Hint

When possible, protect wood furniture from strong sunlight, temperature extremes, abrasive objects, and humid conditions. Place drinks on coasters.

Wood-Furniture Stain Removal Guide

A small amount of mild liquid detergent in water can effectively remove many stains. Test in an inconspicuous area to ensure it doesn't leave a film behind. For more stubborn stains, try the remedies presented below.

Stain	Treatment
Adhesive tape	Apply a little rubbing alcohol, then rub with a soft cloth moistened with a mild solution of dishwashing liquid. Dry and polish if necessary. Or try WD-40 or a citrus-based cleaner.
Alcohol	Rub on the grain with cream polish.
Burns, scorches	If the mark has bubbled or blackened, use a sharp knife to scrape the surface, then sand with extra-fine sandpaper. If the burn is deep, use wood filler, smoothing it to match the surface, then use a repair crayon to match the wood color. For cigarette burns, use the same procedure.
Candle wax	Carefully chip off any excess after hardening the wax with ice cubes. Use a hair dryer to soften the remaining wax. Rub with an absorbent soft cloth to remove excess.
Dents	Cover with several layers of brown wrapping paper and a damp cloth, and apply a warm, dry iron. Repeat until the wood swells and the dent disappears. Remove old polish, apply fresh polish, and buff. If furniture is veneered or is a badly dented antique, hire professional help.
Scratches	Try a product that claims to hide surface scratches. Or use a repair crayon. If these don't work, use wood filler stained to match the wood and apply a similar finish.
White marks	Wet glasses, alcohol, medicines, and perfume can cause white marks. Blot with an absorbent cloth, wipe with a damp cloth, then dry with a soft cloth. If the stain remains, rub in (with the grain) a little non-gel toothpaste or liquid or cream car polish. Wipe with a dry cloth and polish, if necessary. If the ring won't yield, you need a refinisher.

Furniture handles, locks, and knobs

Remove the hardware from the piece of furniture before cleaning so you don't damage the surrounding area. Wipe away all
residue, and dry the hardware thoroughly before replacing it.

Manufacturers apply a lacquer seal to brass or copper handles, locks, and knobs on wooden furniture to prevent tarnishing. Occasionally wipe these with a damp cloth, and buff with a
dry one. Restorers often apply lacquer-seal fittings on antique
furniture. For fittings made of unlacquered silver or gold-plated
bronze, use a silicone wax polish to protect them. If the lacquer
starts to peel or is damaged, remove it with a lacquer stripper,
then reapply.

Commercial polishing may be too harsh and can do harm
when what appears to be bronze is actually gilded brass that
is dirty. Clean gilded brass with a soft brush, removing the
dirt with a mix of equal parts acetone and alcohol. Dry it, then
polish with a jeweler's polishing cloth, using a little alcohol or
turpentine as a lubricant.

Fur rugs

Occasionally dust a fur rug with a soft brush or take it outside
and shake it. To brighten it, rub in an absorbent powder, such
as fuller's earth or cornmeal, leave the powder in for a couple
of hours, then take the rug outside and brush it with a soft
brush, or hang it on a clothesline and beat it gently with a tennis racket. Repeat several times if necessary. Or use a vacuum-
cleaner attachment with an old nylon stocking over the nozzle
to prevent the fur from being sucked up into the appliance. Or
wipe the rug with a damp sponge dipped in a mild detergent,
then brush it with a clean brush and allow it to dry. If the rug
is worn, delicate, or valuable, have it cleaned professionally.

Furs

Hang a fur coat on a well-padded hanger in a cotton bag, never
in plastic. Valuable furs should be put into cold storage during
the warm months. Periodically shake out a fur that isn't worn
regularly. If you are caught in the rain or snow, let the fur dry
on a hanger away from direct heat and light. If you spill something on fur, blot it up with a clean white towel and have the
garment professionally cleaned.

Futon covers

Futon covers—removable outer coverings that protect the futon casing and keep it clean—should be washed according to the care label. Wash dark-colored ones separately two or three times or until you are sure they are colorfast. A blended fiber cover (such as cotton-polyester) won't need ironing if it is folded promptly. Others should be ironed when slightly damp, then aired thoroughly before being put back on the futon.

Futons

Fabrics on futon casings vary—follow the manufacturer's care instructions. Most futons used in North America are as thick and substantial as a mattress and require similar care.

Turn a futon at least twice a year—alternately side over side and end over end. When you turn the futon, air it outside or near a window where sunlight comes in.

Use a mattress pad between the futon and the bottom sheet to absorb moisture. Launder the pad occasionally. Dust the futon when you change the pad, using the upholstery attachment of the vacuum cleaner or a stiff brush.

To remove a musty smell, sprinkle baking soda over the futon. Leave it undisturbed for 24 hours, then vacuum it away. Or use a commercial pet-stain and odor-removal product. For most stains, use a minimal amount of liquid upholstery cleaner. If possible, turn the futon on its side so it will not soak up too much liquid. Speed drying time by using a hair dryer. For urine stains, use a pet-odor-removal product.

If you have a futon that is lightweight and not very deep, loosely roll it up as often as possible—daily is best—so that air can circulate through it and moisture can dry out.

Putting on a Futon Cover, Made Easy

While some futon covers are user-friendly and open along more than one side, some open only along one of the long sides. If you have one of these, open the cover and turn it inside out. Place the long side of the inside-out cover (the side that doesn't contain the opening) next to one of the futon's long sides, and turn the cover right side out while drawing it around the futon.

Garbage disposal units

To avoid buildup, grind only small amounts at one time; run the unit whenever you put waste in it. Periodically leave it on for a few extra moments so the grinding totally empties it. (Always run water while a garbage disposal unit is turned on.) Most manufacturers suggest allowing the unit to run for 20 to 60 seconds after audible grinding is finished.

Break up grease deposits by occasionally grinding ice cubes, fruit pits, or small chicken bones.

Deodorize as needed by pouring ½ cup of baking soda into a sink filled halfway with water, turn on the disposal, and pull up the stopper. Or grind citrus peelings through the unit.

Garbage pails

You should probably have at least two pails to collect kitchen refuse—one for trash and another for recyclables. If you have a garden, it's nice to have a third pail to collect materials for composting. Line the pails with plastic bags. When the pails are empty, wipe them out with mild detergent and water. Use a plastic scrub pad on stubborn stains.

Glass beads

Put the beads in a shallow bowl and spray several with glass cleaner. Then dry them with a soft cloth. Repeat, cleaning several beads at a time, and making sure each bead is thoroughly dry. Buff gently to the desired shine. If beads are very soiled, soak them in water with a little ammonia and water. However, soaking may cause stringing material that's old or dry to weaken and break, so you may need to restring the beads.

Glassware

Wash everyday glassware in the dishwasher, but take care to load the machine carefully, particularly if the glass is thin, so items don't chip or break. Position wineglasses that have fragile stems so they won't be knocked about.

Etching of glassware—scratching that irreversibly mars the surface—is the result of a chemical reaction between the water, the glassware, the detergent—especially in areas with "soft" or "softened" water—and the heat of drying. To reduce the likelihood of this problem, use only a small amount of detergent,

experimenting with the quantity. Underload the dish-washer to permit proper rinsing and draining, and dry dishes without heat.

You should hand-wash crystal, other delicate glassware, and antique and cut glass separately from other dishes in warm water and a mild detergent. Wash these items in a plastic bowl to prevent chipping, and wear rubber gloves for a stronger grip. A few drops of ammonia in the water will help remove any stains. After washing, polish with a soft, lint-free cloth. Do not immerse gilt-edged and enameled glassware in water or clean it with ammonia. Just wipe items with warm, soapy water, rinse, and polish with a soft, lint-free cloth.

Gold jewelry

Soak for no longer than a minute in a solution of one part ammonia to six parts warm water. Or use mild detergent and water. Then clean with a facial tissue or a jewelry-polishing cloth. Rinse thoroughly in warm water, and wipe again. Do not use harsh or abrasive cleaning products.

Gold- and silver-plated finishes

Dust gold plate with a soft brush. Do not rub because the plating is usually very thin and soft, and can be worn off with rubbing. Wash gold-plated or gold-colored faucets and fixtures with warm water and mild detergent. Rinse with warm, clean water. Dry with a soft cloth after cleaning—and after use—to prevent marks from appearing. Do not use a commercial cleaner, which eventually will wear away the surface.

Gilded picture and mirror frames need frequent light dusting. Use a soft watercolor brush, the soft attachment of a vacuum cleaner, or a cotton swab. Occasionally gently wipe frames with a cloth dipped in warm water.

To remove discoloration from gilt, use a weak solution of water and ammonia applied with a soft cloth, being careful to not rub too hard. Rinse, air-dry, and polish gently. Art-supply shops sell wax gilt as a touch-up for small scratches or chips, but the color may not match perfectly. You may prefer to leave minor damage alone. If the frame is valuable or an antique, have a professional picture framer or restorer clean it.

Gold leaf, often used for picture frames, requires dusting only. You can use gold-leaf paint for a touch-up, but note that the color rarely matches precisely.

Carefully wash silver-plating in hot water with a few drops of mild detergent. Do not rub it too hard. Rinse and drain dry, then polish gently with a soft cloth.

Gore-tex

Dry-clean this breathable, waterproof fabric brand used for outdoor clothing and tents, or machine-wash it in warm water. Dry with medium heat. If the garment's outer shell is made of another fabric, follow the care instructions on the label.

Granite countertops

Granite is increasingly popular as a counter surface. It is very resistant to scratches, nicks, and scorching and, since a granite countertop is almost always treated with a protective seal, is easy to clean. Just go over it with a sponge dipped in water and mild detergent, and gently use a plastic scrub pad to remove stubborn surface dirt.

In bathrooms, wipe down granite surfaces frequently to minimize soap scum. If scum does build up, clean the surface with a special product sold just for this purpose or with a solution of ½ cup of ammonia and 1 gallon of water.

Granite floors

Granite floors scratch easily, so try to keep sand, dirt, and grit to a minimum by using door mats and area rugs. Go over the floor frequently with a dry dust mop. You can also vacuum occasionally, but use only the floor-nozzle attachment so you don't scratch the granite. Wipe up any spills immediately because liquids, especially oil and grease, can seep deep into the floor and leave a nasty stain. For regular cleaning, mop as necessary with detergent and warm water, making sure to mop up all the dirt you raise in the process; if you don't, any remaining dirt will sink back into the floor as the surface dries.

Handbags

Evening bags, usually made of delicate fabrics, should be professionally cleaned. When other fabric bags are new, treat them with a stain-repelling spray before using them. To remove common stains, use warm water and mild soap on a clean cloth, or use a spot-removing product. First thoroughly test the soap or the product in an inconspicuous area. If the fabric is washable, very dirty, and not too delicate, use a nailbrush and a solution of gentle laundry detergent. Scrape or wipe off the residue, then wipe the bag with a cloth and allow it to air-dry. You may need to use upholstery cleaner for some nonwashable bags.

Leather handbags and accessories are generally made of finished leather. Clean them once a year with saddle soap, lathering it into the leather with a damp cloth or sponge. Use another damp cloth to wipe away the lather. Wipe the item dry and use a leather conditioner.

Cleaning Caveat

Do not assume that the technician who does the annual or semiannual tune-up of your furnace changes the filters. This is generally considered to be a home-owner's responsibility.

Heating systems

If you have a forced-air system, change or wash the air filters regularly (see **Air cleaners**, page 192). A dirty filter can prevent proper airflow. Make sure the filter fits. It should occupy the entire filter cavity and prevent air from bypassing it. Vacuum the outside of the furnace or heat pump once every month or so. If there are radiators, clean them regularly to keep them at their optimal operating efficiency (see **Radiators**, page 113).

A furnace should be properly maintained. Consider a service contract that includes an annual inspection of your furnace. The service technician should check electrical connections and wiring and gas piping for deterioration and leaks.

Despite the improved efficiency and comfort of most new furnaces, it's generally more cost-effective to repair a furnace than replace it. But if a key component such as the heat exchanger or control module fails, you're probably better off replacing the furnace, especially if the unit is more than 15 years old. The average furnace typically lasts about 18 years.

Humidifiers

Humidifiers and cold-mist vaporizers may harbor molds and bacteria that trigger allergy symptoms. Ultrasonic models do not emit fine microorganisms but have been implicated in spraying fragments of bacteria and molds into the air. Clean all these items scrupulously and frequently, as the manufacturer directs. If you've misplaced the manufacturer's instructions, empty the appliance, rinse the tank with a solution of 1 table-spoon of chlorine bleach in 1 pint of water (or, for large units, 1 cup of bleach in 1 gallon of water), then rinse again with copious amounts of fresh water.

Steam vaporizers don't create mold and bacteria problems. However, you should clean them regularly to remove accumulated harmless but unsightly rust and mineral deposits, which can reduce efficiency and output. Rinse out these appliances before storing them.

Inkjet printers

If print quality deteriorates and the print cartridge isn't out of ink, follow the manual's maintenance instructions for using the cleaning cycle. If printing quality is still a problem, check the manual to see whether it's safe to clean the printhead manually with a soft, lint-free cotton cloth or with a cotton swab dipped in water.

Ironing boards

To keep moving parts flexible, use an all-purpose lubricant spray. Launder removable fabric covers occasionally. Put them back on the ironing board while damp (they may shrink), or replace them with new covers. Metalized covers are more effective than cotton in reflecting heat and speeding up ironing.

Irons (steam)

Follow the manufacturer's instructions for cleaning both the inside and the base of an iron. Descaling may be necessary if you live in an area where the water is hard. Your iron may have a built-in cartridge that needs to be changed when color-coding indicates a scale buildup. Use the product your manufacturer recommends.

Clean coated (nonstick) sole plates with a warm cloth and detergent. Do not use abrasives. Clean uncoated sole plates with metal polish, baking soda, or extrafine steel wool. If steam vents are clogged, use a cotton swab and warm soapy water, or water and vinegar. Remove melted plastic from the sole plate by ironing a piece of aluminum foil sprinkled with salt.

Helpful Hint

Sun keeps ivory from yellowing, but too much sun—and too much cold and soaking in water—can cause ivory to crack. Perfume and hair spray can cause discoloration.

Ivory

Dust ivory pieces regularly with a soft cloth, using a clean, soft toothbrush to reach into carved areas. Wipe such items as mirrors and hairbrushes with rubbing alcohol. Dry them with a soft cloth. Take care not to remove an original patina or coating. Hire a professional to care for valuable ivory objects that are soiled or discolored.

Jade

Add 1 tablespoon of ammonia to 1 cup of hot water. Place the jewelry in a cup, swish it around, and dry it immediately, using only a soft cloth. Jade scratches easily.

Jet

Never soak an object or a piece of jewelry made of jet in water or any chemical solution. Just wipe it with a damp soft cloth.

Jewelry

First check valuable or antique pieces to see if stones are loose or fittings are broken. Have a jeweler make any needed repairs and clean the pieces.

Jewelry made with some stones (amber, jet, amethyst, diamond, ruby, sapphire, and emerald that is not cracked) and with imitation gold and silver can be washed in a solution of mild dishwashing liquid and warm water. Wash the pieces in a bowl, not the sink, to prevent them from disappearing down the drain. If you wash more than one piece of jewelry at a time, don't allow them to come into contact while they are soaking.

After soaking the jewelry for a few minutes, brush an individual piece with an old, soft toothbrush, and dry it with a chamois cloth or facial tissue. Before discarding the water in which you've cleaned the jewelry, pour it through a sieve in case a stone has become dislodged from its setting. Avoid using bleach to clean jewelry because it may damage metal mountings.

The Mohs' Scale

Developed in the early 19th century and named after a German mineralogist, the Mohs' Scale is a measure of the hardness of stones and metals, which are assigned a rating from 1 to 10, from softest to hardest:

Stone	Rating
Diamonds	10
Rubies and sapphires	9
Emeralds and topaz	8
Garnets, tourmalines, and quartz	7
Coral, lapis lazuli, opal, pearl, and turquoise	6
Gold, silver, and platinum	$2\frac{1}{2}$ to 4

Stones rated 6 and lower are easily scratched. Gold, silver, and platinum, as their rating suggests, require the most care when cleaned, worn, or stored.

Helpful Hint

Use chamois cloth to clean jewelry because it's very soft and won't scratch. If chamois cloth is not available, facial tissue will do. Or purchase a special jewelry-cleaning cloth.

Do not use a chemical jewelry cleaner unless you are sure it will not discolor or take the lacquer off an individual piece. Test on a hidden area.

Cameos need special treatment and should not be washed or immersed in anything. Clean them with a soft brush dipped in a jewelry-cleaning solution. Never wash opals, turquoise, or pearls because water will damage them.

See also **Cloisonné**, page 52; **Diamonds**, page 64; **Enamel**, page 72; **Glass beads**, page 83; **Gold jewelry**, page 84; **Gold- and silver-plated finishes**, page 84; **Ivory**, page 88; **Jade**, page 89; **Jet**, page 89; **Mother of pearl**, page 100; **Onyx**, page 103; **Opal**, page 103; **Pearls**, page 107; **Platinum**, page 110; **Rubies**, page 117; **Sapphires**, page 118; **Silver jewelry**, page 125; **Turquoise**, page 135; **Wooden jewelry**, page 149; and **Zircon**, page 151.

Jute

A natural fiber, jute is most often woven into tote bags, rope, and rugs. Jute rugs have no pile and therefore trap very little dirt from regular traffic. Vacuum jute rugs periodically to remove dust.

Blot liquid spills from jute items immediately with a clean white cloth, working from the edges of the spill in toward the center. To remove stains, saturate the area with a mild detergent solution or white vinegar, then blot up immediately with a clean white cloth. Do not rub, which will damage the fibers. Test on an inconspicuous area first.

Kerosene heaters

Wipe a kerosene heater regularly with a damp cloth dipped in mild detergent. Make sure the wick is trimmed.

Keyboards (computer)

To remove dust and dirt from the keyboard, hold it upside down and brush between the keys with a soft watercolor brush or the soft-brush attachment of a vacuum cleaner. To remove visible dirt from the keyboard, shut down the computer, unplug the keyboard, and wipe with a soft, lint-free cloth lightly moistened with mild detergent and water or rubbing alcohol, or use a commercial keyboard wipe. Keep a dust cover on the keyboard when not in use to prevent dust from settling on it.

See also **Computers**, page 53; **Inkjet printers**, page 88; **Laptop computers**, page 93; **Monitors**, page 100; and **Mouse (computer)**, page 100.

Knives

Hand-wash kitchen knives. Even though many have plastic handles that stand up to machine washing, dishwasher detergent can pit the blades, and the machine's heat may cause wooden handles to crack. If handles and blades are made separately and glued together, machine washing may loosen the adhesive.

Never put bone, ivory, and other decorative handles in water. Wash only the blades with soap and water. Use a sharpening steel to keep a fine-edged knife in top shape, honing the edge with a few strokes before each use.

Wash knives with carbon-steel blades immediately after use. Also dry them right away or they will rust. Remove rust and stains with scouring powder you've rubbed onto a plastic scrub brush or scrub pad or a piece of cork.

Lace

Soak delicate white lace in a mild solution of cold water and borax (not bleach, which may damage it). Pin the lace, in the desired shape, to a pillow or a piece of heavy cloth before air-drying so it won't shrink or curl. Do not dry lace in the sun. If ironing is necessary, lay the lace face down on a cloth, put another cloth on top of it, and use the iron on top of that. To store and preserve white lace, wrap it in acid-free paper to prevent discoloration. Valuable or antique lace should be cleaned by a professional.

Lacquered items

Dust boxes, lamp bases, trays, and other lacquered items regularly, and occasionally wipe with a damp, soft cloth. Sometimes, serving pieces of silver, brass, and copper are lacquered to prevent abrasion through constant polishing or to eliminate the need to polish. Relacquer such items and metal lamp bases every five or 10 years, or when they start peeling. You can do relacquering at home, but note that a new coating may not hold if the previous one has not been completely stripped or if there is any trace of cleaner or fingerprints. Consider having a professional do it.

Laminated countertops

To preserve the appearance of laminated countertops, you need to exercise a little care when working on them. Laminates nick and cut easily, so you should never chop directly on them, and hot dishes and open flames can leave scorch marks. The advantage of laminated counters is that they are easy to clean. Simply sponge surfaces with warm water and mild detergent, and use a soft brush in a circular motion if the laminate has a textured surface. While cleaning, never allow standing water to remain on the countertop because it can seep through the seams or between the countertop and backsplash, weakening the material underneath.

To remove stains, apply white vinegar, full-strength detergent, or diluted bleach directly on the spot, leave for a few minutes, then rinse. A nonabrasive cleaning-type wax will help prevent further staining and will brighten up a laminate surface that is dull and worn-looking.

Lampshades

Dust or vacuum a lampshade regularly. Use a hair dryer or compressed air to get into tight spots if necessary.

Laptop computers

Unlike desktop computer monitors, the screens of laptops are not made of glass. They are easily damaged, and replacing them is expensive. Some can be cleaned with a barely moistened, soft, lint-free cloth, but follow the manufacturer's instructions in the manual.

See also **Computers**, page 53.

Laser printers

Clean the housing with a dry cloth moistened with rubbing alcohol. A toner spill is a health hazard. If you have to vacuum the printer, use a toner vacuum with a micro-toner filter. Follow instructions in the manual for checking the fuser wand and ozone filter. Use only alcohol to clean the plastic rollers. Rubber rollers can be cleaned with Goof Off, which is available from office supply stores. Caution: It can damage plastic parts.

Lawn mowers

The maintenance required for your model will be affected by its power source (gasoline or electricity) and whether it is a push or self-propelled lawn mower or a riding mower.

Push or self-propelled gas-powered mowers. Clean beneath the deck. According to manufacturers, built-up clippings interfere with airflow and hurt performance. Especially in damp conditions and at the end of the mowing season, disconnect the spark-plug wire and remove the clippings with a plastic trowel. Sharpen the blade at least once each mowing season. A dull blade tears grass rather than cutting it, and can cause the lawn to become diseased. Remove the blade and sharpen it with a file, which costs about $10, or pay a mower shop to do it. Once each mowing season, change the oil.

Drain a four-stroke engine's crankcase and refill it with the oil recommended in the owner's manual. Check the level before each mowing and add more if needed. Two-stroke engines require no oil changes. Clean or replace the air filter when it's dirty—as often as once each mowing season in dusty conditions. Some mowers have a sponge filter you can clean and re-oil, though most now use a disposable paper filter. Replace the spark plug when the inner tip has heavy deposits—sometimes as often as once a mowing season. A new plug makes for easier starts and cleaner running. At the end of the mowing season, be sure to store the mower properly. There are two ways to deal with gasoline remaining in the tank. With many mowers, you can drain the gasoline from the tank into an appropriate storage container and then run the engine to eliminate any gas remaining. But some manufacturers recommend filling the tank with gasoline and a gasoline stabilizer and running the engine for a few minutes so the treated gasoline gets into the fuel line and carburetor.

Electric mowers. Disconnect the cord or, on cordless models, remove the safety key, and clean beneath the deck. Keep the blade sharp, following the procedure for gas mowers. To extend the life of your mower, save the power cell. With cordless models, stop mowing and plug in the charger when the battery starts running down. Draining a battery completely shortens its life. New ones cost about $100. Manufacturers also suggest leaving the battery on "charge" whenever you're not using the mower.

Riding mowers. Clean beneath the deck a few times each season; remove the housing according to the manufacturer's instructions. Sharpen the blades and scrape off grass a few times each season; if it's a mulcher, clean the blades after each use. Take the mower to a professional lawn-equipment service company for servicing before each mowing season.

Leather clothing
Keep leather clothing away from heat, and don't store it in a plastic bag. Avoid getting perfume or hair spray on it since the alcohol may ruin the color. Don't rub leather excessively.

Light switch plates

Make a cardboard template so you don't get the cleaning product on the wall around the switch plate. Clean plastic switch plates with a light all-purpose cleaner. If the plate is badly fingerprinted, use a degreasing all-purpose cleaner or a little rubbing alcohol on a soft cloth. Use metal polish to clean metal fittings. To clean the switch itself, turn off the power, and take care not to get the liquid on the wiring.

To clean an area of painted wall around a switch plate, use a warm solution of dishwashing liquid or, for very dirty areas, a weak solution of TSP (trisodium phosphate) or a heavy-duty all-purpose cleaner. Extremely dirty patches may require undiluted cleaner. Avoid cleaners with pine oil, which may damage painted surfaces. Rinse with clean water. To clean an area of wallpaper, apply an all-purpose cleaner without bleach and sponge-clean or scrub with a soft brush. Rinse with a damp cloth dipped in clean, warm water. Don't apply too much liquid which may work its way into the seams.

Linen

Made from the stems of the flax plant, linen is similar in many ways to cotton. But it is not as strong or resilient and doesn't hold dyes as well. Still, linen is pretty durable, and its appearance and "feel" improve with laundering. Linen-polyester is a blend often used in tablecloths, napkins, and place mats, which can be treated with permanent-press and soil-release finishes.

Some linens—most commonly drapery, upholstery, and decorative fabrics—may be dry-cleaned only. Linens that have been chemically treated for wrinkle resistance may withstand warm-water washing. Follow the instructions on the care label. Before washing colored linen, be sure to test for colorfastness. If possible, dry white linens in the sun to help them stay white. Linen should be ironed while damp, although wrinkle-resistant linens may not need frequent pressing.

Lingerie

The material that your lingerie is made of will determine its care and cleaning. Hand-washing directions can usually be found on the label. If the label recommends machine washing, use a lingerie bag and the Delicate cycle of your washing machine. Always wash garments unbuttoned and do not machine-dry. To dry, hang garments or lay flat.

Steaming is recommended to remove wrinkles, but if you iron lingerie, turn the garment inside out and use a gentle heat setting. See individual materials for specific care directions and stain removal.

For specific fabric care, see **Acetate,** page 28; **Cotton,** page 57; **Lace,** page 92; **Linen,** page 95; **Lyocell,** page 97; **Nylon,** page 102; **Polyester,** page 111; **Polyolefin (olefin),** page 111; **Rayon,** page 115; **Satin,** page 118; **Silk,** page 123; **Spandex,** page 129; **Triacetate,** page 135; and **Velvet,** page 142. See also **Laundry,** page 224.

Litter boxes

A clean litter box tends to make both cats and humans happier. Remove solid matter daily with a plastic scoop and dispose of it in the trash. Change the litter every few days or so. Before pouring in fresh litter, wash the litter box with hot water, detergent, and a few drops of ammonia. You will not need to change the litter and clean the box as often if you use scoopable litter. Never clean a litter box with chlorine bleach. Urine contains ammonia that can react with the bleach to produce extremely toxic fumes.

Lizard and other reptile skins

Dust gently to avoid loosening scales. To maintain the item's sheen, carefully apply leather conditioner, rubbing it in carefully.

Locks

Polish a lock using the appropriate metal cleaner. Avoid getting polish in the works. Occasionally use a general-purpose lubricant such as WD-40. If you have difficulty getting keys into a lock, use a graphite spray.

Luggage

To clean soft luggage—usually made of nylon, polyester, or polypropylene fabric—use a cloth dampened in a solution of mild liquid detergent. Treat fabric luggage with a spot- or stain-resistant spray when new. If badly soiled, try an upholstery shampoo or a spray powder cleaner that brushes off. Use a spot-removal product for hard-to-remove stains.

Leather luggage is generally made of finished leather. Follow the manufacturer's instructions. Clean pieces once a year with saddle soap by lathering it into the leather with a damp cloth or sponge and wiping it away with another damp cloth. Wipe the piece dry and use a leather conditioner.

Check manufacturer's instructions when preparing to clean metal or plastic hard luggage, though most types can be sponged clean with a solution of mild detergent, then rinsed and dried. A spray cleaner and polish will help protect the surface, but once scratched, it usually cannot be fixed and wears its scars like a war hero.

Lyocell

Lyocell is the generic fiber name for a form of rayon that is often marketed as the brand Tencel. In 1996, it became the first new generic fiber group in 30 years to be approved by the Federal Trade Commission. Strong and easy to care for, Lyocell is used in woven and knitted fabrics (often blended with cotton) including jersey, sweaters, hosiery, denim, sueded fabrics, chinos, sheets, and towels. A few lyocell fabrics should be dry-cleaned only. But some lyocell fabrics should not be dry-cleaned. Check the care label. If the care label permits machine washing, wash warm, rinse cold, and dry on a permanent-press setting. Wrinkles may hang out. If your garment needs a slight touch-up, use an iron set on medium; don't iron fabric made from fine yarns or microfibers.

Marble

Since marble is extremely porous, it stains easily. Don't even think of using a marble surface in a kitchen or bathroom until it's been treated with a penetrating stone sealer. A marble tabletop on which you serve food should be sealed as well. Depending on the product you use and the amount of wear and tear a marble surface undergoes, you may need to re-apply the sealer as frequently as every six months to ensure the surface remains resilient to stains.

Wipe down marble counters, tabletops, and walls routinely with a clean cloth or a sponge dipped in warm water and mild liquid detergent or stone soap, and dry the surface with a soft cloth. Be careful not to use too much soap, and rinse thoroughly, because soap can leave a film on marble and cause streaking. Soap buildup, in fact, is a common problem in marble baths and showers. Wipe these surfaces down with a soft cloth or a squeegee after each use, and occasionally clean them with a commercial bathroom cleaner that's safe to apply to marble.

It's important to keep marble floors clean because dust and grime can abrade them quite easily. Keep a door mat or an area rug near the entrance to a room floored in marble (make sure it has nonskid backing) and go over the floor frequently with a dry dust mop. You can also use a damp mop and a solution of mild detergent and warm water, but wring the mop thoroughly so it's barely damp, rinse thoroughly, and dry the floor with a soft cloth.

If for some reason you choose not to seal a marble surface, be ever vigilant for spills, and be prepared to act quickly. Even water can seep into marble and leave a telltale mark, and substances that are oily and greasy are almost sure to stain badly. Blot up spills immediately (don't wipe them because you will only spread them and cause further damage). As soon as possible, apply a paste of baking soda and water to the area, let dry, wipe off with a damp cloth, and polish the marble with a soft, dry cloth. You may be able to minimize damage from oil and grease by sprinkling the area of the spill with cornmeal, leaving it for several hours, then wiping it up with a warm, damp cloth. Some food stains can be removed with hydrogen peroxide.

Cleaning Caveat

Marble is very vulnerable to "etching" by any type of acidic cleaner, including vinegar and lemon. Since many cleaning products include acid, read labels carefully before using them on marble.

Mattresses

Use a mattress pad between the mattress and the bottom sheet to absorb moisture. Launder it occasionally.

Turn a mattress at least twice a year—side over side, then side over side again, then head over toe. At the same time, vacuum the mattress with an appropriate attachment, and air the mattress outside, if possible, or near a window where sunlight comes in.

To remove a musty or unpleasant smell from a mattress, sprinkle baking soda over it and leave it undisturbed for 24 hours, then vacuum it away. Or use a commercial pet-odor-removal product.

To remove most stains, use a small amount of upholstery cleaner. If possible, turn the mattress on its side when applying spot cleaner so the mattress does not soak up too much liquid. Speed the drying process with a hair dryer. For urine stains, use a pet-odor-removal product.

Microwave ovens

Use a mild cleaner and soft cloth to clean the exterior. Wipe up any spills in the interior immediately. To remove cooking stains, wipe the walls and floor of the oven with a hot, damp cloth. Wash removable parts, such as the turntable, in hot water and dishwashing liquid.

To remove odors, place a bowl of water containing ¼ cup of lemon juice in the oven and run it on high for one minute. Remove the bowl and wipe the oven cavity, using the condensation that will have formed to clean it. Wipe stains, using plain water. Repeat if necessary. Scrape off stubborn stains with a plastic credit card.

Mirrors

Use a commercial glass-cleaning product or one part vinegar or ammonia and eight parts water, and wipe dry with a damp, lint-free cloth. Polish with old newspapers or a lint-free cloth, or dry with a squeegee. In areas where mirrors tend to fog up—bathrooms and kitchens—use a product (formulated for automobile windshields) that contains an anti-mist chemical. Remove hair spray residue with a cloth dampened with rubbing alcohol.

Modacrylic

Lightweight, bulky, and warm, it's often used for stuffing toys and for fake fur. Hand- or machine-wash it on a gentle setting.

Monitors

Unplug the monitor from the power source and disconnect from the computer. Wipe a CRT screen with a dampened cloth. Use a soft, dry cloth for an LCD screen.

See also **Computers**, page 53, and **Laptop computers**, page 93.

Mother of pearl

Wipe with a soft cloth dipped in a solution of mild liquid detergent. Rinse well, and wipe with a soft cloth. If the item has lost its luster through incorrect cleaning, take it to a jeweler.

For inlays, usually found on tabletops and ornamental boxes, apply cream furniture polish with a cloth or a cotton swab, being careful not to touch other parts of the object if they are to be cleaned with another product.

When cleaning a decorative ornament, make a paste of water and powdered chalk available in art-supply shops. Apply it with a soft cloth, then wash the item briefly in warm, soapy water, and rinse in warm water. Gently polish.

Mouse (computer)

Remove the mouse ball, and use a wooden toothpick and a cotton swab dampened with rubbing alcohol to clean out any debris on the rollers. Clean the ball with a cloth moistened with rubbing alcohol.

See also **Computers**, page 53; **Inkjet printers**, page 88; **Laptop computers**, page 93; and **Monitors**, above.

Naugahyde

Naugahyde is a brand of vinyl-coated fabric used chiefly in upholstered seating, but such items as handbags and clothing are also made from Naugahyde.

To maintain Naugahyde's luster and to prevent cracking, periodically spray the surface lightly with furniture polish and buff with a clean, white cloth.

To remove stains, use a solution of mild liquid detergent and warm water applied with a damp cloth. Blot the stain and wipe away any residue with a damp cloth.

Needlework and embroidery

Dust lightly on a regular basis. Vacuum on low with the attachment nozzle covered with an old nylon stocking.

Hand-wash an item that you are sure is colorfast (test in an inconspicuous spot if you are unsure) in a mild detergent, and dry flat between two absorbent towels. Press gently with a warm iron between two clean, dry dish towels. If you are not sure an item is colorfast, have it dry-cleaned by a professional upholsterer or dry cleaner. Store in acid-free paper to prevent discoloration.

Brush chair or stool seats with beading or raised thread-work with a baby's hairbrush. Or vacuum them with a piece of nylon hosiery over the nozzle. If a seat is badly soiled, consult a professional upholsterer and have it removed for cleaning.

Nickel

Nickel will darken if not cleaned regularly. Wash with a mild detergent and warm water. Polish with a soft, clean cloth.

Nonstick pots

Check care instructions. Most are not meant to be washed in the dishwasher but are easily cleaned with hot water and dishwashing liquid. Use plastic or nylon scrubbers to remove any burned-on food. To remove stains, soak the pan in a solution of 1 cup of water, ½ cup of chlorine bleach, and 2 tablespoons of baking soda.

Nylon

This strong, lightweight fabric may yellow if dried in direct sunlight. It may fade, look gray, or attract dyes when washed with other garments. Hand-wash nylon stockings and other garments or machine-wash them in warm water on a gentle cycle with similarly colored items and fibers. Add a fabric softener to the final rinse cycle if you plan to air-dry. If you machine-dry, use a dryer sheet to reduce static electricity and remove garments as soon as they are dried. (Don't use softeners in both washing and drying; they can build up.) Use a warm iron.

Cleaning Caveat

Wash nylon after every wearing—it's hard to keep clean once soiled. Rinse off oily substances immediately after contact.

Oil lamps

When the inside of an oil-lamp chimney becomes coated with smoke residue, wipe it out with newspaper. Handle delicate chimneys carefully. Trim the wick after every use.

Oil paintings

Entrust an oil painting that's of commercial or sentimental value to a professional for cleaning and restoration. Also rely on a professional for any varnished oil painting. After it's cleaned, it will have to be revarnished.

For routine care, simply dust an oil painting occasionally with a soft cloth, a fluffy, long-handled brush, or a soft water-color brush that's been thoroughly cleaned. You can also use special painting cleaners that are available at art-supply shops; be sure to follow instructions.

Onyx

A very porous material used in jewelry, onyx can even absorb sweat from hands, so hold an item in a cloth while you wipe with another. Light marks can be removed with cotton moistened with rubbing alcohol. Blot up any spills on onyx table surfaces immediately. If liquid is absorbed, the onyx will need professional refinishing and repolishing.

Opal

Wipe opal jewelry with a soft cloth. Use a soft toothbrush to clean out any dirt caught in settings. Never soak opal jewelry in anything—moisture will damage them.

Oriental rugs

Because these rugs are generally handmade, are frequently old, and may not be colorfast, they need special care. The rotating brush of a newer upright vacuum cleaner is too harsh, so use a canister cleaner or an upright vacuum with a beater bar (not found on newer models). To prevent the fringe along the edges from being sucked up, cover the attachment nozzle with an old nylon stocking. Always vacuum in the direction that the pile is supposed to lie. If the rug is small enough, take it outside, hang it on a clothesline, and dust it with a soft brush. Because gritty dirt abrades a rug's backing, vacuum the back of the rug occasionally. Remove grease stains with a dry spot cleaner, testing first in an inconspicuous place—perhaps the edge or back.

Every one to three years, depending on your household traffic, hire a professional to clean the rug (see **Professional-cleaning tips,** on page 241). Labels on oriental rugs do not always give information about the backing fiber. CONSUMER REPORTS tests have found that a handmade rug labeled "100 percent wool" may have a fringe or a foundation made of cotton, and machine-made rugs may have a fringe made of synthetic fiber or wool. The presence of other fibers—which you may need a professional to identify—can become significant during cleaning.

Rugs with wool pile should generally be wet-cleaned; silk-pile rugs generally should be dry-cleaned; and rugs with rayon pile must be dry-cleaned exclusively. Rub a damp white cloth over dark portions to check colorfastness. If color comes off on the cloth, the rug will bleed during cleaning.

For more information about caring for your rugs, see **Carpeting**, page 239.

Ormolu

True ormolu is gold leaf overlaid on brass or bronze as a decorative element on furniture, clocks, and candelabra. Imitation ormolu may be brass coated with a colored lacquer. Dust either type infrequently with a natural-bristle hairbrush. Handle only with cotton gloves. Do not wash, rub, or polish ormolu.

Outdoor (vinyl) furniture

Dust with a soft, damp cloth, and vacuum in all the crevices. Remove marks with a damp cloth dipped in baking soda. Abrasives and strong detergents can abrade vinyl-strap furniture. Protect poolside pieces with a large towel, since suntan lotion can stain them and chlorine can bleach them. Clean vinyl furniture regularly with a mild detergent solution, then rinse with water and dry. Otherwise, buildup of soil, oil, and lotion will make it vulnerable to mildew. Treat mildew with vinegar or a bleach solution of one part chlorine bleach and three parts water. Try this in an inconspicuous spot first.

Ovens

For light soil on an oven door, use dishwashing liquid or a mild all-purpose detergent and hot water. Do not use an abrasive powder or an abrasive pad or steel wool. Clean oven shelves in the dishwasher, or hand-wash them in the sink or the bathtub, protecting the sink or tub surface with towels.

Always check the manufacturer's care manual before cleaning an oven's interior. The type of oven you own will determine how you clean it.

Self-cleaning ovens. Use the cleaning cycle of self-cleaning ovens as often as necessary—it turns the most stubborn spills into a powdery, gray-ash residue. At the end of the cycle, wipe off the residue with a damp cloth. Ventilate the kitchen during the cleaning cycle to prevent smoke and fume residue from coating walls and ceilings. If vaporized soil leaks through, use the mildest nonabrasive cleanser to scrub the oven's door and the frame outside the door seal. Avoid scrubbing the gasket itself, except very gently with a sponge dampened with a solution of dishwashing liquid; rinse with a sponge damped with plain water. Never use any abrasive tool or product or a commercial oven cleaner on the interior surface.

Continuous-cleaning ovens. These have a special speckled, rough-texture porcelain finish that, like self-cleaning ovens, is meant to gradually burn off combusted foods—but at normal oven temperatures. You should never use commercial oven cleaners, harsh abrasives, and scouring pads on these ovens. All you should need to do is wipe down the interior with a damp cloth as soon as the oven cools.

Non-self-cleaning ovens. Wipe up standard ovens after use with a hot, damp cloth. Clean up spills on the oven floor immediately so cooked-on food will not build up. Cover the oven bottom with aluminum foil to protect the surface, but don't block any vents. Loosen grease by placing ½ cup of cloudy ammonia in a warm oven. Turn the oven off and close the oven door. Leave it for several hours or overnight, then wipe it out with hot water and detergent. For stubborn stains, use a commercial oven cleaner and a plastic scrub pad or brush.

Helpful Hint

If oven shelves are too soiled to be cleaned with hot water and detergent, soak in a mixture of one part washing soda and four parts hot water, and use a plastic scrubber on stubborn spots.

Painted walls

To prevent dirt from building up, make it part of your routine to clean walls from time to time with the dusting brush of your vacuum cleaner or a soft, long-handled brush. You may occasionally also want to wash the walls, either to freshen them or to prepare them for painting.

To wash, first pull furniture away from the walls, and lay plastic sheeting to protect the floor and carpets. Wash by dipping a sponge or cloth in a solution of dishwashing liquid and warm water. Rinse with clear warm water. Because dirty streaks that dribble down are much easier to wipe off a clean surface than a dirty one, wash from the bottom up. Do a section of about a square yard or so at a time, overlapping sections slightly as you work. Don't stop washing until you have done the entire wall. That way you will avoid leaving hard-to-remove watermarks.

If the walls are very dirty, use a mild solution of TSP (trisodium phosphate) or a heavy-duty all-purpose cleaner; try applying undiluted cleanser to especially stubborn dirt (see **Wall cleaner** in **Homemade cleaning products**, page 271). Be careful, because a strong cleanser may cause the painted surface to streak or fade; test it first in a hidden spot.

Cleaning Caveat

If there are light switches or electrical sockets in the wall you are washing, turn off the electrical supply and keep the switches or sockets dry.

Choosing an Easy-to-Clean Paint

The type of paint you use determines how easy your cleanup will be.

• Flat paint is harder to clean than glossier formulas and picks up more dirt and holds it more tenaciously.

• Semi-gloss paint is easier to clean than flat paint but may be too shiny for larger surfaces.

• A low-luster finish—often called eggshell or satin—is easy to clean and reflects less light than semi-gloss paints do.

• Most top-quality interior paints—which include all-purpose flat and low-luster wall paints, glossier trim enamels, and fairly or very glossy kitchen and bath paints—hold up well when scrubbed with a sponge and powdered cleanser.

• Start off with a light touch when cleaning low-quality paints—if you're not careful, you may remove the paint itself with minor rubbing.

dampened. Wipe with the grain or the pattern, and make sure you leave no moisture behind.

When heavier cleaning is required, wipe the surface gently with a cloth dipped in a solution of warm water and a small amount of mild cleaner such as Murphy Oil Soap, then wring so it is just damp. Test the solution on a small area to make sure it doesn't leave white marks or soften the finish.

If care instructions call for waxing, do so sparingly to avoid a waxy buildup. Wipe off unsightly old wax with a mild solution of Murphy Oil Soap and warm water.

Dust the keys occasionally with the brush attachment of a vacuum cleaner or a soft cloth, and wipe them with a cloth that you've dipped in warm water and wrung thoroughly. Make sure that water doesn't trickle between the keys because moisture can loosen them.

Clean plastic keys as needed with a soft cloth that's been dipped in a solution of mild detergent and water and wrung out. Wipe again with a second cloth dampened in water. Then dry with a third one.

Don't use detergent on ivory keys because it can cause them to discolor. Instead, go over the keys gently with a soft cloth or a cotton swab that you've barely dampened in a solution of equal parts rubbing alcohol and warm water. If ivory keys are badly discolored, have them professionally scraped and repolished.

Your piano tuner should ensure that the interior of your instrument is kept clean, but you can occasionally vacuum it with the crevice tool, making sure not to touch the strings.

Picture frames

For routine care, simply dust with a soft brush or cloth. Occasionally wipe metal, plastic, and treated-wood frames with a damp cloth. Gently remove any marks with a cloth that you've dipped in a solution of warm water and mild detergent and wrung until just damp. Clean a frame of untreated wood with a soft cloth dipped in teak oil. Wipe off any oil that's not absorbed in 20 minutes.

Wipe protective glass with a soft cloth onto which you've sprayed glass cleaner; never spray cleaner directly onto the glass because it can seep beneath the surface.

Pillows

Fluff pillows daily to restore their shape, and air them occasionally to remove dust. Hang them outdoors on a clothesline, the sunnier and breezier the day the better. If this isn't possible, run them through the dryer on a no-heat cycle.

Launder pillows only when necessary, since even the most careful washing can break down the texture of the filling. Follow care instructions on the label carefully. You can machine-wash most foam-filled or synthetic pillows, using a gentle cycle, lukewarm water, and mild detergent. They can become very heavy when wet; if your home machine is not able to accommodate them, wash them in a large machine at a coin laundry.

Down- and feather-filled pillows can often be hand-washed. Fill a basin with warm water and add a powdered detergent, hold the pillow under the water so it is completely soaked, and knead gently. Drain the basin and press down on the pillow to get as much liquid out of it as you can, then roll it in an old towel to prevent it from dripping on the floor. Spin the pillow in the washing machine for two or three cycles to extract as much water as possible.

Dry pillows thoroughly to prevent mildew by hanging them on a clothesline or running them through a dryer set on moderate heat. If you machine-dry a pillow, add a couple of towels to hasten drying and a tennis shoe to keep it fluffed.

To protect a pillow from such substances as hair oil and face cream, use a pillow cover, available at department stores and bedding shops, as an inner layer between the pillow and the pillowcase. Launder both the pillowcase and the pillow cover frequently.

Plastic furniture

Plastic scratches very easily, so you should never clean it with abrasive cleaners or scrub pads. Use only a soft brush or cloth dipped in a solution of water and mild liquid detergent. Apply a coat of automobile wax for extra protection.

Platinum

This metal is deceptive in that, with its rich color and smooth sheen, it doesn't show dirt. Even so, clean a piece of platinum jewelry frequently by soaking it in rubbing alcohol for a minute, then rinsing and drying with a soft cloth. Polish with a chamois or other soft cloth.

Polyester

Quick drying and resistant to wrinkling, shrinking, and fading, this synthetic material is nonetheless difficult to maintain. It pills easily when laundered with other fabrics and attracts oil stains like a magnet. Hand-wash or gently machine-wash a polyester garment, turning it inside out to reduce the visibility of pilling. Let it drip dry or use a low temperature setting on your dryer and remove the garment as soon as the tumble cycle is complete. If ironing is needed, use a medium setting. Dry cleaning is OK for most items. If you want the convenience of polyester without its drawbacks, look for a garment made from a blend of polyester and natural fibers. Such a blended garment will be more durable and much easier to care for than an all-polyester or all-natural-fiber garment.

Cleaning Caveat

This fabric attracts oil stains and soiling from other items in the wash. Wash oily stains as soon as you notice them by rubbing them with liquid laundry detergent or a paste of powdered detergent, then with a wet towel, and rinse.

Polyolefin (olefin)

This fabric is often used in underwear, socks, sweaters, pantyhose, and swimwear. Items can be hand-washed or machine-washed in warm or cold water. Air-dry or tumble-dry on a gentle cycle. Avoid ironing, but if it's necessary, use the lowest temperature setting.

Prints and drawings

If a print or drawing is of sentimental or commercial value, turn it over to a professional for cleaning. If you feel confident undertaking the task yourself, rub dirty spots with fresh white bread crumbs until the crumbs do not absorb any more dirt. Use an artist's kneadable eraser to remove stubborn dirt that remains. To remove grease spots, lay blotting paper over the grease and apply the tip of a warm iron to the paper to help draw out the stain.

When storing prints and drawings that aren't framed, cover with acid-free paper and lay flat in a dry place. Place some mothballs nearby to deter insects.

Quarry tile floors

These thick, unglazed tiles are intended for long wear and heavy-duty service. Treat a newly laid floor with an approved sealer as soon as it is laid. Once the sealer has properly dried, mop as needed with a solution of hot water and liquid detergent. Apply all-purpose cleaner to stubborn dirt spots and scrub vigorously with a brush.

Quilts

Check the manufacturer's instructions, if you have them. Have a hand-stitched patchwork quilt, a quilt made of silk, or any antique quilt professionally laundered or dry-cleaned.

If the manufacturer says a cotton quilt is washable, test it first for colorfastness, then machine-wash it on a gentle cycle with a mild detergent.

Clean a wool quilt at the end of the cold weather, before storing it. Soak it first, then hand- or machine-wash it on a gentle cycle in a detergent designed for use on wool. Thoroughly rinse it, adding a cup of white vinegar to the final rinse. Also see **The Soak and Spin Method**, page 150.

Air-dry a quilt outside, hanging it between two clotheslines to speed drying.

Radiators

Dust regularly with a cloth or the brush attachment of a vacuum cleaner. Do so when the furnace is off to avoid burning yourself. To clean hard-to-reach places behind a radiator, use a long-handled brush, or bend a wire coat hanger to make a loop and tie a dust cloth over it. Wash radiators as needed with a solution of heavy-duty cleaner and warm water. Apply the solution to an inconspicuous spot first to make sure it won't cause a colored surface to fade.

Ranges and cooktops

A good wipe-down after every use and an occasional thorough cleaning will ensure that this equipment looks good and will keep grease, dirt, and grime at bay. New designs and materials are making these tasks easier all the time.

Clean enamel surfaces with a plastic scrub pad dipped in a solution of mild detergent and water. Don't use abrasive cleaners because enamel can scratch. Vinegar, milk, citrus juices, and other acidic substances can leave stains, so wipe up spills right away.

Pull off control knobs and clean behind them, then clean the knobs in the dishwasher or in the sink with water and dishwashing detergent. Be careful not to scrub off markings on the knobs or on the control panel behind them.

If the cooking surface can be raised, do so occasionally; wipe up food that's fallen beneath the cooking units and scrub dirty parts and surfaces. Make sure the cooking surface is cool, and be careful not to wet any electric elements.

Electric coil and gas ranges. Electric coils are self-cleaning, since spills burn off quickly. This is not the case with the burners on a gas stove, on which spills can form a stubborn burn deposit. To clean, immerse the parts in a solution of hot water and dishwashing detergent, let soak to loosen encrusted dirt, then scrub with a plastic pad. If this doesn't do the job, scrub with an abrasive cleanser. You can also clean the parts in the dishwasher, but it may still be necessary to scrub them by hand to remove burn deposits.

Wipe down drip pans and reflector bowls beneath coils and burners with a cleanser that is abrasive enough to remove

More and more, ranges and cooktops are being designed with easy cleaning in mind. Touch-pad controls put an end to greasy knobs, and smoothtops do away with pesky nooks, crannies, and drip bowls. New designs also include some relatively low-tech innovations such as raised edges around cooking surfaces to keep spills off the floor. If you're outfitting your kitchen with a new stove, you'll probably be delighted with the array of labor-saving options that are now available.

stubborn spills but not so abrasive that it will scratch the surface. Or soak them in a sink filled with hot water to which you've added dishwashing liquid. Or clean them in the dishwasher. Make sure these parts are cool before touching them. You may occasionally want to spruce up your cooktop by installing a new set of drip pans and reflectors.

Smoothtop. On these cooktops, a sheet of ceramic glass covers the electric heating elements. With a smoothtop, it's easy to wipe up most spills because no burners get in the way. But it's important to keep food spills, especially those containing sugar, off the surface, because they can cook on and cause pitting. Take care, too, not to scratch the surface. Use a spoon rest, cook in tall-sided pans to prevent overflows, and don't set aluminum foil, pot covers, or pots with dirty cooking bottoms on the surface.

Wipe up spills immediately with a damp cloth, and wipe down the surface after using it with a solution of water and a mild, nonabrasive detergent. For routine cleaning and to remove stains and marks, use special cleaners recommended by the manufacturer. These will not harm the surface and are formulated to leave a protective coating.

See also **Ovens**, page 105.

Rattan

Vacuum furniture made from the fibers of this plant with the upholstery attachment of the vacuum cleaner, or dust with a feather duster. If the piece is still dirty, use a brush to scrub it with a solution of ¼ cup of borax and 1 tablespoon of liquid detergent mixed in 1 quart of warm water. Rinse with clear warm water, giving it another scrub with a brush as you rinse.

To prevent rattan furniture from drying out, cracking, and darkening, once a year wet the piece with warm salted water, and allow to air-dry. When dry, apply lemon oil or a little furniture cream, following the label's instructions.

Rayon

Also known as viscose, this fabric is lightweight and strong when dry but weak and flimsy when wet. It's prone to wrinkling and doesn't hold its shape particularly well. Dry cleaning is recommended for most rayon items. If the care label permits, hand-wash with mild suds in cool or lukewarm water, or machine-wash using the gentle setting. Do not twist or wring wet items. Lay sweaters flat to dry, but air-dry other items using nonrust hangers. Damp items can be ironed using a low or medium setting. Begin with the garment turned inside out; finish ironing it right side out with a pressing cloth. Dry items should be pressed with a cool iron only.

Redwood furniture

See **Furniture,** page 76.

Refrigerators

Spill-proof, pull-out shelves and other handy features that make cleanups easier are almost standard equipment in new refrigerators. Even so, ongoing maintenance and a little elbow grease is required to keep refrigerators sanitary, odor-free, running efficiently, and looking good.

To avoid scratching, clean soft plastic surfaces inside the refrigerator with a damp sponge dipped in a mild solution of ¼ cup of baking soda mixed with 1 quart of water. It's especially important to keep the door seal clean because dirt impairs its ability to hold in cold air.

Remove glass or wire shelves and other fittings—including the removable drip pan at the bottom of some older-model refrigerators—and wash them in the sink with hot water and liquid detergent. Use baking soda on stubborn stains.

Leave an open container of baking soda on a refrigerator shelf to keep odors down. If strong odors persist, switch off the refrigerator, remove all food, and wash the interior with a solution of baking soda and water. Leave the door open and repeat the washing once or twice a day until the odor is gone.

The exteriors of many refrigerators are surfaced with baked enamel, though many new models have vinyl and sometimes stainless-steel surfaces. You can clean most with a sponge dipped in a solution of dishwashing liquid and hot water. Remove stains with a little baking soda applied to a damp cloth. Don't use abrasive cleansers because they can scratch the surface. For stainless-steel refrigerators, use a specially formulated cleanser. See also **Metal cleaners,** page 179, and **Stainless-steel countertops,** page 129.

The condenser coil helps disperse heat and is outside the cabinet. Since it tends to collect dust, which lowers the refrigerator's efficiency and raises energy costs, it should be cleaned once or twice a year. This is especially important before the onset of summer, when high temperatures impose heavy demands on the refrigerator. The condenser is usually located behind or beneath the refrigerator, though on built-in models it is on top of the unit. To clean the condensers on all but built-in models, turn off and unplug the refrigerator, then pull it out so you can easily reach the back. (You may have to remove the "service access" panel to reach the condenser.) Use a condenser-coil cleaning brush (available in hardware and appliance stores) to dust the condenser, then vacuum it with the crevice tool. To clean the condenser of a built-in unit, consult a professional.

See also **Freezers,** page 76.

Rubber tile floors

Strong and acidic cleaning solutions and excessive scrubbing can harm the surface of rubber tile. To clean safely, sweep the floor, then mop with a solution of clear water and mild detergent. Don't allow the soapy solution to dry on the rubber. Rinse immediately with clean, cold water and buff dry with a dust mop or a sponge mop to which you've tied a clean towel. To remove gum or other soft, sticky substances from the floor, cover the area with ice, scrape the substance off with a plastic spatula or scraper, and dab any remaining residue with a cloth or cotton swab dipped in turpentine.

Rubies

Place a ruby or piece of jewelry set with this stone in a bowl filled with a solution of 1 tablespoon of ammonia and 1 cup of hot water. Swish the piece around, then dip it in another cup or bowl into which you've poured some rubbing alcohol. Pat dry with a paper towel. Or clean these stones with a commercial jewelry cleaner, following instructions carefully.

Rugs (dhurrie, kilim, Navajo, and rag)

Vacuum these reversible, tightly woven, long-wearing rugs as you would carpets. If the rug is small enough, take it outside and shake it, or hang it over a clothesline and brush it with a soft brush. Check the label for care instructions before washing, shampooing, or dry cleaning. Such rugs can often be washed by hand or machine. The Navajos recommend sweeping fresh snow over the rug and air drying. Test a rag rug for colorfastness, then put it in a pillowcase and machine-wash it. Or hand-wash it in warm water with soap powder. After washing, gently pull the rug back into shape, and air-dry it flat.

For more information about caring for your rugs, see **Carpeting**, page 239.

Sapphires

Pour 1 cup of hot water into a bowl and add 1 tablespoon of ammonia. Immerse a sapphire or a piece of jewelry into which a sapphire is set in the solution and swirl it with your finger. Remove, dip in some rubbing alcohol, and pat dry with a paper towel. You can also use a commercial jewelry cleaner.

Satin

Wash or dry-clean according to the instructions on the care label. Dry-clean satin upholstery.

Scanners

Follow the instructions in your manual. It is usually recommended that you leave the scanner flat and lock the scanning device, if possible. Moisten a soft, dry, lint-free cloth (not a paper towel) with streak-free window cleaner, camera-lens-cleaning fluid, white vinegar, or rubbing alcohol, and wipe the glass gently. Only if necessary—that is, if there is dirt or moisture on the underside of the glass—refer to the manual to see how to take the scanner apart and clean that surface. Reassemble the scanner and unlock the device (if necessary) before plugging it in again.

Sealed wood

See **Flooring,** page 260.

Seashells

To clean and disinfect shells you find on the beach, put them in a pot of water to which you've added a few drops of bleach and bring it slowly to a boil. Simmer for about 10 minutes, turn off the heat, and let the shells cool in the water. Rinse thoroughly to remove any flesh still clinging to the shells, then set them on a soft cloth to dry. Dust regularly, and wash in a solution of warm water and mild detergent if they become dirty and greasy.

Seersucker

Wash or dry-clean, according to instructions on the care label. Drip-dry after washing. Don't iron seersucker because you will flatten the finish.

Sewing machines

Clean a sewing machine after every use to prevent lint from building up. Follow manufacturer's instructions for other maintenance tips. Keep in mind, though, that many electronic machines do not need to be lubricated.

Don't apply cleanser directly to a sewing machine because it can get onto the parts and rub off on fabrics you sew. Instead, clean the casing with a soft cloth that you've sprayed with an all-purpose cleaner. Rub the cleanser in well, and use a clean cloth to remove any excess.

Use the brush supplied with the sewing machine to remove residues of lint that collect under the bobbin. If you no longer have this tool, you can purchase one at a shop that sells sewing supplies.

Shag

For shag or other high-pile carpets, use a canister vacuum or an upright model with a beater bar. An upright cleaner with a rotating brush can damage shag or become entangled in loop or pile carpeting. A carpet rake (purchased from a rug retailer) can be used on shag rugs to loosen tangles. To have all the pile lie in the same direction, rake the carpet after vacuuming.

For more information about caring for your rugs, see **Carpeting**, page 239.

Sheepskin

Shake a sheepskin rug outdoors, or vacuum with an old nylon stocking covering the nozzle of the attachment. If the rug has a backing, rub in an absorbent powder, such as fuller's earth or cornmeal, and let it stand for a couple of hours. Then take the rug outside and brush it with a soft brush, or hang it on a clothesline and beat gently with a tennis racket. Repeat several times if necessary. Some sheepskin rugs can be machine-washed (check the label): If it permits, use plenty of fabric softener, and keep the water temperature cool or lukewarm; then air-dry. If the rug has no backing, sponge carefully with a cleaning product made for wool, applying it with a damp sponge. Don't wet the skin because it can shrink. Hang the rug outside to dry, and when it's still damp, brush the pile up. Or use the absorbent-powder treatment described above.

For more information about caring for your rugs, see **Carpeting**, page 239.

Sheets

Wash new sheets before you use them to remove creases from the packaging and to determine if they shrink or fade, in which case you should return them.

Follow the manufacturer's instructions for care. You can safely wash and dry just about all sheets in a machine, though you should wash dark colors separately if you are not sure they are colorfast.

Ironing should not be necessary if you remove the sheets from the dryer promptly and fold them immediately. However, sheets made from linen and such premium cottons as Egyptian and pima look and feel better if ironed. Do so while they are still damp. Store cotton sheets and towels in a dry place.

Shoes

To preserve the appearance and longevity of shoes or boots, apply a water- and stain-repelling product every few weeks and clean them regularly.

Wipe dirt and mud from shoes and boots as it accumulates. Use the blunt edge of a knife and a sponge on most leather, and a soft brush on suede and other fabrics. If shoes become wet, let them air-dry and clean as soon as possible to remove dirt and grime that might damage the shoe. To ensure shoes made of soft leather and fabric keep their shape while drying, stuff them with paper towels or newspaper.

A quick and effective way to shine leather shoes and boots is to apply polish with a soft cloth, let it soak into the leather, and buff with the same cloth. Wipe patent-leather shoes clean with a soft cloth and polish with an instant-shoe-shine pad. Treat leather shoes and boots regularly with one of the many conditioners available; these waterproof the leather and keep it supple. Leave the conditioner on for 12 hours or so, then buff. If leather shoes are scratched, apply polish directly to the area and buff. Repeat until the scratch is no longer noticeable.

Use a commercial stain remover to take oil and grease stains out of suede shoes, repeating the application several times if necessary. Test it first on the tongue to make sure it doesn't leave a mark. To restore flattened nap, hold the shoe 3 inches from the spout of a steaming (not boiling) kettle, then brush in a circular motion. Use an emery board or a blunt knife to raise small areas of badly flattened nap. You can purchase products that restore color to faded suede.

Clean fabric shoes and canvas sneakers with a commercial upholstery cleaner, following instructions on the container. You can also hand- or machine-wash canvas sneakers; remove the laces, place the shoes in an old pillowcase to protect the washing drum, and wash in cold water and mild detergent on a gentle cycle. Hand-wash sneakers made of leather and synthetic materials in a solution of warm water and sneaker shampoo or dishwashing liquid, using a soft brush to remove grime and reach into crevices. Stuff the sneakers with paper towels or newspaper and let them air dry.

Showers

To prevent soap and dirt from building up on surfaces, wipe down or squeegee shower walls and doors each time the shower is used. Or spray on a special shower-cleaning product that's intended for use after every shower. Clean showerheads regularly with cleanser to prevent deposits from building up. If a metal showerhead becomes clogged with scaly deposits, place it in a pot to which you've added a solution of one part vinegar to eight parts water, bring to a boil, and simmer for

How to Prevent and Remove Mildew

Mold and mildew grow on bathroom tiles and grout, shower curtains, walls, and in any other damp, dark place.

- Keep a window open or use a fan to reduce moisture. After a steamy shower, leave the shower door or curtain open and the door to the room ajar.

- Don't use wall-to-wall carpeting in a damp bathroom.

- Spray mildew with a diluted bleach solution (one part bleach and four parts water) and let sit for half an hour. Scrub off, then rinse. When working with bleach, make sure the area is well ventilated. Wear a mask and eye protection if you are sensitive to the fumes.

about 15 minutes. Soak a plastic shower head in a solution of equal parts vinegar and hot water.

If you use a shower curtain, protect it with a plastic liner. Machine-wash the liner frequently, using a detergent that contains chlorine bleach to remove mildew. You can also machine-wash most shower curtains. Follow care instructions. If the curtain is colored, be sure to use only bleach that is safe with colored fabrics. See also **Bathtubs and sinks**, page 37, and **Ceramic tile**, page 48.

Shutters

Once a week, dust shutters with a soft, clean cloth, or vacuum them with the dusting attachment. If the shutters are wooden, you can use an appropriate wood oil every six months, although some of these can make surfaces sticky and more prone to fingerprints and dust. Do not use furniture polish, which may muddy the finish.

Siding

With regular cleaning and maintenance, siding can keep a house looking like new.

Vinyl. This is the most popular choice for siding material, and little wonder: It's low-maintenance, holds color well, and is fairly resilient. Though it may crack in extreme cold and if struck by a hard object, it generally lasts 20 years or more. Clean with an all-purpose cleaner. Use a long-handled brush, working from top to bottom, or a power washer. Be sure to point the power washer straight ahead, not upward, to ensure that water doesn't seep beneath the siding. You may also use a home-washing kit that attaches to a garden hose, but the job will take much longer than it will with a power washer. Cover

Eliminating Mildew From Vinyl Siding

To eliminate mildew, spray an all-purpose cleaner or a solution of one part bleach to three parts water onto the mildewed surface. Do not use cleaners that can harm the surface of the siding, such as those containing organic solvents and undiluted chlorine bleach.

vinyl siding when working in the vicinity with sealant or any other substance that might disfigure the surface.

Aluminum. While aluminum siding is easy to maintain when new, over time it may fade, dent, and lose its color. In regions near salt water and where salt is used on roads in the winter, aluminum can corrode. Clean with a commercial cleaning solution that contains agents that kill mildew. Apply it by hand or with a power washer (but be careful not to dent the aluminum) and rinse thoroughly. Before painting, clean thoroughly and apply a suitable primer to any bare spots. The coat should last for many years.

Cedar clapboard. This long-popular choice can last from 10 to 100 years. But it requires time-consuming and costly upkeep, including regular painting or staining. On a regular basis, use a stiff brush to clear away leaves and other debris from shingles and the gaps between them because they may trap water and cause a leak. To treat mildew, spray a solution of 1 quart of bleach, 3 quarts of water, and 3 ounces of TSP (trisodium phosphate) onto the area and scrub with a soft brush. Rinse thoroughly with fresh water. Apply a solution of one part household bleach and three parts water to kill moss, which can loosen shingles. Take care not to let these cleaners get on plants. When doing repairs to cedar clapboard, use rust-resistant nails; others may stain the wood.

Sieves

Clean immediately after each use, before any residue can harden and dry. Hold the sieve upside down under running water and use a medium-bristle brush dipped in mild detergent and hot water, making sure you remove all food matter from the holes.

Silk

Silk thread, secreted from the larva of a moth, is the strongest of all the natural fibers. It is usually wrinkle-resistant and elastic, holds shape well, and, cool and light, is ideal in hot climates. When the natural gum is not cleaned from the fiber,

Helpful Hint

Protect silk by storing it away from light and insects. Since perfume, strong deodorant, and perspiration can damage silk fibers, always clean your silk garments after wearing them.

the material is called raw silk. Shantung, pongee, and tussah are all unevenly woven silks and are usually not dyed. A few special silk fabrics—crepe, chiffon, organza, voile, georgette, grosgrain, moiré, taffeta, and satin—are used for evening wear.

Most care labels recommend dry cleaning only because some silk dyes will dissolve in water, causing "bleeding" and color transfer. Some unlined silk items can be hand-washed in lukewarm water using dishwashing liquid or other mild soap, or machine-washed using a gentle cycle.

If the care label recommends hand washing, test for color-fastness by washing a small, inconspicuous area first. Knead the item gently in clear water to rinse, hang and let air-dry.

Store silk in a dark place because sunlight can weaken the fabric and fade the color. Do not try to spot-clean stains, which also can weaken the fabric and cause permanent marks. Never use bleach on silk.

Silver

You can safely hand-wash most silver, but take care to protect the surface when doing so. Avoid detergents with chlorides, which can damage silver, and don't let detergent powder come into contact with silver, because it can pit the surface. When hand-washing silver, use mild detergent, rinse thoroughly, and dry immediately with a soft cloth to prevent streaking. Don't let stainless-steel and silver items touch each other; a chemical reaction between the two metals may cause silver to become pitted.

Replating and Other Restoration Services

Whatever the problem, professionals can restore silverware and silver hollowware, which is a term for tea and coffee services, trays, pitchers, candelabras, and other pieces that serve as containers.

Breaks and dents can be repaired, bristles and blades can be replaced in old hairbrushes and knives, and, if the backing of a silver-handled mirror is peeling, a new mirror can be installed.

Companies that do replating often restore silver as well. They will also relacquer silver and other metals so they won't tarnish.

To prevent tarnishing, store silver in a dry, airtight container lined with anti-tarnishing flannel. Remove tarnish regularly by applying silver paste with a damp sponge and using a toothbrush on pieces that are deeply patterned. Buff to a polish with a dry cloth. Be extremely gentle when polishing Sheffield plate and electroplated silver because the layer of silver is so thin that harsh polishing can remove it.

Dip cleansers are convenient because they don't require tedious rubbing. You just dip the silver into them or spread them on silver surfaces. However, dips don't remove heavy tarnishing and can leave pale stains on silver pieces. They can damage antique finishes, even when carefully applied, and can dull satin finishes; use a paste cleaner for these finishes instead. Dip cleansers can also cause the stainless blades of silver-handled knives to spot or pit. Rinse these promptly after using a dip cleaner.

Silver jewelry

A quick way to clean a piece of silver jewelry is to treat it in silver dip. But you'll get a softer finish with silver polish or even a little non-gel toothpaste. Apply them with a damp sponge or cloth, rinse, then buff the piece to a polish with a soft cloth.

Sisal, coir, rush, and split-cane rugs

All of these rugs are made from plant fibers. Most are sold with a rubber backing. Vacuum regularly to remove dirt and debris caught between the fiber and the backing. For spills, first blot, then apply an absorbent dry powder. Check with the manufacturer for the best way to shampoo or dry-clean. Deep-clean or shampoo about once a year.

For sisal or coconut mats, shake to remove dirt and dust, vacuum both sides, and occasionally take them outside and sponge them with warm soapy water. Rinse with a garden hose, and leave them in a warm spot to air-dry. Note that water may darken the color.

For more information about caring for your rugs, see **Carpeting**, page 239.

Skunk odor

To deodorize the coat of a dog or cat that has been sprayed by a skunk, try the following: In a large, open container, mix a quart of 3 percent hydrogen peroxide, ¼ cup of baking soda, and 1 teaspoon of liquid soap (be sure your container is large—the mixture will produce a great deal of foam). Then work the mixture into the animal's hair, making sure to keep it out of the eyes—the mixture is nontoxic, but the salt from the baking soda will sting. Let it sit until the odor has abated and then rinse thoroughly. Repeat if necessary.

Skylights

How often you wash a glass skylight depends on where you live, but the inside usually needs cleaning twice a year. Be sure that the stools or ladders you use are safe; if the skylights are way out of reach, hire a professional window washer to do the job. If you decide to do it yourself, work on a cloudy day or when windows are in shade because direct sun will cause streaking. You'll need two buckets, a sponge, a rubber squeegee, a clean, lint-free cloth, a chamois cloth, and a commercial cleaning solution or one you've prepared (see **Homemade cleaning products,** page 271.) Clean from the highest point down, using a slightly dampened sponge to apply the solution. Wipe across the window with the dampened squeegee blade, then wipe the blade. Use the chamois to rinse with clean water. Remove remaining moisture with the dry cloth. Check for caulking that needs replacing, paint in need of a touch-up, and cracks in the glass.

See also **Windows,** page 147.

Slate

For easy maintenance and to prevent unsightly stains, seal slate countertops and floors with a penetrating commercial stone sealer and reapply it about every six months. Make sure, though, that the product you use is recommended for use with slate because some sealers can cause darkening. Sponge-clean slate countertops with a solution of mild detergent and warm water, and gently use a plastic scrub pad to remove most stains. Never apply white vinegar or any other acidic cleaner to slate because it can etch the surface.

Go over a slate floor frequently with a dry dust mop to pick up dirt and grime, which can scratch the surface. Vacuum occasionally with the floor-nozzle attachment. Mop as necessary with a mild detergent and warm water. Wring the mop so it's barely damp because excess water can seep into pores and imbed dirt and grime. To restore shine to a dull surface, mop the floor with a water-based, self-polishing wax, or use an electric polisher to apply a coat of solvent-based wax.

Slipcovers

Rotate the cushions of a piece of furniture with slipcovers so they all get regular wear and maintain a uniform appearance. Remove the cushions and vacuum them with the brush attachment frequently, using the crevice tool to get into indentations around seams and other hard-to-reach places.

Before attempting to clean a slipcover, read the fabric-care label. If the slipcover is fitted, you may want to shampoo it while it's in place on a piece of furniture to ensure it maintains its shape and tight fit. Don't attempt to shampoo only a portion of the slipcover; unless you shampoo the entire piece, there can be a noticeable difference in color. Test a shampoo for colorfastness by applying it first to a hidden swatch of fabric. If you don't feel confident you can do a competent job, call in a professional furniture-cleaning service.

It's safe to hand-wash or machine-wash many loose-fitting slipcovers. Follow care instructions carefully to avoid shrinking or fading them. If the slipcovers are too large to fit into your washing machine, take them to a coin laundry. Gently iron them inside out, using a spray starch to protect them and make them easier to iron. Put the covers back on the piece of furniture while they are still slightly damp to ensure they dry to fit. See also **Upholstery**, page 137.

Smoke alarms

Smoke alarms run on batteries or a house current and typically are installed on ceilings or high on walls. Ionization alarms, better at detecting flames, are more common than photoelectric alarms, which are better at detecting smoke, although a home needs both types of protection. Battery-powered dual-detection alarms combine ionization and photoelectric technologies and provide the most complete coverage.

Whichever type of smoke alarm you have, press the Test button at least monthly to make sure the unit is working. If your smoke alarm runs on batteries, replace them once a year on an easy-to-remember date such as the weekend in October when clocks return to standard time.

Regularly vacuum a smoke alarm with an attachment; insects, dust, or cobwebs may reduce a unit's effectiveness or cause false alarms. Remove grime from the exterior by wiping with a paper towel sprayed with an all-purpose cleaner

Replace a smoke alarm every 10 years. New alarms have a date stamp to help you keep track.

Solid-surface synthetic countertops

These materials imitate marble and other types of stone and consist of polyester or acrylic resins combined with mineral fillers. They are sold under various brand names that include Avonite, DuPont Corian, Formica Surell, Nevamar Fountainhead, and Wilsonart Gibralter.

Solid-surface synthetics are much easier to maintain than the stone surfaces they imitate. However, knives can easily scar the surface, and the countertop may discolor when exposed to prolonged heat.

Clean this type of countertop with a sponge dipped in a solution of warm water and detergent or an ammonia-based cleaner. It's generally safe to apply a liquid scouring cleaner to stubborn stains, but if the counter has a high-gloss finish, use a sponge instead of a plastic scrub pad when working with these cleaners. A solid-surface synthetic surface can withstand light sanding. To remove shallow scratches, nicks, gouges, and burn marks, use 400-grit sandpaper for semi-gloss and high-gloss finishes and 180- or 220-grit for matte and satin finishes. Call a professional if the surface is deeply scratched or badly burned.

Spandex

Also known as the brand Lycra, spandex is used in swimwear, sportswear, underwear, and other garments and provides shape and elasticity. Some fiber blends may be dry-cleaned, but usually hand or machine washing is preferable. To ensure that spandex maintains its elasticity, hand-wash items in luke-warm water, or machine-wash on a gentle cycle, using a low temperature setting and a mild detergent. Never wash spandex with chlorine bleach or a detergent that contains it. Be sure to rinse well. Drip-dry, or use a low-temperature set-ting on your dryer. It's usually not necessary to iron clothes made from spandex, but if you need to remove wrinkles, set the iron on a low temperature setting only. Don't leave the iron on one spot for long.

Stainless-steel countertops

Stainless steel is quite easy to clean and maintain, but unfor-tunately, water is your No. 1 enemy with these otherwise serviceable surfaces. It leaves spots, so you should wipe a stainless-steel countertop with a clean, dry cloth every time it gets wet.

Stainless-steel surfaces usually come clean readily with hot water and detergent. But if a simple wipe-down doesn't do the job, apply undiluted liquid detergent directly to a trouble spot, or clean the area with a soft cloth to which you've applied rubbing alcohol. Don't use abrasive scouring pow-ders or scrub pads, which can scratch the surface. Be careful, too, when using special stainless-steel cleaners because many are formulated for industrial use and can harm a home coun-tertop; wipe these cleaners off as quickly as possible and rinse thoroughly.

See also **Metal cleaners,** page 179.

Straw handbags

Vacuum a straw handbag for routine cleaning, using low suc-tion and placing an old nylon stocking over the end of the nozzle to protect the straw. Use a soft cloth or cotton swab to apply undiluted detergent to dirty or greasy spots, then wipe with a clean cloth dampened in cool water and leave to air dry. Don't use warm water, which can distort the straw. If the straw is reasonably firm, you can apply an aerosol fabric protector to help keep the bag from becoming soiled. Let the coating dry thoroughly before using the bag or it will rub off on your clothing.

Suede

Some suede garments are now washable, but some can only be sponged or dry-cleaned. Check the care label. If you decide to clean suede, test any detergent or product you plan to use in an inconspicuous area first. Dry-clean all the pieces of a suede outfit at one time because the suede will change color during the cleaning process. Rub suede occasionally with a suede brush or another piece of suede. To protect the finish, spray on a special suede fabric protector or have one professionally applied.

See also **Furniture**, page 76; **Shoes,** page 120; and **Ultrasuede**, page 136.

Swimsuits

Always rinse a bathing suit in cool, clean water after a swim to remove chlorine, salt, and residue from suntan preparations that may stain it permanently. Follow the instructions on the care label for laundering, which will vary according to the material. Most suits are machine-washable but should be air-dried and never wrung out, put in a dryer, or dried on a radiator. Don't leave a damp suit in a plastic bag because it can mildew.

Teak

Teak requires little care and is extremely durable, making it ideal for outdoor use. Scrub it periodically with a bristle brush dipped in a soapy solution of one part bleach to four parts water to which you've added a mild detergent. Rinse and allow to air-dry. For deeper cleaning, use a product formulated for cleaning teak.

As teak weathers and turns silver-gray, some small cracks and spots may appear on the surface. Do nothing about them; they will disappear as the piece continues to age.

Tea kettles

Wash dirt and grease from the exterior of an aluminum, cast-iron, stainless steel, or plastic-coated tea kettle with dishwashing liquid and hot water. Remove mineral deposits from the interior by filling with equal parts white vinegar and water, bringing it to a boil, and allowing it to stand overnight.

Telephones

Dust with a soft cloth as needed, and remove visible grime on the instrument with a cotton ball or cotton swab that you've barely moistened with rubbing alcohol. Take special care to wipe down earpieces and mouthpieces with the alcohol, or use a special antiseptic cleanser on these areas.

Television sets

Regularly dust plastic cabinets. An anti-static product sprayed on a cloth, then wiped on the cabinet, will reduce dust collection. Or use a pre-treated anti-static dusting cloth. Clean nonplastic cabinets with a product recommended by the manufacturer. Spray nonabrasive window cleaner on a cloth and apply it to the screen, then buff with a paper towel.

Tents

Tents are made with a variety of fabrics and should be cleaned according to the manufacturer's care instructions. Follow them carefully because improper cleaning can destroy the fabric and remove waterproofing. To prevent mildew, make sure a tent is dry when you store it. If you must leave a campsite with a wet tent, erect it again as soon as possible and let it air-dry.

Terrazzo

Extremely durable, terrazzo is traditionally made from a combination of 80 percent marble chips and 20 percent Portland cement and is so porous it requires professional cleaning and stain removal.

Modern terrazzo is made with urethane, epoxy, or other synthetic resins instead of Portland cement, making it far less prone to staining. Even so, have a terrazzo floor sealed after installation and resealed periodically. Damp-mop regularly, and clean as needed with a mild dishwashing detergent or a solution of 3 gallons of water and 1 cup of a cleaner made especially for terrazzo. Never use an acidic or alkali cleaner because they damage the surface. If the floor is heavily stained, have it cleaned professionally.

Terra-cotta

Scrub terra-cotta pots using only water and a brush. Then disinfect with a sponge or cloth dipped in a solution of one part chlorine bleach to nine parts water.

For easy maintenance of tile floors, have the terra-cotta sealed. Damp-mop regularly, and clean as needed with a commercial stone-cleaning product or a cleanser formulated especially for terra-cotta.

Thermoses

Wash a thermos the same way you would glassware—in warm water and dishwashing detergent. To remove lingering odors, fill the thermos with hot water and ¼ cup baking soda; close, leave overnight, then rinse. Store a thermos with the top off and a little baking soda inside to keep it fresh, rinsing it thoroughly before use.

Ties

Ties are normally made of one of seven materials: silk, wool, cotton, rayon, acetate, nylon, or polyester. For specific care information or stain removal for any of these fabrics, look under its individual entry heading.

Ties generally do not need to be ironed. Their edges are rolled, not creased, which contributes to the body of the tie. If a tie must be ironed, use the setting indicated on your iron for the tie's fabric. A better option might be to steam the tie with a handheld steamer.

To keep ties in good condition, store them either hanging or rolled. Bleeding of a tie's pattern is probably due to the lack of colorfastness of the dyes used in its manufacture. Nothing can be done when this happens. The dyes used in higher-quality ties tend to be more resistant to bleeding. It is best, as a general rule, not to soak ties in water to clean them, even if they are stained.

Lower-quality ties are also more susceptible to rippling or puckering, which are also problems that cannot be fixed.

Tiles

See **Ceramic tile,** page 48; **Quarry tile floors**, page 112; and **Terra-cotta**, opposite page.

Tin

Metal bakeware can rust easily, so it must be washed and dried carefully. Don't use abrasive cleaners because they can scratch and pit the surface, allowing rust to form. Wash in a solution of hot water and mild detergent. Dry immediately with a cloth, or place in a hot oven for a few minutes. Wipe with oil regularly to prevent rust.

See also **Bakeware,** page 36.

Toilets

Brush the toilet bowl regularly to remove any stains and hard-water deposits, making sure to clean beneath the rim. Clean the brush afterward by leaving it in the bowl while flushing the toilet. Once a week, use the brush to clean the bowl with a disinfectant cleanser you've poured into the water, making sure to clean the brush by running it through the soapy water, then rinsing it during a flush. Use a sponge dipped in a solution of hot water and disinfectant cleanser to wipe down the rest of the toilet and the toilet seat.

To remove hard-water deposits deep inside the bowl, pour a gallon of water into the bowl to make it empty out without refilling. Apply a commercial rust remover or a scale and hard-water cleaner, leave for half an hour, then flush away. An in-tank cleaner will slow the buildup of new deposits, but an occasional thorough cleaning will still be necessary.

Tortoiseshell

To clean a comb or other object made with this material, wipe it with a soft cloth or cotton swab dipped in rubbing alcohol. Rub with a soft cloth dipped in borax to polish.

Towels

Towels absorb large amounts of dirt and body oils and should be laundered frequently. Machine-wash and dry according to care instructions, and fold as soon as possible to prevent wrinkling. Wash darks separately because they can bleed, and add bleach to a whites-only load to restore brightness. Don't use fabric softeners. They help ensure towels remain soft but also leave a waxy film that makes them less absorbent.

No matter how well you care for your towels, don't expect them to hold up to repeated washings. Even when washed in cold water, they're likely to shrink over time. Colored towels, blue and green especially, can fade.

Consider buying an extra washcloth when purchasing towels and storing it with the receipt. That way, you can demand a refund if your towels fade.

Toys

Occasionally washing small plastic toys in the dishwasher is an excellent way to keep germs at bay. Use a twist tie to keep the toys in place on the upper rack or in the silverware basket. Clean marks off plastic toys with a toothbrush to which you've applied a solution of baking soda moistened with some dishwashing liquid, then sponge it off. Use rubbing alcohol to remove tough stains.

If a stuffed toy is marked "all new materials," you can safely machine-wash it. If it has long hair or other long fibers that might get caught in the agitator, put it in a mesh bag before placing it in the machine. If a stuffed toy can't be washed, put it in a plastic bag filled with baking soda and shake thoroughly, then brush off the powder over a sink or outside. Or rub cornmeal into the toy, let stand, and shake out.

Triacetate

Triacetate is used in sportswear and clothes in which pleat retention is important—such as robes, dresses, and skirts. It is shrink-resistant, heat-resistant, and easily washed. Pleated items should be hand-washed. Nonpleated items that are 100 percent triacetate can be machine-washed. Air- or machine-dry. Check the care label before you iron—tri-acetate usually needs only touch-up ironing, but some garments or blends may be no-iron.

Turquoise

Water can damage turquoise. Clean by simply wiping with a soft cloth, and use a soft, dry toothbrush to clean settings around the turquoise.

Typewriters

Typewriters usually come with a cleaning kit consisting of brushes and cleaning fluid for cleaning the type. Use either the supplied brush or a small, synthetic, fluffy brush to remove dust. Use rubbing alcohol on a cotton swab to clean keys and in between them, and to remove any ink stains in or on the machine. A typewriter that is used frequently should be serviced and cleaned professionally once a year. When the typewriter is not in use, cover it to protect it from dust.

Cleaning Caveat

Do not use nail-polish remover or other cleaners that contain acetone for removing stains from triacetate. Acetone will dissolve it. Perfumes containing organic solvents may also harm it.

Ultrasuede

Ultrasuede is a brand of synthetic, suede-like fabric made of polyester microfibers in a polyurethane backing. Maintain the nap by lightly brushing with a medium-bristle clothes brush. Machine-wash Ultrasuede on Delicate, and tumble-dry on the lowest heat setting. Press on the lowest heat setting, turning the garment inside out, and use a pressing cloth to avoid damaging the nap.

The fabric is supposed to be stain-resistant, but if stains do occur, remove them by blotting with a solution of 1 teaspoon of liquid detergent and 1 cup of warm water. Blot again with a wet cloth or paper towel to rinse with a dry cloth or paper towel to remove excess moisture. Most Ultrasuede garments can also be dry-cleaned; check the label to be sure.

Umbrellas (outdoor)

Use a sponge dipped in mild detergent and water to clean canvas and vinyl umbrellas. Rinse with a hose, and then leave open to dry thoroughly. Apply automotive vinyl finish to a clean, dry vinyl umbrella to keep soils and stains to a minimum. Remove built-up grime with a cleaner sold for the vinyl tops of cars. Keep an umbrella closed during inclement weather, but open it afterward and clear away any dirt and debris that might have blown or washed into the folds. Clean the umbrella before putting it away for the winter, and make sure it is completely dry before storing it.

Upholstery

Vacuum upholstered furniture regularly to prevent dirt from building up. To clean up a spill, blot the wet areas immediately with a white towel or paper towel; dyes in a colored towel or paper towel can bleed and leave a stain on the upholstery.

To clean upholstered furniture, you can buy a cleaning product and apply it by hand; buy or rent a machine that cleans both upholstery and carpeting; or call a professional cleaning service.

Hand cleaning. Generally, cleaning by hand means spraying upholstery cleaner on the fabric, gently rubbing the resulting foam with a damp sponge, cloth, or brush, and then vacuuming the residue. The job can be time-consuming and may not yield the results you expected. Any hand-cleaning product is likely to work better if the job is done before the upholstery becomes badly soiled.

Machine cleaning. Setting up the machine, cleaning the piece of furniture, and then disassembling and cleaning the

Cracking the Furniture Label's Code

Many furniture manufacturers have adopted a standard labeling system that uses letter codes to indicate how furniture should be cleaned. If you purchased your furniture within the past few years, the label that includes these codes may have been attached to the fabric sample, to the tag hanging from the furniture, or to one of the cushions of the upholstered piece. Here is what the letter codes mean:

W—Use a water-based cleaner. Spot-clean only with the foam of a commercial upholstery shampoo or foam of a mild detergent. (Add some to water, shake it up, and use foam only.) Use very little foam. Too much moisture may create a mildew problem.

S—Use a solvent cleaner. Use a commercial dry-cleaning solvent for spot cleaning. Use very little and observe the cautions on the label about the flammability of the product. Solvent cleaners will NOT remove water stains and must be water-free; otherwise they will cause spotting or shrinking. Do not use with latex foam rubber.

S-W—Use either a water-based or a solvent cleaner.

X—Vacuum only. Use of any cleaning agent may cause excessive shrinking, fading, or spotting.

Guide to Cleaning Upholstery Fabric

The chart below shows how upholstery fabrics respond to both wet and dry cleaning and can help you decide whether to dry-clean with solvents or "wet-clean" with a water-based solution. Most upholstery fabrics can be dry-cleaned. Many fabrics can be cleaned effectively by steam-cleaning with detergent and water, but not all fabrics react well to water—some shrink, some become mottled by water spots, and some turn brown. Additionally, some fabrics may bleed with both wet and dry cleaning. Also, while oil-based spills are likely to stain all fabrics, water-based spills can stain many fabrics too. If your fabric is a blend of fibers, base your decision on the most sensitive fabric in the blend. However you clean, test on an inconspicuous spot first.

FIBER	Wet-Cleaning Only Tendency to: Shrink	Water-spot	Brown	Wet- and Dry-Cleaning Cautions	Tendency to Bleed
Cotton	Moderate	Low	High	Fabric may contain glazing, sizing, or other finishes that can run or be removed during cleaning.	High
Linen	High	Low	High	Fabric may contain glazing, sizing, or other finishes that can run or be removed during cleaning. Fabric darkens when wet, making it hard to assess quality of cleaning.	High
Rayon	Very High	High	High	Fabric may contain glazing, sizing, or other finishes that can run or be removed during cleaning. Fabric has a tendency to shrink, even when preshrunk.	High
Silk	Low	High	High	Water marks may be difficult to remove without damaging fabric. Fabric may stretch with excessive agitation.	High
Wool	Moderate	Low	Moderate	Darkens when wet, making it hard to assess quality of cleaning.	Moderate
Acetate	Low	Low	Low	Fabric has a tendency to shrink, even when preshrunk. Dissolves in acetone. Avoid nail-polish remover or commercial ink removers.	Low
Acrylic	Low	Low	Low	Spots reappear after cleaning.	Low
Nylon	Low	Low	Low	Fabric dissolves in strong acids.	Low
Olefin	Low	Low	Low	Spots reappear after cleaning. Age, sun, and chlorinated solvents may weaken latex backing; resists bleach.	Low
Polyester	Low	Low	Low	Spots reappear after cleaning.	Low

machine can be difficult and time-consuming. You may find that the results are not worth the effort.

Professional cleaning. Professional cleaning may seem expensive, but it's far less costly than replacing a soiled piece of furniture.

To find a professional cleaning service, get a personal recommendation, look under "Carpet Cleaners" or "Upholstery Cleaners" in the yellow pages, or check with the Association of Specialists in Cleaning and Restoration (800-272-7102 or *www.ascr.org/cuci.asp*) for a member company that has passed a test on cleaning upholstery, adheres to the group's code of ethics, subscribes to its educational programs, and has its technical support.

A cleaning service should be able to provide a preliminary estimate over the phone. Request that a technician come to your home to evaluate the job and spot-test the cleaner the company uses by applying it to an inconspicuous piece of fabric. A reputable company should explain the procedure, tell you what kind of results you can expect, outline guarantees and other policies, provide references, and give you a firm quote. Check references the company provides.

Some professionals may prefer to steam-clean with water and detergent because the results are generally better than they are with dry cleaning. But cleaning with water—even by a pro—can be risky, so make sure the cleaning professional does a spot test and is prepared to switch to dry cleaning or a foam-based cleaner.

Chemical fabric protection. If fabric protection was applied at the mill where the fabric was made, the fabric should not need to be treated again until it has been cleaned two or three times. Stain repellents such as Scotchgard protect against both oil- and water-based stains, while silicone stain repellents protect only against water-based stains and may yellow with exposure to ultraviolet light. If you don't know if the fabric has been

Helpful Hint

Check the following before using any upholstery cleaner:

• Shrinkage. Try a bit in a hidden spot. If fabric is tighter or pulled together when it dries, do not use.

• Colorfastness. Apply the cleaning solution to a white rag and press it on a hidden spot. If the color bleeds, use another method.

treated with a stain repellent, apply one after cleaning.

A professional can apply stain protection for an additional charge. If you decide to apply one yourself—not an easy task—you must make sure you apply it evenly. Use an electric spray or aerosol can rather than a pump sprayer. Check the label to make sure the protection is advised for your type of fabric, and apply a small amount in a hidden place first to make sure the fabric doesn't bleed.

See also **Cushions**, page 61.

Vacuum cleaners

Change the paper bag or clean the cloth bag as soon as suction drops noticeably, even if the bag is only halfway full. Small quantities of fine, dense dirt can reduce a bag's efficiency and consequently a cleaner's suction. Some newer-model upright vacuum cleaners have, instead of a bag, a see-through dirt-collection container. To minimize mess when emptying the container, place a plastic garbage bag over the opening before tilting the unit. Do this outside if possible. Many new vacuums—with or without bags—have filters that require periodic cleaning or replacement. Check your users' manual for specific instructions for your machine.

Be careful about what your vacuum takes in. Objects such as coins and paper clips can damage the motor fan. A regular vacuum has no tolerance for wetness and should never be used outdoors. Even moisture from a recently shampooed carpet may cause damage. String can snarl up the works as it winds itself around the rotating brush. If your vacuum swallows something hard or stringy, turn off the power and disconnect the electric plug before trying to dislodge the foreign object. When clumps of dust or other debris clog the hose, insert a broom or mop handle into it, being careful not to puncture the hose cover.

Vases

Wash a glass vase with mild detergent and water. If the vase is stained or has accumulated sediment at the bottom, mix equal parts vinegar and warm water, add a few drops of mild detergent, pour the solution into the vase, and let stand overnight. Brush out the sediment with a bottle brush. Or add crushed eggshells and shake until the sediment loosens. Empty the vase and rinse. (If the neck of the vase is narrow, use dry rice grains instead of eggshells.) Or pour water into the vase and add a denture-cleaning tablet, following the instructions for soaking on the package. Empty the vase and rinse.

VCRs

Cover VCRs when they're not in use to prevent dust from getting into the ports. Use a dehumidifier in a room that is prone to condensation. Dust the case regularly. Do not use liquid cleaning products. To clean smudgy or sticky spots, dip the edge of a cloth in a detergent-and-water solution and spot-clean only. If the picture is deteriorating, use a special VCR cleaning tape, but only if the manufacturer recommends this. If this is not successful, servicing may be required.

Velvet

Check the care label. Some types of velvet can be machine- or hand-washed, but velvet brocades and garments that may be damaged or that may bleed color should be dry-cleaned.

Venetian blinds

See **Blinds,** page 40.

Videotape cassettes

Store tapes in a cool, dry place where they aren't likely to gather a lot of dust. Stand them on end, so that weight is taken off the tape edge, preventing jamming.

Viyella

This brand of fabric is half cotton and half wool. Machine-wash it on a delicate setting. Use a cool iron while the fabric is still damp.

Wallpaper and wallcoverings

Most wallpaper sold today can be washed and in some cases scrubbed. Do not leave paper uncleaned for a long time, since it may absorb the soiling.

Washable. Most wallpaper is paper or fabric coated with vinyl, which may be described as paper-backed vinyl, vinyl-coated paper, expanded or textured vinyl, or even (incorrectly) solid vinyl. Vinyls can be smooth like plain-paper wall coverings, textured like leather or fabric, or embossed. Vacuum them regularly with a brush attachment, or use a dust mop with a disposable pad, working upward, since drips onto soiled areas can cause streaks that are hard to remove.

Nonabrasive bleaching cleansers may fade some colors. Instead use an all-purpose cleanser without bleach, and sponge-clean or scrub with a soft brush. Rinse with a damp cloth dipped in clean, warm water. Take care not to apply too much liquid because it may work its way into the seams.

To remove a greasy spot from washable wallpaper, blot it and rub with cornstarch, allowing it to absorb the grease. Then gently brush or vacuum the cornstarch away. Or sponge on a solution of liquid household cleanser, first testing to make sure it won't stain. Remove crayon with a lubricant such as WD-40, and take off ink with rubbing alcohol; blot afterward. Spot-test to avoid discoloring or staining wallpaper.

Nonwashable. Plain paper—often a reproduction of an antique pattern—has no protective coating and can't tolerate scrubbing. Dust it regularly with a vacuum brush, or use a dust mop with a disposable pad. Textured wallpaper is easily damaged.

To remove a stain, gently rub it with kneadable wall-covering cleaner, or dab powdered borax into the mark, then brush. To remove grease, rub cornstarch on the spot and allow it to absorb the grease, then gently brush or vacuum it away.

Fabric. Gently dust with a soft brush or damp cloth. Spot-clean carefully with a solvent suitable to the material. Test first in a hidden area. Check with the manufacturer or the wallpaper hanger to see how to deep-clean a fabric covering.

Grass cloth. Heavily textured wall covering made of jute, linen, or grass woven and bonded to a backing is easily stained. It is best cleaned with a vacuum rather than a sponge or rag since the grass can work loose easily. Use a soft vacuum-cleaner brush on low suction. Treat marks with an aerosol solvent made to remove grease. Don't allow furniture to touch this material since it can rub the grass loose and leaves marks.

Walls
See **Ceramic tile,** page 48; **Cork,** page 56; **Painted walls,** page 106; and **Wood paneling**, page 148.

Washing machines
Usually made of baked enamel, the exterior of a washing machine can be cleaned with a mild detergent solution. Leave the door of the washing machine open for a while after removing a wash load so that the interior can dry out and odors do not build up. Sponge off detergent accumulations from around the opening. Follow the manufacturer's instructions for cleaning underneath the agitator. In areas where water is hard, add a little water softener to the detergent to remove any built-up scale.

Water
Most drinking water in the United States is safe. But if you have any qualms about the purity of your tap water—or simply don't like its taste or smell—you may want to consider getting a water filter. Alternatives include bottled, boiled, or distilled water.

Facts about your water supply can help you decide. A federal law requires water utilities serving more than 10,000 people to send an annual report to their customers that clearly explains exactly what's in the water when it leaves the treatment plant. Some states have required such reports for years. If your water utility serves 10,000 or fewer, you may find information at a public library or in a local newspaper. People with a well or on a very small system must have testing done on their own.

If you decide that your water does need filtering, don't stop with the filter. Compare notes with neighbors and notify the water system as well as local health officials. When the source of a problem can be found, it should be eliminated.

See **Water filters,** page 218.

Water Pollutants to Watch Out For

A few pollutants can pose a risk even if they're under the government's legal limit. They are especially dangerous to vulnerable groups, such as pregnant women and people with cancer or AIDS. Be especially alert for the following:

Arsenic. The element occurs naturally in the Earth's crust and shows up mainly in water supplies drawn from wells. If your water supply has an arsenic level higher than 10 micrograms per liter—the World Health Organization safety limit—use a distiller, the only product currently certified to remove arsenic.

The Environmental Protection Agency (EPA) is moving ahead with plans to lower the safety limit for arsenic. At the current maximum level of 50 micrograms per liter, arsenic carries a lifetime cancer risk of at least 1 in 1,000 and perhaps as high as 1 in 100, according to a recent assessment by the National Research Council.

Chlorination byproducts. Chlorination kills germs, but it also reacts with organic matter in water to form chloroform and other trihalomethanes, which are suspected carcinogens and have been recently linked to an increased risk of miscarriage. If the level of trihalomethanes in your water is higher that 75 micrograms per liter, drink filtered water, especially if you're pregnant or planning a pregnancy.

Cryptosporidium. This tough microscopic parasite was responsible for the single-largest outbreak of disease from a contaminated public water supply in U.S. history. Healthy adults generally recovered from infection, but the parasite was fatal to about half of those with cancer or AIDS. If your water system is required to test for cryptosporidium, your water report will note that. The cysts can be filtered out or killed by boiling water that you use for drinking or cooking.

Lead. Water that leaves the treatment plant relatively free of lead can pick up hazardous amounts from lead or lead-soldered pipes and some brass faucets by the time it emerges from your tap. The only way to be sure your own water is lead-free is to have it tested. To find a certified testing laboratory in your area, call the EPA's Safe Drinking Water Hotline, 800-426-4791, or go to *www.epa.gov/safewater*. If the lead level is more than 15 parts per billion, consider filtering your water. Most filters effectively remove lead.

Watercolor paintings

As is the case with all paintings, watercolors are best turned over to a professional for cleaning. If you want to attempt cleaning one yourself, first try to remove spots by rubbing them with fresh white bread crumbs until the crumbs do not absorb any more dirt. Very gently rub any stubborn marks that might remain with an artist's kneadable eraser. If you detect grease spots on the painting, apply some acetone solvent, available in art-supply shops, to a soft, clean cloth and gently dab the stain. Then lay a piece of blotting paper over the area and gently go over it with the tip of a warm iron to help draw out the stain.

Unframed watercolors are quite fragile, so you should store them with care. Cover with acid-free paper, lay flat in a dry place where the painting will not be crushed or wrinkled, and place mothballs nearby.

Waterproof fabric

Brush this fabric well when it's dirty. Apply a waterproofing agent or have a professional do it from time to time.

Wicker

Wicker is not a material but a technique of weaving synthetic material or long strips of plants—such as rattan and reed—into furniture. All-weather wicker may be left outside year-round. Follow the manufacturer's instructions for cleaning. If wicker is treated—sealed with lacquer, varnish, or shellac, then coated with liquid furniture wax—it should need only regular dusting.

Untreated wicker should be kept inside during inclement weather. For routine cleaning, use the upholstery attachment of a vacuum cleaner or a feather duster. In the winter, dryness may cause it to crack, so wipe with a damp sponge occasionally or give it a very light coating of lemon oil. Once a year, if a piece has no wooden parts, scrub it with warm water and detergent, spray it with a garden hose, or put it under a shower. Dry it as quickly as possible by putting it in the sun or using a hair dryer or floor fan. Don't sit on it until it's thoroughly dry. Sand away any rough edges with fine paper.

An alternative is wiping with a clean, damp sponge, trying not to let wooden parts become too wet. For visible dirt, add

1 tablespoon of liquid detergent to 1 quart of warm water, or use the foam from a solution of detergent and water.

Wash and rinse painted wicker the same way you would painted wood. If you get a painted wicker piece too wet, the paint may crack and peel.

Wigs and hairpieces

Clean a synthetic wig with mild dishwashing detergent or a wig shampoo. Use cool water—hot water takes out the styling. Air drying is recommended, but you may use a hair dryer on a cool setting. Clean machine-made human-hair wigs with shampoo for normal hair plus conditioner since they lack natural oils from the human head. You can use a hair dryer for styling. Hand-knotted human-hair wigs require the services of a professional wig cleaner. Though they can be washed like human hair, they must be blocked into position when shampooing is over or they will lose their shape.

Window frames and door frames

Dust regularly. Clean very dirty frames before the windows are cleaned. Vacuum the runners of aluminum window frames and doors, then polish the frames with silicone car polish, which can also be used in channels to help windows slide smoothly. Or lightly oil the channels. Wash painted frames with a sponge dipped in warm water and detergent. Rinse with warm, clean water, and towel dry, if necessary.

Windows

How frequently you need to clean your windows depends on where you live, but the insides usually need cleaning twice a year. Wash windows on a cloudy day or when the windows are in shade because direct sun will cause streaking. If you live in a home with many windows, divide the job into segments rather than attempting to do them all in one day. You'll need two buckets, a sponge, a good-quality rubber squeegee, a clean, lint-free cloth, a chamois cloth, and a commercial cleaning solution or your own (see **Homemade cleaning products,** page 271).

Loop curtains over a hanger, and hang them out of the way. Clean windows from the top down. Use a slightly dampened sponge to apply the cleaning solution. Wipe across the window with the dampened blade of the squeegee, then wipe the blade. Follow with a rinse of clean water applied with the chamois. Polish off any remaining moisture with the dry cloth. While cleaning, check any putty that needs replacing; paint repair that might have to be done; or cracks in any glass.

Remove new paint spatters with a cloth dipped in turpentine (for oil-based paint) or water or glass cleaner (for water-based paint). Use a single-edged razor to scrape old paint, holding it at an angle to avoid scratching the glass. Leave $\frac{1}{16}$ inch of paint on the edge of the glass to protect the frame from condensation inside and rain outside. Note that glass cleaner can soften water-based paint. If you spray it onto a painted surface, blot, don't rub; the paint will harden once dry. Wipe away putty marks with ammonia.

Clean small windows or stained-glass windows with a damp sponge first, then wipe with a clean, damp chamois. Polish with a clean cloth. Treat delicate stained glass with care. Painted glass should be gently cleaned with a damp chamois.

Most new double-hung windows have tilting sashes, a handy feature that lets you pivot them inward for easier cleaning. With most, you simply flip a lever or two to tilt the sash inward. But with some, you must pull the sash out of the track.

Some high windows and skylights can be cleaned with special extension tools, but it may be practical to hire a professional window cleaner, if only for the out-of-reach windows.

See also **Skylights,** page 126.

Wood furniture

See **Furniture,** page 76.

Wood paneling

Dust or vacuum-clean wood paneling regularly with a vacuum cleaner's soft brush attachment or a ceiling brush. Remove dirty fingerprints with a damp cloth dipped in a mild detergent solution.

For lacquered, varnished, or waxed wood finishes, you can use an appropriate wood oil every six months, although some of these can make surfaces sticky and more prone to fingerprints and dust. Do not use furniture polish, which may muddy the finish.

Occasionally wipe painted wood paneling with a barely damp cloth. If the wood has been sealed, dampen it with a sponge, and wipe dry. Maintain shine with occasional use of an aerosol cleaner or polish.

Dust oiled or untreated wood regularly, and wipe it occasionally with a light coating of Danish oil or a commercial polish such as Scott's Liquid Gold applied with a soft cloth. Wipe again to remove excess.

Polish wax-finished wood paneling with a good-quality paste wax once or twice a year. When wax builds up and starts to smear, remove it with turpentine and reapply. To improve the appearance of faded and scratched paneling, apply turpentine on fine steel wool and rub in the direction of the grain. Polish and buff.

Wooden jewelry

Wipe beads, brooches, and bangles with a damp chamois cloth, then polish with a little olive oil. Rub the oil in well, then buff with a soft cloth.

Wooden salad bowls

Wipe a bowl out with a nonabrasive pad or a cloth dipped in warm, sudsy water. Rub until food particles are removed, and dry the surface immediately. Never soak a wooden bowl in water, put it through the dishwasher, or leave it in direct sunlight. If the wood appears to be dry, rub in some vegetable oil to season it. Use a paper towel to remove the excess.

Wool

Made from the fleece of animals, wool is water-repellent and wrinkle-, stain-, and soil-resistant. It is warm and retains color well. Types of wool include alpaca (from alpaca goats), angora (angora rabbits), camel hair (camels), cashmere (Asian

Helpful Hint

You can prevent stored wool from being damaged by using moth repellent.

goats), lamb's wool, llama, mohair (angora goats), and pashmina (Himalayan capra goat). Wool fabrics include jersey, gabardine, crepe, twills, and broadcloth. Recycling wool is an old practice, and items made of recycled wool may be less expensive. "New" or "virgin" wool is made from wool that has not previously made up another product. It may be softer than other woolens, but a garment made of "100 percent new wool" is not necessarily a superior product because it may include some inferior grades of wool.

All wool garments can be dry-cleaned, but check your item's care label before hand or machine washing. "Dry-clean only" means just that—no wet washing. Some garments may be hand-washed carefully in cold water with a mild wool-washing product. Wools that can be machine-washed should be cleaned on a gentle cycle.

Turn a washable wool garment—one that does not contain mohair or angora—inside out before hand-washing. Wash carefully in cold water with a mild wool-washing product. Do not wring wool items. Instead, lay hand-washed garments on a dry towel and then roll up the towel to remove excess mois-

Washing Wool: The Soak and Spin Method

Simple wool garments that can be hand-washed, such as sweaters, can also be laundered in a top-loading washer, using it as a washbasin that spins. Here's how:

• Be sure the sweater has no buttons or decorative trim and doesn't contain angora or mohair, which are difficult to clean. Keep light colors separate from darks, and wash reds by themselves. Turn the sweater inside out before washing.

• Fill the tub with an appropriate amount of warm or cold water, add a mild detergent, and run the machine just long enough to mix.

• Shut off the machine and immerse the sweaters. Do not agitate them. Let them soak for 10 to 20 minutes, then set the machine to the Spin setting to extract the soapy water.

• Remove the sweaters from the tub and refill it with plain water. Let the sweaters soak for another 10 to 20 minutes with no agitation, then spin to extract the water. Repeat if they still feel soapy.

• Lay the sweaters flat to dry, and reshape them as needed.

ture. Unroll the now-damp towel, remove the garment, and lay it flat to dry on a new towel so it will retain its shape.

Machine-washed garments should also be dried flat. They should be placed in a dryer only if the care label permits machine-drying. You might want to forgo machine drying altogether, however—in CONSUMER REPORTS tests, machine drying damaged some sweaters made of machine-washable wool.

Don't press wool with a dry iron—use the Wool or Steam setting. To avoid a shine, iron the garment inside out or use a pressing cloth.

Wrought iron

This hardy material usually needs only a dusting with a clean cloth. If it seems dirty, clean it with mild detergent and hot water, then rinse and dry. To prevent rusting on wrought iron, apply a liquid wax polish or paste wax or use a rust-inhibiting paint. If rust has formed, use a commercial rust-removing product, then paint or wax.

Zircon

Zircon is somewhat soft, so avoid scratches and sharp blows. Clean with a solution of one part mild detergent, one part household ammonia, and three parts water. Dry the jewelry with a lint-free towel.

Cleaning Agents

Acetone

A solvent used to remove nail polish and animal and vegetable oils, acetone is normally sold in the form of nail-polish remover or as a solvent for paint or for varnish. Do not use on acetate fabrics; it will dissolve them. Highly flammable, acetone should be used only away from an open flame and in a well-ventilated area. Alternatives for stain removal are mineral spirits and Murphy Oil Soap.

Air fresheners

Normally available in aerosol, block, and plug-in forms, air fresheners contain solvents and perfumes and may contain hydrocarbons as propellants. A well-ventilated home probably doesn't need an air freshener. Instead, leave in a room overnight a bowl of hot water containing a few drops of household ammonia, a tablespoon of bicarbonate of soda, or a few drops of lavender oil. To remove bathroom odors, light a match, burn a candle, or use aromatherapy oils and a burner.

All-purpose cleaners

All-purpose cleaners are good for many home-cleaning tasks, particularly in the kitchen and bathroom (see also **Bathroom cleaners,** page 160). Most all-purpose cleaners are usually either "pourables" (liquids applied on grime) or spray cleaners. They can also be found in a variety of forms including pow-

ders, gels, and pastes. Brands include Ajax, Comet, Fantastik, Formula 409, Lysol, Mr. Clean, Soft Scrub, and Spic and Span.

All-purpose cleaners are good for mopping, washing, and spot-cleaning hard surfaces such as walls, floors, appliances, kitchen cabinets, and countertops. Other tasks are best handled by specialized products. For example, glass cleaners are generally the best choice for cleaning glass because they streak the least, bathroom cleaners are generally most effective on bathroom grime, and lye-based oven cleaners provide the oomph needed for standard, non-self-cleaning ovens.

What CONSUMER REPORTS tests have found

Most commercially available all-purpose cleaners were shown to be effective and versatile cleaning agents in CONSUMER REPORTS tests that subjected a range of products to tough cleaning tasks on a variety of surfaces.

Pourables generally have different formulations, and they may do better overall spot cleaning than spray cleaners. The best cleaning pourables often contain pine oil, an effective cleaning ingredient with a distinctive "clean" scent.

Though chlorine bleach is limited in effectiveness and may be difficult to handle for most cleaning jobs, it is a useful ingredient in an all-purpose cleaner. Whether pourable or a spray, an all-purpose cleaner containing bleach is often the best choice for attacking mildew and some stains.

When diluted in a bucket of water, a pourable product can be effective for mopping floors. Few spray products suggest that their liquid contents can be used in this manner. Effective pourables for this purpose often claim to contain pine oil, citrus oil, or oil soap.

When used at full strength, an all-purpose cleaner should be used gently, then promptly and carefully rinsed off. Otherwise, you may risk marring the surface being cleaned. Check the label for precaution, and, if in doubt, test in a hidden area before using the cleaner.

Cleaners for the Kitchen

For most routine kitchen cleaning tasks, you'll need little more than a bleach-powered all-purpose cleaner, dishwashing liquid, and a commercial spray cleaner.

Most of the bleach-fortified all-purpose cleaners CONSUMER REPORTS tested did a fine job on common kitchen stains, such as juice and red wine, and baked-on grime. And a product with bleach— a powerful bacteria killer—is a fine choice for wiping away mildew or cleaning a kitchen surface after preparing raw meat or fish (see also **Disinfectants**, page 165). Products that performed well on kitchen stains and were relatively gentle to surfaces include Fantastik All Purpose Cleaner with Bleach, a spray; and Soft Scrub with Clorox Bleach, an antibacterial paste.

Although most kitchen messes require little more than a wipe with water or perhaps the application of a little dishwashing liquid, commercial spray cleaners such as Earth Rite and Goo Gone are convenient for quick swipes and are aggressive grease cutters as well.

Alkalies and Acids

Many cleaners contain acids or alkalies. On a pH scale of 1 to14, with 7, like pure water, considered neutral, acid solutions fall below 7 and alkaline solutions are above 7. Highly alkaline cleaners are considered caustic and highly acidic cleaners are corrosive.

Generally, grease- and oil-based soiling are best treated with alkaline cleaners, which separate heavy soil and grease from surfaces and fabrics so they can be rinsed away. Common alkaline cleaners are ammonia, borax, chlorine bleach, detergents and soaps, TSP (trisodium phosphate), and washing soda.

Particulates (such as smoke) and mineral deposits left by hard water (such as the lime scales formed by calcium and magnesium) are best treated with acidic descaling cleaners. Common acidic cleaners include white vinegar, lemon juice, commercial rust-removing products, and many metal cleaners (which remove tarnish and corrosion from metals).

Some products are caustic enough to warrant that you wear rubber gloves when cleaning or at least that you avoid prolonged contact with the skin. Since the solvents and other ingredients that dissolve, emulsify, suspend, or otherwise loosen grime are powerful chemicals, any cleaner should be used carefully in accordance with its labeled precautions and kept out of the reach of children. To avoid potentially hazardous chemical reactions, never mix any cleaner with ammonia or chlorine bleach. Just mix with water.

CONSUMER REPORTS tests have reinforced the importance of carefully reading the product label. Some cleaners are more appropriate for certain surfaces than others. You must consider possible surface damage before using any all-purpose cleaner; the most effective cleaners also tend to be those most likely to leave their mark.

Don't assume that "green" claims mean a lot. Products that are supposed to have an "environmentally sensitive formula" or be "environmentally certified" might indeed by kinder to the Earth. But claims like these are too vague to be meaningful, verifiable, or useful when you buy.

Ammonia

This strong alkaline cleaner is also a mild grease solvent. Soapy or sudsy ammonia, which contains about 5 percent ammonia in addition to a little detergent, is a useful version. Never mix ammonia with products containing chlorine bleach. Such a mixture gives off dangerous fumes. Dilute full-strength ammonia with water. One effective mixture is eight parts water to one part ammonia; check the label of your ammonia bottle for other recommended solutions. When working with ammonia, wear protective gloves, and make sure the area you are cleaning in is well ventilated.

Auto polishes

Over time, sunlight, water, air pollution, and other contaminants oxidize car paint. Eventually the gloss fades and the finish is no longer able to shed such contaminants as water and dirt. At this point, auto polish can make a dramatic improvement.

Most manufacturers of car-care products use the terms "polish" and "wax" interchangeably. Both usually refer to a liquid, paste, or spray that adds luster to the finish and sometimes removes oxidation and embedded grime. None of these products is all things to all people, though. What you choose may depend on how much elbow grease you want to put into the job. Before buying, make sure that you actually need auto polish. Some abrasive products might do more harm than good when paint is new or nearly new.

To check to see if you need polish, study the way water beads on the surface of your car. The beads of water that form on a protected surface are relatively small and rounded and sit high on the surface. If the beads of water on your car's finish are the size of a quarter or smaller, you don't need to wax. As the polish wears away, though, the beads spread and flatten. Eventually, when the polish is completely gone, water doesn't bead at all; it lies in a sheet on the surface. This is the time to apply auto polish.

What CONSUMER REPORTS tests have found

One-step applications contain abrasives or solvents to remove stubborn stains or oxidation from a car's finish and waxes or silicones that can fill tiny cracks and renew the water repellence of the finish. Sprays are easiest and fastest to use, but they don't typically clean very well or have a lasting effect, especially on cars with a very dirty or oxidized finish.

CONSUMER REPORTS has found that waxing a medium-sized sedan with a spray polish typically takes one person about 25 minutes. Shake a liquid or spray container before you begin; some of the ingredients may have settled to the bottom.

Liquid and paste polishes take about twice as long to apply, but they usually can remove oxidation and dirt and last a relatively long time. Manufacturers use a variety of ingredients, from traditional carnauba wax (which comes from a Brazilian palm) to "space age" polymers. An applicator included with some liquids and pastes can make the job easier. Most products instruct you to let the polish dry to a haze after application, then buff with a dry, soft, cotton cloth. Buffing is likely to be fairly easy with most products, but some dry into a rather stiff coating that needs more effort to buff.

If you're using a polish for the first time on a dark-colored car, test it on an inconspicuous part of the car, such as the doorjamb. The polish should remove any oxidation or contaminants without leaving a haze or scratches. Owners of cars with a light-colored finish don't have to worry too much because imperfections caused by scratching or hazing will be hard to see.

For an extremely weathered finish, even the most abrasive polishes may not be adequate. You may need to start off with a special, highly abrasive polishing or rubbing compound, usually found next to auto polishes at auto-parts, discount, and department stores. But if you use a polishing compound, be wary about rubbing too long or too hard—you could rub through the paint to the primer.

Nearly all the polishes produce a good or very good shine, but none are miracle workers. No polish will make a weathered finish look like new, or make a new car's glossy finish even glossier. Some actually make the finish look worse, leaving behind fine scratches or a residue that's hard to remove. The stains that some polishes leave on a car's plastic trim are a related problem. Products that warn users not to get polish on the trim tend to be the worst offenders, while those that promise not to stain are true to their word.

Some polishes promise to protect a car's finish from the ravages of nature. Such claims are often not inaccurate, just overly dramatic. It stands to reason that a layer of wax may

Helpful Hint

Always wash a car before polishing, to avoid grinding the dirt into the paint and scratching the finish. And never polish a car in direct sunlight or when the surface is hot to the touch. That's when the paint can soften and be susceptible to scratching.

provide a measure of protection from tree sap, road tar, bird droppings, and sunlight.

Claims made by some polishes to last up to a year did not stand up to CONSUMER REPORTS tests. Even the most durable products lasted only about two months with normal use. Some liquids and pastes were most durable; the durability of the spray products tested was only fair.

Whether you choose a spray product or a liquid or paste product, the results will depend on several factors, including the condition of your car's finish, the climate, and where you store your car. The relative ease of a spray may be appropriate if your car's finish is in good shape and you wash your car regularly and park it out of the elements in a garage. A liquid or paste may be best for an older car with a weathered finish that is parked in the street, rain or shine.

Baking soda (bicarbonate of soda)

Sold in powder form, this is a mild alkali. It can be used for a variety of household cleaning purposes, such as removing stains from tiles, glass, oven doors, and china; cleaning out refrigerators; helping to remove odors; and removing baked-on food from pans. It acts as a stain remover for fruit juices and other mild acids.

Bathroom cleaners

Cleaners used in the bathroom—from all-purpose cleaners to specialized bathroom cleaning products—should be able to prevent and remove soap scum in showers and bathtubs, remove mildew from grout, remove unusual stains, and clean metal fixtures and surfaces. Some of the products promoted as bathroom cleaners derive most of their strength from old-fashioned pine oil; others rely on a mix of other chemicals. Because damp bathrooms are fertile grounds for fungi, specialized bathroom cleaners often claim to contain a mildew cleaning agent, which some all-purpose cleaners lack. Often this agent is a form of chlorine bleach.

What CONSUMER REPORTS tests have found

All powdered cleaners and some all-purpose and bathroom cleaners are effective at cleaning soap scum. You can improve the product's performance by leaving it on the soap scum longer than the time recommended on the label, but be sure to rinse it off before it dries out.

A product's effectiveness in removing mildew that accumulates in the grout on a tiled surface seems to depend on whether or not it contains bleach. In CONSUMER REPORTS tests, almost all products did an excellent job of cleaning and killing mildew. However, few bleach-free cleaning products, despite what their labels may claim, are effective mildew killers.

Tough stains such as lime scale, formed when hard water leaves a deposit,

Helpful Hint

Never mix a bathroom cleaner containing bleach with a product containing ammonia. The resulting mixture can form toxic fumes.

Daily Shower Cleaners

Ads for daily shower cleaners suggest that keeping soap scum and mildew off a shower wall is as easy as squirt, squirt. The four products CONSUMER REPORTS tested did prevent soap-scum buildup by removing a mixture of soap and hard water that we spritzed on black ceramic tiles. But no daily shower cleaner was very good at removing mildew. If mildew is your problem, look for a cleaner designed for that purpose, or use your own mixture of bleach and water. If the mildew is chronic, try improving the ventilation in your bathroom and wiping down the tiles and curtain after showering.

Before using a shower cleaner, read the product's label carefully. All are relatively gentle to surfaces, but some are harmful to marble, some to stainless steel, some to latex paint, and some to granite. Additionally, some products warn that they may irritate your eyes, which is a concern if you're cleaning a small, enclosed shower.

You can avoid possibly harming your shower's surface (and save money at the same time) by simply wiping down the tiles after showering. If you don't have hard water, soap scum won't be much of a problem anyway.

and the rust that can drip from aging fixtures proved a hard match for most bathroom cleaners.

Many cleaners dull or discolor brass and painted trim. Some also mar stainless-steel surfaces, and you may find a cleaner that mars vinyl shower curtains.

Some cleaning products can irritate skin and eyes, and a few are acidic or alkaline enough to warrant the use of rubber gloves. Some pump sprays can irritate lungs; labels may caution against use by people with heart or respiratory problems.

Many cleaners claim to disinfect, and they may indeed get rid of some microorganisms for a while. But you should not put too much faith in the long-term disinfecting powers of your bathroom cleaner. Any germs you eliminate from an unsterile environment will soon be replaced by others.

See also **All-purpose cleaners,** page 154; **Disinfectants,** page 165; and **Window cleaners,** page 189.

Bleach

Bleach removes color, stains, and mildew and also disinfects household items. The two main types used around the house are chlorine bleach and oxygen bleach. The chlorine bleach

Cleaning Caveat

Wear rubber gloves when using bleach. Always dilute it, be careful not to spill it, and make sure to replace the cap properly. Bleach can damage skin and cause serious injury if swallowed. Store out of the reach of children and pets.

you can buy at the grocery store is the chemical sodium hypochlorite mixed with water in a 5.25-percent or 6 percent solution. Don't use chlorine bleach on fine washables such as wool and silk. Chlorine bleach is a useful ingredient in an all-purpose cleaner, especially useful for disinfecting cutting boards that come in contact with raw meat.

Most oxygen bleaches come in powdered form. Often labeled "all-fabric bleaches," they may contain other agents, including optical brighteners, perfumes, and sometimes enzymes. They are safe for virtually all fabrics and help maintain whiteness but are not as effective at restoring it as chlorine bleaches are. They take longer to work than chlorine bleaches, so pre-soaking is often advisable.

Hydrogen peroxide (actually an oxygen bleach) is normally sold through drug stores and is used as an alternative for stain removal and mild bleaching and sterilizing. You can release hydrogen peroxide in water by adding powdered sodium peroxicarbonate or sodium perborate. There are also powdered bleaches containing sodium perborate or calcium peroxycarbonate that are good for some surfaces, such as decks, as well as for laundry. Lemon juice is a mild bleach that is safe to use.

Bleach can be used to disinfect surfaces, but remember that airborne bacteria are always present. You may decide that disinfecting with bleach is really not worth the bother. Household items can be sterilized with bleach, but a less-toxic alternative is to use boiling water or to dry things in a hot oven. You can use sunlight to sterilize and bleach cloth diapers.

Borax

This is a water softener, disinfectant, and, when mixed with sugar, a safe and effective ant killer. Sold in powder form or as colorless crystalline salt, it is not an especially strong cleaner but does make an excellent freshener when added to laundry, and it is an all-around deodorizer. Borax can be bought at supermarkets, hardware stores, and drug stores.

Brass and copper cleaners

Brass and copper can be cleaned with commercial cleaners available in the supermarket. Some of these products must be washed off thoroughly because they can stain or etch metals if left in contact with them. Others may be wiped or rubbed off. It is a good idea to restrict your choice to a wipe-off polish for objects that can't be readily rinsed or submerged.

Some wipe-off brands may produce a better shine. Wash-off products, however, require less elbow grease to remove tarnish— an important consideration if you have to clean a heavily tarnished surface. For objects that may be only thinly coated with brass or copper, use a cloth dipped in a mixture of dishwashing liquid and water.

Before any polish can work, the metal surface must be free of any lacquer. Clean, but do not attempt to polish, any metal that has a lacquered finish.

Carpet cleaners

These contain detergents and solvents and are usually sold as a powder or foaming aerosol. Powdered cleaners are best if you don't want to wet the carpet, which may lead to mildewing. But the powder is difficult to remove without a commercial vacuum cleaner. The use of powdered cleaners may actually void some consumer vacuum-cleaner warranties. Aerosol cleaners were found to be ineffective in CONSUMER REPORTS tests. The sponge used to clean the spot floated on top of the foam created by the aerosol cleaner and was unable to reach into the carpet.

Special carpet-stain cleaners are also available. These can be very effective on stubborn stains. To avoid damaging the carpet or affecting its color, you should test any stain remover on an inconspicuous spot before applying it to a prominent place. Additionally, try patting with brush bristles instead of scrubbing, which may damage carpet fibers. Be sure to rinse out and blot up any residual detergent.

See also **Carpeting,** page 239.

Compressed air

Available from photography-supply shops, this is air in a can, usually with a tube-type device that can direct a burst of air to a particular spot. The pressure from the released air can be used to chase dust from hard-to-reach spots, such as spaces beneath computer keys. But it can also drive dust farther inside. Instead, consider vacuuming with a crevice tool covered with an old nylon stocking.

Cream of tartar (potassium bitartrate)

This common baking ingredient is a mild acid, usually packaged as odorless and colorless translucent crystals or powder and often used in home cleaning when a mild acid is called for. It is an ingredient of baking powder and cosmetics. To use as a bathtub stain remover, sprinkle cream of tartar on the stain and then rub with lemon wedges. To remove spots from aluminum cookware, mix 2 tablespoons of cream of tartar powder and 1 quart of water in the stained item. Bring the solution to a boil and simmer for about 10 minutes. Wash and dry the item as you usually would.

Descaling cleaners

Containing strong acids, these are used to remove mineral deposits or stains from appliances, sinks, baths, and bathroom accessories (alkaline cleaners are ineffective on mineral deposits). Less corrosive alternatives are white vinegar, lemon juice, and commercial products such as CLR.

See also **Bathroom cleaners,** page 160.

Disinfectants

The makers of home-cleaning products appear to be committed to making your house not only clean and sparkling but also downright antiseptic. In recent years, manufacturers have introduced hundreds of everyday cleaning agents labeled "antibacterial" or "disinfectant." There are now antibacterial products for almost every kind of cleaning you might want to do.

What CONSUMER REPORTS tests have found

A variety of disinfectant products are used to kill bacteria and germs on dishes, household surfaces, and household fabrics. Disinfectant cleaners for hard surfaces—such as floors, sinks, and countertops—contain chlorine bleach, quaternary ammonium compounds, pine oil, or ethyl alcohol as the active ingredients. All work against common disease-causing viruses and bacteria. Strictly speaking, antibacterials kill only bacteria, while disinfectants kill viruses and mildew

The Limits of Disinfectant

Enterprising manufacturers have incorporated the antibacterial chemical triclosan in dozens of durable products–cutting boards, shower curtains, knife handles, socks, pillows, mattress pads, underwear–usually under the trade name Microban.

But these impregnated products offer minimal advantage, say experts CONSUMER REPORTS consulted. The triclosan does inhibit the growth of bacteria and mildew within the product; the main effect is to prevent bad odors. But there's not enough Microban on the surface of these products to stop the accumulation of bacteria there, where they pose the greatest hazard. So even if your cutting board or mattress pad is impregnated with Microban, you still have to clean it properly if you want its surface to be free of disease-causing germs.

as well. Many products that carry the label "antibacterial" are actually disinfectants.

Bleach and ethyl alcohol tend to act faster than ammonia products, and bleach works particularly well on food or dye stains. Ethyl alcohol is flammable until it dissipates. Pine oil should not be used on surfaces touched by food.

When you want instant disinfecting because you need to prepare food on a surface that was just touched by raw meat or meat juices, use a disinfectant appropriate for the surface, preferably a product containing chlorine bleach. Be sure to read the product's labeling carefully and follow any instructions about use on surfaces that touch food.

Disinfectants may make you feel that your home is safe from germs, but because most bacteria are airborne and most disinfectants can cause problems in waterways by killing helpful bacteria (especially in septic tanks), use disinfectants with discretion. Focus on controlling viruses and bacteria where they are most likely to cause illness.

Normal cleaning is sufficient for walls, draperies, bedding, floors, and other dry surfaces where germs do not survive long. Ordinary cleaners can suffice even for toilet bowls; there's little chance that germs lodged there can infect you and your family. Unless mold or mildew is a problem, you generally don't need disinfectants in your bathroom at all. Cleaning thoroughly with an all-purpose cleaner or bathroom cleaner and hot water is usually sufficient.

Dishwasher detergents

Sold as a powder, a gel, or tablets, they are usually composed largely of phosphates and silicates, though a few brands are phosphate-free. Phosphates help detergents do their job, especially in hard water, but they also promote algae growth in rivers and lakes. Even so, phosphate pollution from dishwater detergent is still considered relatively minor and insignificant, and dishwasher detergents with phosphates are permitted. Effective nonphosphate formulations aren't widely available.

Dishwasher detergents containing enzymes aren't new, but they are increasingly popular. The enzymes break down food particles so the other ingredients in the detergent can remove

In most areas of the country, household water is hard, meaning it's high in calcium or magnesium salts. Hard water is more likely to leave spots or film on glassware and dishes after a wash. If your dishwasher leaves spots or film, you can change your brand of detergent or try a rinse agent. A rinse agent is designed to lower the surface tension of water, causing it to sheet off the dishes. This helps the dishwasher rinse away spots and film.

them. While they don't ensure excellence, six of the eight enzyme detergents CONSUMER REPORTS tested cleaned far better than all of the nonenzyme detergents tested.

Over time, detergents can erode glasses, giving them a hazy or iridescent look. The problem is most severe in areas where the water is soft. Most detergents tested by CONSUMER REPORTS left glasses very hazy.

Machine washing can also damage silver. Chlorine bleach discolors silver, and most regular dishwasher detergents contain it to aid in the removal of stains and act as a disinfectant. (Enzyme detergents do not, since enzymes are incompatible with chlorine bleach.) All of the chlorine-containing products tested by CONSUMER REPORTS discolored silver, while none of the enzyme products did. If you must machine-wash silver, use a chlorine-free product, follow label instructions, and keep the silver away from stainless steel and other metals to prevent pitting.

Dishwashing liquids

Dishwashing liquids are synthetic-based cleaners that may contain degreasers and enzymes as well as emollients for the hands. Some products may also include alcohol to keep the surfactants dissolved, along with preservatives, fragrances, and colorants. Dishwashing liquids containing the chemical triclosan promise to kill bacteria on your hands as well as dishes and other surfaces. But such "antibacterial" products aren't really needed. Hot-water washing and

rinsing and air drying will get your dishes clean enough.

Dishwashing liquid does not have to produce any meaningful amount of suds to be effective at removing soil. The most important characteristic of a good dishwashing liquid is its ability to facilitate removal of tough soil. Some elbow grease and the help of a dish cloth, sponge, steel wool, or plastic scrub pad are needed. A small amount of dishwashing liquid can be used for household cleaning jobs, but its soil-attracting sticky residue means you should rinse well.

You need only a few drops of dishwashing liquid on a dish-cloth or sponge to wash an individual item. For a sinkful of dishes use about 1 tablespoon of liquid for every 3 gallons of water. Water for washing and rinsing dishes should be as hot as you can bear. Wear gloves to protect your hands from the hot water.

Drain cleaners

There are two main types of drain cleaners—biological treatments and chemical treatments. Biological treatments are supposed to work best as a preventive measure, helping you keep your drain pipes free and clear. The powerful ingredients in chemical treatments can damage some surfaces and pipe materials, as well as cause serious harm if accidentally inhaled or brought into contact with the skin and eyes. Consequently, they should be thought of as a last resort, to be called upon when prevention has failed and when a mechanical device such as a plunger or a snake (plumber's auger) has been unable to budge the clog.

What CONSUMER REPORTS tests have found

Biological treatments help to keep pipes clean and clear by introducing bacteria that feed on the organic matter in drain accumulations. Some are sold via catalogs that specialize in "environmentally friendly" products; others in hardware and grocery stores. Enzymes are used to stage an initial attack on organic matter such as grease and soap, but the real muscle comes from microorganisms that are supposed to break down and digest that organic material. They're supposed to flourish in the pipes to provide a continuous, live-in cleanup crew, pick ing away at the sticky stuff that often binds hair and other materials together or the material that holds it to the pipes.

Biological treatments take time to reach their full effectiveness. All the ones CONSUMER REPORTS tested require at least one overnight application, during which the drain cannot be used, and most require two to five applications to get the colony established. Since some bacteria are washed out as the drain is used, all treatments recommend a monthly maintenance application. Also, you should not pour boiling water, bleach, disinfectants, solvents, and other enemies of bacteria into a treated drain. If an obstruction is caused by wood, plastic, or other material not on the microorganisms' diet, don't expect results. And while noncorrosive, the biological treatments are not entirely benign. The packaging for most of them warns that they're harmful if swallowed. Some labels also recommend avoiding contact with skin, eyes, and respiratory passages.

Chemical drain openers are among the most hazardous products sold for home use. Even diluted, they may attack metal pipes and porcelain surfaces. The heat they release as they work may weaken plastic pipes and joints, and even send a geyser of corrosive liquid back into the room. If they're unable to reach the clog, you'll have a blocked drain full of corrosive liquid; and if they do work, mediocre results may require a reapplication.

Fabric softeners

Fabric softeners are related to soap. They work by coating your laundry with waxy lubricants that let fibers slide past each other, reducing wrinkling and alleviating the scratchiness of freshly washed clothes. The lubricants also separate a napped fabric's fibers and stand them on end, which makes a towel, for instance, feel fluffy. They also reduce static cling caused by the clothes dryer's tumbling.

There are two types of fabric softeners: rinse liquids and dryer sheets. Liquid softeners are added to the wash during the rinse cycle; many washing machines automatically add them from a dispenser atop the agitator. Dryer sheets are impregnated with softener; when you put a sheet into the dryer along with the laundry, the softener is released through contact and heat.

What CONSUMER REPORTS tests have found

The wax coating left by fabric softeners may eventually make clothes dingy-looking and towels less absorbent. If whiter whites and brighter brights are important to you, use a high-performing laundry detergent with high brightening ability before you add a fabric softener. The wax coating may also interfere with the way high-performance sports clothing "wicks" body moisture. The softener's fragrance (which may be there both to please consumers and mask chemical ingredients) is muted considerably by the time the wash is done. There are some that are perfume-free.

Floor-care products

There are three basic categories of floor-care products: products that clean, combination products that both clean and shine, and products that add a protective film to the floor.

Many floor cleaners can effectively remove soil from resilient floors but usually contain detergents that may damage surface-finished wood floors. Some cleaners can leave a dulling residue that must be rinsed away. A surface-finished wood floor can usually be cleaned by damp-mopping sparingly with hot water and no detergent. For no-wax flooring, be sure to use a product especially formulated for that purpose. For a penetrating-sealed floor, remove sticky marks with a damp

....

Helpful Hint

CONSUMER REPORTS has found that liquid fabric softener builds up in clothes over time and can cause all-cotton clothing like fleece or kids' sleepwear to become more flammable. If you want to use a fabric softener with your all-cotton clothes, use a dryer sheet if their labels say it's OK.

cloth that has been wrung out. Do not mop.

Combination products combine cleaning agents for dirt removal and polishing agents that add protection and shine. Since there are many types of combination floor-care products, read the recommendations pertaining to the types of flooring they claim to be good for. Some combination products are self-removing. Others should be stripped periodically.

Even polishes labeled as self-cleaning may leave a small amount of old polish behind, usually most noticeably in corners where the polish isn't worn away. Strip the old wax after six or eight coats, or at least once a year. (For a homemade remedy, see **Floor-wax stripper**, page 271, in the **Special Cleaning Advice** section.) There are also wax removers on the market. Some are recommended on the labels of their brand-mate floor polishes.

Some floor polishes are formulated for no-wax floors. But before deciding to wax a no-wax floor that looks dull, attempt to remove any residue buildup that might be the cause. Use a no-rinse floor cleaner, scrub with a mop or stiff-bristle brush, and wipe up the loosened soil as you clean. You may have to clean the floor three or four times to remove the residue. Then use the polish.

If you have surface-finished wood floors, don't use polish. For a penetrating-sealed floor, apply a coating of wax with fine-grain steel wool from time to time. On no-wax vinyl-surfaced floors, on which the shine is a bit less glaring, polish can add a touch of gloss, but little more. The amount of protection offered by a thin film of polish is insignificant compared with the protection offered by the vinyl flooring itself.

For plastic-laminate flooring, follow the manufacturer's

To Wax or Not to Wax?

An accumulation of tiny scratches will eventually dull no-wax flooring made of vinyl. The polishes in combination floor cleaners may have some ability to fill in tiny scratches, which might improve the shine of worn areas. But until a no-wax floor is worn, don't waste your money on floor polish. You'd be better off saving that money to make up for the extra cost of the no-wax flooring.

recommendations. For stone, masonry, or resilient floors, use conventional polishes or sealers to protect and add or restore shine. Apply them after the floor has been cleaned and rinsed, and has dried. These polishes dry shiny and require periodic removal. (See also **Flooring**, page 260)

Fuller's earth

This clay mineral powder is a useful absorbent for a variety of materials and surfaces. It is used to absorb oil and grease from nonwashable fabrics, such as wool, and from porous flooring such as concrete (see **Concrete**, page 53). It's good for removing stains from wallpaper. And it can help brighten and maintain difficult-to-clean carpets (see **Animal skins**, page 30; **Foam-backed carpets**, page 76; **Oriental rugs**, page 103; **Rugs (dhurrie, kilim, Navajo, and rag)**, page 117; **Shag**, page 119; **Sheepskin**, page 119; and **Sisal, coir, rush, and split-cane rugs**, page 125).

Furniture polishes

There are five types of furniture polish: aerosol, silicone cream, cream, liquid wax, and paste wax. Aerosol polish is typically silicone-based. It's best on hard surfaces and should not be used for fine furniture. Silicone cream is similar to aerosol but is intended especially for use on high-gloss furniture. Cream is often made up of wax, water, and oil emulsion. Liquid wax contains natural and synthetic wax as well as a cleaning solvent. Paste wax is similar in composition to liquid wax but may also contain silicones. It should be applied sparingly, in small circles, and rubbed in the direction of the wood grain.

What CONSUMER REPORTS tests have found
At one time, spring cleaning involved the herculean task of rewaxing the furniture, usually with paste wax. The wax was supposed to "feed" the wood. But CONSUMER REPORTS tests have found that in general

the need for waxing and cleaning with a brand-name product is often unnecessary.

The surface of much new furniture has been sealed at the factory with a durable finish that keeps the wood from drying out and, to some degree, protects against spills and minor scratches. Oils and waxes don't penetrate this finish. The minuscule residue left behind by most polishes after application and buffing contributes nothing.

While older furniture and well-worn furniture may require occasional polishing, most furniture just needs careful cleaning to remove the dulling film, created by dust, smoke, and greasy fumes and fingerprints, that builds over time into a grimy coating. You can use dust-removing products and wood cleaners. These may be needed especially on old pieces of furniture on which the original finish may not have sealed the wood very well.

French chalk

Actually, it's a fine, powdery talc used to absorb grease and oil spills on fabrics and paper products.

Glass cleaners

See **Window cleaners** on page 189.

Glycerin

A byproduct of fat or oil in soap making, glycerin is a sweet, syrupy, water-soluble liquid. It is used to help loosen stubborn stains on washable fabrics. After applying the glycerin to the stain, launder the stained item. Also known as glycerol, it is sold at pharmacies.

Hand soaps

Hand soap is usually found in either bar or liquid form. Bar soap is made from animal fat or vegetable oils with the addition of caustic soda. Liquid hand soap is tidier and doesn't leave the messy residue of bar soap.

Many liquid hand soaps are also marketed as "antibacterial" soaps. This usually means that they contain triclosan, a household germ killer that's strictly an antibacterial and that works like an antibiotic drug, killing most types of bacteria. Many medical experts are not enthusiastic about hand washes containing triclosan. For one thing, it is useless against viruses, which are responsible for most diseases transmitted by the hands. There's also evidence that triclosan could make bacteria more resistant to certain antibiotics.

Ethyl alcohol is also found in some "antibacterial" products for the hands. It kills both viruses and bacteria and works much more quickly than triclosan does. Used alone, it dries the hands intolerably. But it's much easier on the skin when incorporated into a gel product, such as Purell.

Jeweler's rouge

Jeweler's rouge is a red powder made from ferric oxide. It is used for cleaning and polishing precious metals and gemstones. Much cheaper than regular polish, it can be found at hobby shops or jewelers' suppliers.

To clean and polish heavily tarnished silver with jeweler's rouge, rub the surface with a piece of flannel impregnated with the rouge until tarnish-free. Then buff with a clean piece of flannel. The result will be silver that's just about as clean and bright as you can get with the best silver polish. This method has a few drawbacks: You may have to rub a lot more than you do with silver polish, and unless you're careful, you may rub away fine antiquing.

Laundry detergents

These can contain a combination of synthetic detergent and a number of other ingredients and agents: brighteners, bleach or bleach alternatives, anticolor transfer or loss agents, builders, antisoil redeposition agents, enzymes, and perfumes. All of these ingredients are formulated in varying strengths. Light-duty laundry detergent for hand-washables is milder than heavy-duty liquid or powder detergents.

In a bid to differentiate themselves from competitors, manufacturers over the years have rolled out products to attack odors, safeguard fabrics, and make clothes smell like "the great outdoors." They have also banished perfumes and dyes and reduced packaging waste.

Today's laundry detergents continue the one-upmanship. There are detergents with "active oxygen"; hydrogen peroxide, touted to "rejuvenate" clothes; and a trademarked substance that supposedly keeps cotton from wearing out in the washer as fast as it would otherwise. But active oxygen is simply a term for chlorine-free bleach; all products can be said to rejuvenate clothes; and washers don't seem to beat up on clothes anywhere near as much as your average 5-year-old.

Some products vow to kill bacteria in your wash load; their maker has sent evidence for that claim to the Environmental Protection Agency. But all detergents formulated in the U. S. will wash away most bacteria. Adding chlorine bleach or drying clothes thoroughly will kill any that remain.

What CONSUMER REPORTS tests have found
Peripheral abilities aside, detergents perform better at their main task—cleaning—than they ever have, CONSUMER REPORTS tests have shown. All make lightly soiled clothes clean. And all

Wrinkle-Reducing Laundry Detergent

Wrinkle-reducing laundry detergents contain an agent that is intended to help untangle clothing fibers and prevent wrinkles from setting. In CONSUMER REPORTS testing, none of the shirts washed using the detergent could go to work without ironing. When the shirts were tested five times in a row on the chance the wrinkle-reducing effect was cumulative, there was no improvement.

Laundry Tablets

Among the latest offerings from the detergent doctors at Tide and Wisk are laundry tablets, which are supposed to make washing your clothes less of a pill by removing any concerns about spilling. They're easy to use. Travelers and coin laundry users especially might like their convenience.

In CONSUMER REPORTS tests, laundry tablets compared favorably with other laundry detergents. They dissolved completely and were effective in cleaning tough stains. But you pay for the convenience. If you don't mind measuring powders, you can wash for much less.

do at least a good job of keeping soil from migrating—you may end up with dingy laundry if the detergent frees soil from one item of clothing only to deposit it on others. But the best detergents are now better at tackling a broad range of tough stains while making clothes brighter.

The low-sudsing powdered and liquid detergents sold for front-loading washers are a major development in the world of detergents. Is this niche really necessary? Yes, because front-loaders do treat clothes differently—they use less water than top-loaders and tumble clothes instead of spinning them.

The front-loader liquids CONSUMER REPORTS tested proved extremely effective, at least in a front-loader. Although at least one provides directions for use in top-loaders, you might think twice about using it that way. Using a top-loading detergent in a front-loader will save you money, but it could produce too much sudsing unless you take care to use a ¼ cup or less per load.

There's good news for people who use liquid detergents, which account for the bulk of detergent sales. Liquids, as a group, now work as well as powders. Formulating an outstanding liquid detergent is tricky, partly because manufacturers can blend only so many ingredients with water before the mixture thickens or separates.

Most detergents contain colorless chemicals called optical brighteners, which make laundry appear whiter in sunlight or fluorescent lighting. CONSUMER REPORTS measured brightening by examining white cotton swatches before and after laundering. There were noticeable differences.

There are plenty of very effective laundry detergents from

Cleaning Caveat

Don't be tempted to use one of those ceramic laundry discs that claim to clean hundreds of loads without detergent. CONSUMER REPORTS tests have found that they don't work.

Detergents for Hand-Washables

Next to the regular laundry detergents, you may find several products, such as Woolite, that make special claims for laundering fine washables of such fabrics as linen, wool, cotton, and silk. These, too, are detergents, and unlike the soap flakes of yesteryear, they won't leave behind a gray scum if you don't rinse well. They have ingredients that lift off soil and keep it suspended in the wash water; others that remove grease; enzymes to help attack stains; and optical brighteners. The brighteners give off a bluish color in sunlight or under fluorescents that make white cloth—especially cotton—appear whiter.

You can also try dishwashing liquid, though it lacks brightener and other helpful ingredients found in specialized products. Use it on your fine washables with water at about 70° F, warm enough to be comfortable to the hands but not so warm as to cause shrinkage. Wash and rinse in just a few minutes; delicate fabrics should not be left soaking for very long. Items that need handwashing should not be put in the dryer.

which to choose. If your laundry needs freshening, not heavy-duty stain removal, just choose a low-cost product.

None of the detergents tested removed very tough stains completely, but most of them left many of the stains far less noticeable. Some products even worked fairly well on motor oil, which used to stump almost all detergents.

Concern over the link between phosphates in detergents and an over-abundance of algae in waterways has led to the elimination of phosphates from major U.S. laundry detergents.

Laundry soap

Before detergent, there was soap. Laundry soap may be hard to find (you can, of course, use hand soap). Soap flakes are history. Most laundry cleaning is better done with detergents.

Lemon juice
See **Bleach,** page 161.

Metal cleaners

Although many metal polishes make broad claims, it's most likely you'll get the best results from specialty products designed for a particular metal surface. See **Brass and copper cleaners,** page 162, and **Silver cleaners,** page 185.

Mildew removers

Commercial mildew-removal products usually consist of chlorine bleach and a thickening agent. You can also make your own solution of 3 to 4 quarts of water, 1 quart of liquid chlorine bleach, and 2 to 3 ounces of TSP (for more on TSP, see **Trisodium phosphate,** page 188).

Mineral spirits

A refined solvent of naphthas, mineral spirits are used for solvent in fats and waxes and as a paint thinner. Pay close attention to the cautions on the label. This product is a fire hazard, and excessive inhalation in a poorly ventilated space may cause central nervous system depression and lung injury.

Neat's-foot oil

This pale-yellow fatty oil is used as a leather conditioner and protector. It is made from the hooves and bones of cattle and similar animals.

Oven cleaners

Most ovens today are self-cleaning, making this harsh product something you can skip. (For more information on cleaning your oven, see **Ovens,** page 105.) Oven-cleaning products often contain lye, one of the most dangerous substances sold for household use. Lye decomposes the baked-on fats, sugars, and oven dirt that ordinary cleaners can't touch, turning them into soapy compounds you can wash away.

Lye-based oven cleaners should be used only on the shiny, porcelain-coated metal surfaces or glass of a standard, non-self-cleaning oven. Never use them on bare metal, on a self-cleaning oven, or on a so-called continuous cleaning oven, which has a special speckled, rough-texture porcelain finish that, like self-cleaning ovens, is meant to gradually burn off combusted foods, but at normal oven temperatures. Even with a regular oven, you might consider skipping an oven cleaner—such an oven in continual use can reach a steady state at which grease and grime burn off at the same rate they accumulate. Once cool, your oven may need nothing more than a wipe-down with a mild solution of dishwashing liquid and water followed by a rinse with a damp sponge.

The high-temperature cleaning cycle of self-cleaning ovens usually reduces stubborn baked-on soil to an easily removable ashy residue. At the end of the cycle, simply wipe off the residue with a damp cloth. If your oven is in good working order, this should be all that you need to do.

Commercial oven cleaners, harsh abrasives, and scouring pads should never be used on continuous-cleaning ovens. All that should be needed to keep them clean is a wipe-down of the interior with a damp cloth or sponge as soon as the oven is cool.

What CONSUMER REPORTS tests have found

Oven cleaners come most often as an aerosol, sometimes as a brush-on jelly. Each has drawbacks.

Brush-on jelly is tedious to apply and difficult to keep from splattering. Be sure to cover your hands and forearms.

Aerosol cleaners are easy to apply but difficult to aim accurately. Clouds of aerosol mist may deposit cleaner not only on oven walls but also on heating elements, thermostats, and light fixtures, and in your lungs. Sprays with a broad, concave button are easier to guide than sprays with a small button.

Aerosols without lye are also available. These often use a combination of organic surfactants activated by heat to break down oven grime. They aren't likely to irritate your skin or eyes (or damage kitchen surfaces).

Oven-cleaning products that contain lye must be used with extreme caution. Labels on such products contain long lists of warnings and should be read carefully. Lye-based oven cleaners are corrosively alkaline and sufficiently reactive to seriously burn skin and eyes if left on for a prolonged time. If droplets are inhaled, lye-based oven cleaners may harm the throat and lungs.

You should don safety goggles, a long-sleeved shirt, and rubber gloves before using any cleaner containing lye. If you're using an aerosol, you should also wear a paper dust mask (to keep from inhaling the droplets) along with protective goggles.

Not only should you take steps to protect yourself from the corrosive effects of lye, but you should also protect nearby floors, counters, and other surfaces. Spread newspaper on the floor in front of the oven. Take care not to splash any of the cleaner on aluminum, copper, or painted surfaces outside the oven, and keep it off the heating element, gaskets, and light fixture inside the oven.

Petroleum jelly

This semi-solid form of mineral oil can be used as a lubricant to assist in removing stubborn stains.

Pre-washers, boosters, and pre-spotters

Today's high-performance laundry detergents remove many common stains, but some stains can be stubborn. Laundry boosters may help. These stain-fighting products contain a variety of chemical ingredients, such as sodium percarbonate, surfactants, perfumes and softeners, hydrogen peroxide, enzymes, and solvents.

Boosters may be available as bars of soap-like solvents, powders, pump sprays, aerosols, liquids, and sticks. Some liquid laundry detergents can work as self-boosters when applied directly to stains before laundering. (Powdered detergents can be mixed with a little water and applied as a paste with a tooth brush.)

The performance of commercially available boosters in CONSUMER REPORTS tests varied from product to product—the best were effective on most common stains, some on only a few. Before turning to a booster, you might first try soaking items in ordinary laundry detergents before washing; overnight soaking can be highly effective.

Never use heat to dry a garment that appears to be stained. The stain will set.

See also **Stain Removal**, page 242.

Rubbing alcohol

This clear, colorless liquid is an effective household cleaner, especially for glass. It is also anti-bacterial; good for chrome, jewelry, and ivory; and versatile as a stain remover. It is particularly effective with ballpoint-ink stains. Rubbing alcohol consists of isopropyl alcohol (70 percent by volume) and purified water. It is flammable and may cause skin and respiratory problems if misused.

Rust removers and inhibitors

Some of the products in this category work like sealers: They can be painted or sprayed onto surfaces to prevent rust. Some are rust converters that form a protective coating. Most contain phosphoric acid, corrosives, oxalic acid, and solvents.

Saddle soap

As its name suggests, saddle soap is a soap and not a synthetic detergent. It is designed for cleaning leather and is especially effective at cleaning polished leather. A leather conditioner should always be applied after using the soap.

Scouring cleansers

It used to be that the more abrasive a scouring powder was, the more effectively it cleaned—and the more surely it eroded porcelain-enamel finishes and the decorative polish of cookware and acrylic vanities.

Today's scouring cleansers claim to remove soil and stains without damaging the surface being cleaned. Liquid cleansers, introduced in the 1910s, replaced gritty particles, such as silica, with softer abrasives like calcium carbonate. Today, both liquids and powders derive much of their cleaning strength from detergent, nonchlorine bleach, and other ingredients. The detergent in the cleanser helps loosen soil and cut grease; the bleach aids in removing many stains, especially from scratched and dented surfaces; and other ingredients enhance a cleanser's effectiveness on a variety of stains.

Cleansers have a range of abrasiveness, with liquid cleansers at the low end and powders at all levels. Whenever possible, use gentler cleaners, such as baking soda, with sponges or plastic scrubbers. The good all-purpose cleaner

Using Scouring Cleansers Safely

Scouring cleansers contain powerful active ingredients and should be used with discretion. To avoid harm to both yourself and what you're cleaning, bear the following in mind:

• Never mix a cleanser containing chlorine bleach with one containing ammonia.

• Read the warnings on any rust-removing cleansers. Some cleansers are irritants, so wear gloves and remove jewelry.

• Try a cleanser in an inconspicuous spot before using it on a new surface.

• Apply the cleanser with a light touch using a soft applicator, such as a cellulose sponge; if this fails, cautiously use a more aggressive applicator, such as a plastic mesh pad.

can take care of ordinary soil floors, walls, countertops, and range surfaces.

The gentlest cleansers will leave few or no marks even on a piece of glass (which is similar in hardness to the porcelain in bathtubs and sinks). A slightly abrasive cleanser leaves light hairline scratches on glass panels and is more likely to erode surfaces over time. Moderately abrasive cleansers leave a silky smooth frosting of scratches.

A good product, if inadvertently spilled and not wiped up, shouldn't leave permanent marks on chrome, imitation marble (usually made of acrylic), fiberglass, glass, or glazed tile. But watch your pots and pans. A number of cleansers dull or discolor aluminum, copper, and other metals if not wiped off after application. Most cleansers do well on difficult-to-remove soil and on a variety of stains, such as pot marks and tea stains on a kitchen sink. Some are especially effective on particular types of difficult stains, such as rust and hard-water deposits, and are labeled accordingly.

Silver cleaners

One type of silver-care product (three-way) removes tarnish and polishes, and it also treats silver with chemicals that retard further tarnish. Another variety (two-way) cleans and polishes but doesn't claim to retard tarnishing. Both types of products include a mild abrasive. You rub on the polish, wipe it off, and then buff the finish to the shine you want.

There are also one-way products that come in liquid form and are used for cleaning only. They don't require tedious rubbing to remove tarnish. You just dip the silver in them or spread them onto silver surfaces.

Acidic dip cleaners, as a class, have some inherent hazards. Wear plastic or rubber gloves to protect your hands while cleaning, since the cleaner may irritate skin. Be careful not to get any cleaner in your eyes. Since excessive inhalation of their sulfide fumes may be disagreeable and may cause headaches, 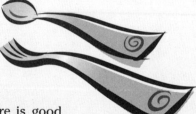 these cleaners should be used only where there is good ventilation. Rinse silver thoroughly after cleaning with acidic dip products.

Three-way products may be higher-priced than others, but they are preferable because they do the job of polishing and do it well, and their tarnish retardant ensures you can wait longer before you need to repolish. Dip cleaners work fast, but you may still need to use a polish afterward—so you're doing the job twice. See also **Jeweler's rouge,** page 175.

Starches and sizing

Starches and sizings restore body to such fabrics as cotton and linen that may become limp after washing or dry cleaning.

Starch is available in spray, powder, or liquid form. The powder should be mixed with a lot of water for light starching, less water for heavy starching. Spray starches are applied to the fabric during ironing. You add the other types to the final rinse when washing cottons and linens.

Sizing is lighter than starch. It is often applied to fabrics by the manufacturer for protection and body, but eventually it breaks down as a result of moisture, perspiration, and cleaning. You apply it to the fabric before ironing.

Toilet cleaners

Toilet-cleaning products come in a variety of forms, including in-bowl powders and liquids, and flush dispensers that clip onto the tank. Some products clean, deodorize, and disinfect. They can contain various amounts of bleach, detergents, disinfectants, and odor-masking scents and deodorizers.

While in-tank cleaners are the easiest to use, liquid and powder in-bowl cleaners that are used with a brush do a better job. Powders are less convenient than liquids to apply around the bowl and under the rim. Don't be swayed by disinfecting claims. A disinfecting cleaner can only temporarily cut the population of some germs.

In-bowl cleaners. Most in-bowl cleaners use acid to dissolve mineral scale and eradicate stains. Active agents may include hydrochloric, phosphoric, or oxalic acid; some granular cleaners use sodium bisulfate, which, when dissolved, works like an acid. Brands with the highest acidity have the greatest potential for cleaning but should be handled with great care. Products with lower acid content may require more cleaner, more time, or more muscle to do the job. Always handle an in-bowl cleaner with care. Never mix it with other household chemicals or cleaners, including in-tank cleaners; toxic fumes may result.

Nonacidic liquids may not be very effective at removing mineral stains but should work well on nonmineral stains and can be brushed away readily. A dash of liquid all-purpose cleaner brushed into the bowl can effectively clean one that is lightly soiled for less than the cost of in-bowl cleaners and does not contain harsh chemicals.

In-tank cleaners. Some in-tank cleaners slowly dispense bleach and surfactants to lighten stains. The amount of bleach released is usually quite small, but it may be enough to bleach out stains when the water stands for hours. If the toilet isn't flushed at least once a day, the bleach may become concentrated enough to damage parts inside the tank, so some plumbing-fixture manufacturers recommend against in-tank cleaners. To determine when it's time to replace a bleach-based cleaner, put a drop of food coloring in the bowl; if the water remains

T

colored for more than a few minutes, the bleach-based cleaner is spent, and needs to be replaced.

Although in-tank cleaners have deodorizing scents that many people associate with cleanliness, these may be imperceptible once the cleaner dissolves in the tank.

Some in-tank cleaners contain blue dye to tint the water and hide accumulated dirt. Such cleaners also contain detergent and other ingredients, but don't actually claim to clean a dirty bowl.

Trisodium phosphate (TSP)

This highly alkaline detergent is used to clean grease, grime, and mold from most household surfaces, such as walls and concrete flooring before they are painted. TSP is sold in hardware stores and home centers. Phosphate-free substitutes are also available.

Turpentine

Turpentine is made from balsam extracted from conifers. It is highly aromatic and used to assist in the drying process of oil paints. Mineral turpentine (turps) is a petroleum-derived solvent with added benzene-type components. Turpentine and mineral turpentine are both found in oil-based house paints and are used as thinning agents for paint, lacquer, and varnish. They can also be used as solvents for stain removal.

Washing soda

It's used as a water softener and will assist with laundry tasks when used in conjunction with soap. Do not use it with silks, woolens, or vinyl.

Water softener

If your garments come out of the wash stiff and look dull and gray, and if soaps and detergents don't lather well, you probably have hard water. Other signs: the presence of bathtub rings and white residue around faucets and on glassware. You can check with your local water-supply company to be sure. You can try adding a packaged water softener to your laundry to remove minerals that can cause yellowing. Follow the instructions carefully.

White vinegar

White vinegar is a solution of at least 4 percent acetic acid. Sold in grocery stores, it's good for a variety of household cleaning tasks, including removing some carpet stains, clearing clogged drains, and cleaning coffeemakers, chrome, cookware, and countertops. Don't use on acetate fabrics; it may dissolve the fibers.

Window cleaners

Squeegee-wielding professionals know that plain water can clean lightly soiled windows. But if you put off washing your windows until they're really dirty, you'll need something more potent. The best cleaner is one that works fast and removes grime with a minimum of help from you.

Almost any cleaner should have enough muscle to clean glass, but few manage it without streaking. However, some of the streak-free formulas are hard on other surfaces; take particular care around aluminum and paint. For a home-made **Glass and window cleaner** recipe that performed well in Consumer Reports tests and will leave few or no streaks, see page 272.

Cleaning Appliances and Tools

Air cleaners

While whole-house and single-room air-cleaning products have their limitations, they can provide significant relief from some indoor pollutants when other measures such as ventilation and frequent vacuuming fall short.

If your house has forced-air heating and cooling, use an appropriate whole-house filter for your system. (A room air cleaner's work would be quickly undone by a central system's continual circulation of unfiltered air from other rooms.) If your home lacks forced-air heating and cooling, you're limited to a room air cleaner, which uses a fan and generally a filter to clean the air of a single room.

What CONSUMER REPORTS tests have found

Whole-house models. Filters for the whole house are generally available in widely used sizes or can be adapted to fit. They range from ordinary fiberglass furnace filters, costing about a dollar, to electronic precipitators, which can cost more than $400 and must be installed professionally in the house's duct system. Many heating systems use plain matted-fiberglass filters that are meant to trap large particles of dust and lint. These filters are flat, 1 inch thick, and need to be changed monthly. Made of fiberglass or another synthetic material, pleated filters have pleats to increase the surface area. They need to be changed quarterly. Electrostatically charged filters are plain or pleated, disposable or washable, and are mostly made of materials with a permanent charge that is supposed to turn them into tiny magnets for pollen, lint, pet dander, and dust. The disposable ones should be changed quarterly; the washable ones should be washed monthly and may last up to 10 years.

Extended-media filters are about the thickness of a box fan and pack a thick ruffle of accordion-pleated fiberglass or other material inside. You need to replace them only once a year. You'll need to have a special holder for the filter installed in the ductwork.

Electronic precipitators are serious-looking units that impart an electrical charge to particles flowing through them and then collect the particles on oppositely charged metal plates or filter media. They must be plumbed into ductwork and then plugged into house current. The collector-plate assembly must be removed and washed every one to two months. Replace filter media about once a year.

CONSUMER REPORTS tests found that the least expensive approach—using a plain fiberglass filter—did little to eliminate dust and smoke particles. Washable electrostatic filters were only about as effective as plain fiberglass filters, though they are more expensive; however, they do last longer. Also more expensive than a plain fiberglass filter are pleated filters with an electrostatic feature. In CONSUMER REPORTS tests, some of them were 10 to 15 times as effective at cleaning the air as plain fiberglass.

An extended-media filter costs hundreds of dollars to install but is only as effective as a pleated electrostatic filter. The most expensive approach, using an electronic precipitator, was by far the most effective. The units tested worked about 30 times as well as a plain fiberglass filter.

Choose on the basis of how large an air-quality problem you have. One of the better pleated electrostatic filters may be all you need. Consider an electronic precipitator if someone in your home smokes or has a chronic breathing problem. Make sure the filter fits snugly in its mount. You can use weather stripping to seal gaps; leaks around the filter's frame can make it less effective. Use of some filters can make it harder for a heating and cooling system to work properly if airflow is restricted too much or is already weak.

Room models. The best room air cleaners work well, even on dust and cigarette smoke, which produce particles that are much smaller and harder to trap than pollen and mold spores. But they aren't good at gases— a telltale odor will linger long after you clear the air of cigarette smoke. Because most room units clean far better at their noisy, high-fan setting, balancing noise and performance can involve a lot of manual switching between speeds.

The Association of Home Appliance Manufacturers, a trade group, tests and rates room air cleaners using a measurement known as CADR (clean air delivery rate), which is determined by how well a filter traps particles and how much air the machine moves. Separate CADRs are listed for dust, tobacco smoke, and pollen. CONSUMER REPORTS advises buyers to pick a unit whose CADRs are at least two-thirds the room's area, assuming an 8-foot ceiling. For example, a 12 x 15-foot room—180 square feet—needs a unit with a CADR of at least 120 for the contaminant you want to remove. For a room with high ceilings, you'll need a unit with larger CADRs. (It's assumed that you'll run the air cleaner at high speed.) You may want to find an air cleaner rated for an area larger than the room where you plan to use it. That way you can have good cleaning performance at a lower, less-noisy setting.

Helpful Hint

The Association of Home Appliance Manufacturers' certification label gives the clean-air delivery rate (CADR), measured at the high fan setting in cubic feet per minute, for dust, tobacco smoke, and pollen. The higher the CADR, the faster a machine will clean the air. CONSUMER REPORTS conducts tests at the low fan setting as well as high.

Most room air cleaners weigh between 10 and 20 pounds. They can be round or boxy in shape and can stand either on the floor or on a table. Tabletop models are typically smaller and thus have correspondingly smaller CADRs. Whatever their configuration, two technologies predominate. More common is a high-efficiency particulate air (HEPA) filter, which mechanically strains the air of fine particles. The other technology relies on electrically charging the particles in the air. As air flows through an electrical field, particles take on a charge; they're then trapped on oppositely charged collector plates inside the machine.

With most room models, a fan pulls air into the unit for filtration. Some room air cleaners with an electronic precipitator or a HEPA filter incorporate ionizing circuitry to improve their performance. Powered needles or wires charge particles, which are then more easily trapped but may also stick to walls or furnishings, possibly soiling them.

Indicators in most models let you know when to change filters. HEPA filters are generally supposed to be replaced once a year. They can cost more than $100—perhaps the same amount as the price of the unit. It's generally recommended that air cleaners' pre-filters, designed to remove big particles and odors, be changed quarterly. Washable pre-filters should be cleaned monthly.

The collector-plate assembly of an electronic-precipitator room air cleaner must be removed from the machine and washed every month or so, or the unit's filtering capabilities may suffer. You slide out the assembly as you would a drawer and put it in a dishwasher or rinse it in a sink.

Most models have a handle, and some of the heavier models have wheels to ease transport. The choice of speeds is usually Low, Medium, and High.

A few units use a dust sensor and an air-quality monitor to raise or lower the fan speed automatically as conditions warrant. Tests of one model with this feature found that it did not respond well to very small particles in the air.

Room air cleaners provided varying levels of performance in CONSUMER REPORTS tests, with no one type—HEPA filter or electronic precipitator—clearly besting the others. When set at high, the best models did a very good or excellent job at clearing a room of dust and smoke. Other models were only good or fair. The tabletop models tested were the weakest performers. Most room air cleaners were easy to use. Electronic-precipitator models are cheaper to run because they don't require you to replace an expensive filter.

Room air cleaners are noisy, especially at the high setting—sounding somewhat like a room air conditioner. Noise is reduced at lower speeds, but performance is also reduced.

Measure the area where you plan to operate the air cleaner, and choose a model that is sized appropriately. Follow instructions when placing any unit so it will work effectively. Some cleaners can sit against a wall; others belong in the middle of the room.

Brooms

There are different types of brooms for different types of jobs. For large areas, such as outside decks, garage and basement floors, patios and terraces, select a push broom. Upright brooms are good in small, narrow spaces and in corners.

Brooms are available in different fibers and textures. Soft brooms are good for light dirt on smooth floors. Brooms with stiffer bristles are appropriate for rougher surfaces. For outdoor use, you need stiff, heavy fibers. Corn brooms, which have uneven straw bristles, are fine for that purpose. Natural fibers (such as straw) are not recommended for use on oil and solvents but are preferable if the surface is hot; synthetic (PVC) fibers are preferred for use with chemicals, oils, solvents, and moisture but may melt when used at high temperatures.

You'll need a whisk broom or brush and a dustpan to collect the dirt before throwing it in the trash can. Or use a broom and a long-handled dustpan.

Wash your broom's bristles from time to time in a mild detergent solution. Rinse in warm water and then (if the broom has natural bristles) in cold, salty water. Hang your broom up by its handle to avoid flattening the bristles.

Helpful Hint

If you need to, you can screw a hook on the end of your broom's handle in order to hang it up.

A Bouquet of Brushes to Have on Hand

The size, fiber texture, and handle shape of a brush will vary according to the task for which it is intended. Most brushes can be cleaned with a mild dishwashing detergent or in the dishwasher. Here's a good selection to have on hand:

• A wire brush for cleaning a barbecue grill.

• A stiff-bristled brush for cleaning burned-on food from surfaces, such as a cast-iron skillet.

• A scrub brush with a handle for miscellaneous cleaning tasks. Synthetic fibers are better for light to moderate tasks, and natural-plant fibers are better with acids or solvents and harder scrubbing, such as removing stubborn food stains ground into the floor.

• A toothbrush for scrubbing hard-to-reach surfaces in silver and other decorative items.

• A tile grout brush—a single row of stiff, synthetic fibers for scrubbing between ceramic tiles.

• A stiff-bristled brush with an extension handle that connects to the garden hose. Sometimes called an "automotive brush," it's better for exterior walls than it is for cars.

Carpet deep-cleaners

Regular vacuum cleaners remove loose dirt, but hardly touch the dirt and oils that stick to carpet fibers. Deep-cleaners (also known as extractors or steam cleaners) are supposed to go a step further: These machines typically spray on a detergent, sometimes working it in with moving brushes, then vacuum the dirty solution up.

What CONSUMER REPORTS tests have found

Available to rent or buy, these machines don't really "deep-clean" or "steam-clean." The dirt they remove is mainly what you see near the surface. And the cleaning solution that sprays from them is hardly steam—it's actually a solution of hot tap water and detergent. (CONSUMER REPORTS tests show that the detergent solution is about 20 degrees cooler when it sprays out at the carpet than when it's put into the machine.)

You'll see two main configurations: canisters and uprights. Canisters have a light wand and a long hose, which are pretty easy to work with, although the large handle may get in the way when you're cleaning tight spots. Changing tools can be a chore. Carpet-cleaning attachments may have moving or fixed brushes. Clear plastic attachments for spot cleaning provide good control and visibility. Most canisters hold 2 to 3 gallons—enough to clean a large room.

Uprights combine into a single unit a tank for dispensing cleaning solution, a tank for holding dirty solution, a vacuum, and a fixed or moving brush. When full, uprights typically weigh about 30 pounds and are cumbersome to push around. Several of the machines have attachments for cleaning upholstery, stairs, and tight spots between furniture. In general, uprights are easier to store than bulky canisters. Most uprights hold 1 to 2 gallons of solution, enough to clean a small to medium-sized room.

In CONSUMER REPORTS tests, no machine was able to remove all the potting soil that was ground into off-white, Scotchguard-treated nylon plush carpet panels, but several did an acceptable job. No deep-cleaner came close to removing all the stains that were applied to carpet samples. The best machines lightened the stains but spread them around somewhat. The worst gave little evidence of cleaning. Admittedly,

Helpful Hint

A carpet should be deep-cleaned or shampooed every 12 to 18 months, depending on the type and color of the carpeting, how much it's walked on, and the carpet manufacturer's recommendations.

the tests were very demanding. On lightly soiled or dark carpeting, you probably won't notice residual dirt after you use a deep-cleaner and fluff up the pile with a regular vacuum. Carpeting that has stain and soil repellent will resist stains somewhat better than the untreated carpet used in the CONSUMER REPORTS stain-removal test.

Deep-cleaners are fairly difficult to maintain. After each use, you must clean brushes and tools, and empty and clean the solution tanks—a messy 15- to 20-minute task.

Other Ways to Keep Your Carpet Clean

A carpet deep-cleaner can do only so much. To keep a carpet looking its best, blot up spills before they set, leave dirt-caked shoes at the door, and vacuum regularly. And consider these other approaches:

Shampooers. Lacking vacuum power, a scrubbing machine simply works the solution or a moist powder into the carpeting. When it dries, you pick up the loosened dirt with a regular vacuum cleaner. Scrubbing machines are a little easier to keep clean than deep-cleaners because you don't have to deal with a dirty solution tank or suction hose. Compared with upright carpet deep-cleaners, they're less bulky but will probably take about the same amount of closet space.

Wet/dry vac. You apply pre-treatment to a stained area, vacuum with the wet/dry vac, and repeat. It's important not to use so much solution at once that you soak carpeting to the point of damaging its backing or the floor underneath it. In CONSUMER REPORTS tests, this method worked better than any of the carpet deep-cleaners for spot cleaning, though it wasn't practical for cleaning large areas.

Carpet-cleaning professional. This no-sweat method produces results similar to those of the best deep-cleaners used with large amounts of cleaning solution.

Carpet stain cleaner or diluted dishwasing liquid. Cleaning manually with off-the-shelf products removes stubborn stains better than deep-cleaning machines. Before applying any cleaner to a prominent place, try it on an inconspicuous spot to make sure it won't hurt the carpeting or affect its color. To avoid damaging carpet fibers, try patting with brush bristles instead of scrubbing. Be sure to rinse out and blot up residual detergent.

Aerosol foam cleaner. This is the most grueling and least effective way to clean heavy dirt. In CONSUMER REPORTS tests of two foam cleaners, the sponge we used floated on top of the foam without reaching down into the carpet. Even after more foam was added than recommended, the results were no better than with the worst-performing machines tested.

Dishwashers

Most dishwashers fit into a 24-inch-wide space under the kitchen countertop and are attached to a hot-water pipe, a drain, and an electrical line. Compact models require less width. Portable models can be rolled over to the sink and connected to the faucet. A "dishwasher in a drawer" design from Fisher & Paykel has two stacked compartments; when one is in operation, the other can be used to store clean dishes.

A dirt sensor found in many middle-range and high-end models is designed to adjust water use to the amount of dirt to be removed. The trade-off is usually higher energy use than with nonsensor models, especially for very dirty loads. Also increasingly common is a sanitizing feature that makes the water extra-hot and is supposed to provide a better wash. But remember that as soon as you touch a dish while taking it out of the dishwasher, it's no longer sanitized.

What Consumer Reports tests have found

Dishwashers offer a choice of at least three wash cycles: Light, Normal, and Heavy. Light may be good enough for many loads, and it uses less water. Rinse/Hold lets you rinse dirty dishes before using the dishwasher on a full cycle. Other cycles offered in many models include Pot Scrubber, Soak/Scrub, and China/Crystal. Pricier dishwashers often distribute water from multiple places, or "levels," in the machine. Dishwashers also typically offer a choice of drying with or without heat.

Some models use two filters to keep wash water free of food: a coarse outer filter for large bits and a fine inner filter for smaller particles. This design has proved effective in Consumer Reports tests. In most such models, a spray arm cleans residue from the coarse filter during the rinse cycle. Some of the more expensive models have a filter that you must pull out and clean manually. A food-disposal grinder cuts up large food particles.

Sensors in "smart" dishwashers determine how dirty the dishes are and provide the appropriate amount of water. Some brands use pressure sensors that respond to the actual soil removed from the dishes. Other brands use turbidity sensors that work by measuring the amount of light that passes from

Helpful Hint

More and more dishwasher detergents contain enzymes to boost performance. Consumer Reports has found that many of them yield a better clean. For more, see **Dishwasher detergents, page 166.**

the sender to the receiver in the sensor. In CONSUMER REPORTS tests with very dirty dishes, models with sensors didn't clean noticeably better than ones without sensors. And with heavily soiled loads, energy use was significantly higher.

A sanitizing wash or rinse option that raises the water temperature above the typical 140° F doesn't necessarily mean improved cleaning. Routine use could cost a small amount more a year in electricity.

More expensive dishwashers have better soundproofing and electronic touch-pad controls (some of them "hidden" in the top lip of the door). Less expensive models have mechanical controls, usually operated by a dial and push-buttons. Touch pads are easier to clean. Dials "chart" progress through a cycle. Some electronic models digitally display time left in the wash cycle. Others merely show a "clean" signal. Some models with mechanical controls require you to set both dial and push-buttons to the desired setting for the correct combination of water quantity and temperature. A delayed-start control lets you run the washer at night, when utility rates may be lower. Some models offer child-safety features, such as a door and controls that lock.

Most models hold cups and glasses on top, plates on the bottom, and silverware in a basket. Features that enhance flexibility include adjustable and removable tines, which flatten areas to accept bigger dishes, pots, and pans; slots for silverware that prevent "nesting"; removable racks, which enable loading and unloading outside the dishwasher; stemware holders, which steady wine glasses; fold-down shelves, which stack cups in a double-tiered arrangement; and adjustable and terraced racks, which accommodate tall items.

Stainless-steel dishwasher tubs may last virtually forever, whereas plastic ones can discolor or crack. But most plastic tubs have a 20-year warranty—much longer than most people keep a dishwasher. In CONSUMER REPORTS tests, stainless-steel-lined models had a slightly shorter drying time but didn't wash any better.

Most dishwashers CONSUMER REPORTS tested did an excellent or very good job, with little or no spotting or redepositing of food. The best performers aren't necessarily the costliest. But high-priced models offer styling and soundproofing that appeal to some buyers. Avoid the lowest-priced models—those without a filtering system. They tend to redeposit tiny bits of food. Foreign brands are often more energy-efficient and quieter, but also pricier and less convenient. Some have spray arms that may hamper loading large dishes and filters that require periodic manual cleaning.

Otherwise, CONSUMER REPORTS tests found that the main differences are in water and energy usage and noise level. The quietest models are so unobtrusive you might barely hear them. Most good performers take at least 90 minutes to complete a cycle. A few even run for about two hours.

CONSUMER REPORTS has concluded that for very dirty loads, a water-adjusting dirt sensor feature significantly increases energy use. Remember that any dishwasher can be made to use less water (and less energy for heat) by simply running it at its lightest cycle.

Dryers

Dryers are relatively simple. Their major distinctions are how they're programmed to shut off once a load is dry (moisture sensor or thermostat) and how they heat air (gas or electric). Both affect how much you'll pay to buy and run your machine.

Dryers are available in different sizes. Full-sized dryers differ only slightly in width (the critical dimension for fitting into cabinetry and closets), from 27 to 29 inches. Front-mounted controls on some let you stack them atop a front-loading washer. Full-sized models vary in drum capacity from about 5 to 7½ cubic feet. (The larger the drum, the more easily a dryer handles bulky items.)

Compacts, exclusively electric, are typically 24 inches wide, with a drum capacity roughly half that of full-sized models—about 3½ cubic feet. They can be stacked atop a companion front-loading washer. Similarly, many full-sized dryers and front-loading washers can be stacked.

Another space-saving option is a laundry center, which combines a washer and dryer in a single unit. Laundry centers come with gas or electric dryers. Those can be full-sized (27 inches wide) or compact (24 inches wide).

What CONSUMER REPORTS tests have shown

Full-sized dryers often have two or three auto-dry cycles, which shut the unit off automatically when the clothes reach the desired dryness. Each cycle might have a More Dry setting, to dry clothes completely, and a Less Dry setting, to leave clothes damp and ready for ironing.

As clothes tumble by a moisture sensor, electrical contacts in the drum sample their conductivity for surface dampness and relay signals to electronic controls. Dryers with a thermostat, by contrast, measure moisture indirectly by taking the temperature of exhaust air from the drum. Moisture-sensor models are more accurate, sparing your laundry unnecessary drying—and sparing you needlessly high energy bills.

Most dryers have a separate temperature control to, say, keep heat lower for delicate fabrics. A cool-down feature helps to prevent wrinkling when you don't remove clothes immediately. Some models continue to tumble without heat; others cycle the drum on and off. An Express Dry cycle is meant for drying small loads at high heat in less than a half-hour. Large loads will take longer.

A top-mounted lint filter may be somewhat easier to clean than one inside the drum. Some models give a warning signal when the lint filter is blocked. Most full-sized models have a drum light, making it easy to spot stray clothing. You may be able to raise or lower the volume of an end-of-cycle signal or shut it off. A rack included with many machines attaches inside the drum and keeps sneakers and other bulky items from tumbling.

CONSUMER REPORTS has found that nearly all clothes dryers handle ordinary laundry loads well. Models with a moisture sensor don't overdry as much as models using a thermostat do, saving a little energy as well as

How to Vent Your Dryer Safely

Dryers vent their exhaust, including lint, through a duct that must attach to the machine. Four types of duct are available, but two of those types may be dangerous. Flexible ducts made of plastic and foil may sag over time and lead to a buildup of lint in the duct. That lint could catch fire. Rigid and flexible metal ducts are much safer choices. You can tell flexible metal ducts from flexible foil ducts because metal ducts, unlike foil ducts, will hold their shape if bent.

sparing fabric wear and tear. If the dryer will go near the kitchen or a bedroom, pay attention to the noise level. Some models are loud enough to drown out normal conversation.

It's worthwhile to spend extra for a moisture-sensor model. More efficient drying can pay for the extra cost over the life of the machine. It typically costs about 30 cents less per load to operate a gas dryer, making up the price difference in a year or two of use. The extra hardware in a gas dryer typically makes it more expensive to repair than an electric model.

Dust cloths, feather dusters, dust mops

As with brooms, the dust cloth, feather duster, or dust mop you choose depends on the job. While all are intended to pick up dust, each tool is geared toward a specific task.

For cleaning easily scratched objects, use lint-free dust cloths. The only acceptable cloths are made from 100 percent cotton material. Other fibers create lint or are too abrasive. If you don't have the appropriate material, buy 100 percent cotton cloths from restaurant-supply houses or automotive-supply shops, or buy cloth diapers for this purpose.

Goose or ostrich feather dusters are good for dusting knick-knacks, photo frames, and other lightweight objects. Shake the dust onto the floor, then vacuum it up. The dusters can be washed in a mild solution of dishwashing liquid and water.

Lamb's wool dust mops or dusters can be used to wipe across large surfaces—even walls—to pick up dust. The lamb's wool "head" can usually be removed and laundered. Dust mops can also be made of cotton-blend looped yarn. These mop heads can also be detached for laundering. Both kinds of dust mops are especially useful in cleaning wood and painted concrete floors, where dust can accumulate easily.

Disposable dust cloths, paper-like cloths made of polyester and polypropylene, can be used for cleaning hard surfaces including wood, ceramic, and vinyl floors; car dashboards; and electronic dust magnets such as TV and computer screens. They can also help you avoid a dust shower when cleaning ceiling fans and vents, and they pick up pet hair as well. They can be used like a dust cloth or attached to a mop handle (sold separately) to do floors. Both are made to be used dry, without furniture polish and cleaners, and both rely on "electrostatic action" to collect dust, dirt, and hair. (A newer "wet" version of the Procter & Gamble product is useful for damp mopping.) A new "mitt" made of the same material as the dust cloths has recently also come onto the market. Instead of attaching the cloth to a mop handle, you wear it on your hand, making it easier to dust objects with intricate designs, such as candlesticks or vases.

CONSUMER REPORTS tests of two brands—Pledge Grab-It by SC Johnson and Procter & Gamble's Swiffer—found that both picked up much more of the fine dust and pet hair than a regular dust cloth, but left a good deal of coarse dirt behind.

Floor polishers

Floor polishers can be used to scrub vinyl, marble, ceramic, terrazzo, and even concrete floors. They are also used to sand and apply finish to wood floors. Polishers are available both in the large commercial size used in office buildings and in a smaller size, intended more for home use.

Floor polishers resemble upright vacuum cleaners. But instead of a rotating, cylindrical beater brush, they have disk-shaped, natural-bristle brushes—from one to three of them—that spin at high speed.

Both the smaller and commercial-sized floor polishers are available at tool-rental sources. Both polishers work the same way, but the commercial polisher has larger pads and brushes that cover a larger area at one time. Renting a polisher for a day costs about a tenth of the purchase price for a home polishing unit.

If the polisher is being used as a waxer, apply the wax to the brushes. The heat of them melts the wax into the floor and gives it a high polish. Disposable waxing pads are sometimes used, in which case wax is applied to them. Run the floor polisher on low speed, moving back and forth with the grain, spreading wax evenly. Overlap your passes slightly. When wax starts to spread spottily, turn off and unplug the machine. Reload wax onto the brushes or pads. Follow label instructions regarding drying time, then polish and buff. Use the same machine in the same way, without the wax, to polish the floor. Then buff the floor using felt buffing pads with the polisher.

If the machine is to be used for sanding, sandpaper disks or screens are attached; for buffing, felt disks are used.

See also **Flooring**, page 260.

Irons

Many businesspeople are hanging up their business suits and dresses in favor of casual attire that is often made of washable fabrics, such as cotton. That means fewer trips to the dry cleaner and more time pressing machine-washed garments so they look presentable.

When buying an iron, budget-priced doesn't necessarily mean bare-bones. Features such as automatic shutoff, burst of steam, and self-cleaning capability are now standard on many models. Higher-priced irons priced tend to be larger, with such innovations as vertical steaming, anti-drip steam vents, and even anti-calcium systems designed to prevent mineral buildup.

What CONSUMER REPORTS tests have found

Steam makes a fabric more pliable so the heat and pressure of the iron can set it straight. Many new irons release more steam than earlier models did. Most produce the best steaming during the first 10 minutes of use and then gradually taper off as the water is used up.

You can usually adjust the amount of steam or turn it off, but models with automatic steam produce more steam at higher temperatures. An anti-drip feature, usually on higher-priced models, is designed to prevent leaks when using steam at lower settings.

"Burst of steam," available on most new irons, lets you push a button for an extra blast to tame stubborn wrinkles. If steam isn't enough to do the job, such as getting wrinkles out of linen napkins, dampen the item using the spray function, available on virtually all irons today. On some irons, burst of steam can be used for vertical steaming to remove wrinkles from hanging items.

A growing number of irons have a hinged or sliding cover on the water-fill hole. The idea is to prevent leaking, but it doesn't always work. Also, the cover may get in the way or can be awkward to open and close. A removable tank is most convenient to use.

Soleplates of steam irons are usually made of aluminum or stainless steel and can have nonstick or enamel coating—all of which performed well in CONSUMER REPORTS tests. Nonstick soleplates are generally easier to keep clean, but they can be scratched by something like a zipper, which could create drag over time. You should clean the soleplate occasionally to remove residue, especially if you use starch, following the manufacturer's directions.

Almost all new irons can use tap water, unless the water is very hard. Most models now offer a self-cleaning feature to flush deposits from vents, but it's not always effective with prolonged use of very hard water. The burst of steam feature also cleans vents to some extent.

Many of the irons on the market will do a fine job of removing wrinkles from clothing. The most significant differences come in ease of use. For example, some controls are easier to see and use. Features also differ from model to model, so determine what is important to you—and be sure to include automatic shutoff on your must-have list. Try out an iron before purchase to see if its size and shape feel right to you.

See also **General rules for ironing**, page 235.

Mops

There are three major types of household mops: swivel-headed flat mops, string mops, and sponge mops. They are intended for different cleaning tasks, and it is helpful to keep one of each major type around to tackle assorted household cleaning challenges.

With a swivel-headed flat mop, the threaded socket of the head fits onto an extension handle. The head can hold an attachment such as a lamb's wool pad for applying wax or a scrubbing pad. A string mop is a water-retaining tool that is used to apply cleaning solutions, absorb spills, and do gentle scrubbing. The strings are made of blended fibers. Sponge mops are also used to apply cleaning solutions and do gentle scrubbing. These mops usually have replaceable heads and wringing mechanisms that save having to bend over to wring out the mop.

Relatively new are Procter & Gamble's Swiffer Wet and Swiffer WetJet. The Swiffer Wet is simply a pre-soaked cleaning cloth similar to dry Swiffer cloths. Using the same mop-style handle as the dry cloths, the wet cloths are for spills and other small mopping jobs, such as a small bathroom. The Swiffer WetJet is sold as a "cleaning system," a sort of self-contained mop and bucket: The handle holds a bottle of cleaning solution that the user sprays onto areas to be mopped via a button on the handle. Eliminating the need for a bucket, rinsing, or wringing, the Swiffer WetJet purports to enhance cleaning convenience.

Paper towels

Paper towels lead a brief and unglamorous life. They're typically called upon to scour a dirty oven, sop up a kitchen spill, or wipe a window. And yet to perform these seemingly unexacting tasks, paper towels have special qualities.

Even when wet, paper towels should withstand scrubbing without falling apart. For mopping up, it can be just as economical to use a costly but highly absorbent towel as it is to use a cheap but less absorbent towel. For spilled salad dressing or motor oil, a poor-quality towel may smear the spill rather than absorb it. But for many other uses, cheaper towels will do the job.

All towels should separate cleanly at their perforations so you won't be left holding a torn sheet or more sheets than you need. Generally, two-ply towels detach more evenly than one-ply towels. Paper towels with short, weakly anchored fibers tend to shed lint, a particular problem when you clean a mirror or windowpane. Soft towels are usually more absorbent but may not hold up as well during scouring.

With paper towels, you get what you pay for. Keep a more expensive brand on hand for more demanding tasks, such as picking up a large spill, and use an economical brand for everyday chores. Some brands are now available with rolls that allow you to tear off half a sheet rather than a full-sized one. These are handy for tasks such as cleaning up small spills or wiping a few crumbs off a countertop.

Relatively new on the market are paper towels that come in a box with a pop-up type dispenser, rather than as a roll. While these are more convenient in some ways—they can be kept in rooms where you might not want a paper towel holder, such as a baby's room or a den—their absorbency is equal to that of a roll towel, but at a much higher price.

If you reserve the paper towels for cleaning cutting boards, countertops, and greasy spills and use a sponge or rag for other cleanup chores, you'll keep the kitchen clean while using less of a disposable product.

Paper shop towels, like cloth shop towels, clean greasy tools and effectively scrub rust. Some ordinary paper towels might tend to shred a bit but should do the job nevertheless. Paper shop towels absorb water faster than their cloth counterparts do, even after the cloth has been laundered, but a cloth shop towel is probably better for motor oil. Cloth shop towels are cheaper if they're used at least 10 times.

Pressure washers

Pressure washers can clean siding, driveways, grills, outdoor furniture, decks, cars, and dog kennels; the most powerful ones can even strip paint. Some machines come with attachments for specific, hard-to-reach places. Cleaning will vary depending on whether you use detergent; the amount of water pressure; the width of the spray angle; the distance from the surface being cleaned; and the surface material and texture.

There are two main types: gas-powered and electric. Gas-powered units are more powerful but must be used outside in well-ventilated areas because they can produce lethal doses of carbon monoxide. You can buy a pressure washer for a few hundred dollars, or rent one for about $30 a day.

Connected to a garden hose, pressure washers use a trigger gun to deliver a jet stream of water that is 10 to 50 times more powerful than the spray from a garden hose alone. The power of the machines varies according to the horsepower if the machine is powered by a gasoline engine or to the amperage (amps) if it has an electric motor.

Pressure washers range from 1,000 to 5,000 PSI (pounds per square inch). As with many cleaning tools, the model you choose will depend on the use for which it is intended. A 1,200-to-1,350-PSI electric machine is fine for cleaning the lawn furniture and car, adequate for the deck, and marginal for the siding and patio. A 1,500-to-2,200-PSI gasoline machine is good for the deck and adequate for doing the siding or the patio. A 2,200-to-5,000-PSI gasoline machine can do all such jobs well. Look for the highest PSI if you need to strip paint or clean roofs and sidewalks, but remember that too much pressure or spraying too closely can damage wood or other materials.

Cautions for Using a Pressure Washer

Because these machines combine pressurized water, detergents or other chemicals, and electricity or gasoline, they are potentially hazardous. Follow manufacturer's instructions carefully. Keep your personal safety and the safety of your property in mind at all times when you use a pressure washer. Here are some other tips:

• This equipment is best used on resilient surfaces. The water is under high-enough pressure to damage surfaces such as wood. Before you begin, always test on a small area first.

• A pressure washer's blast can be so powerful that nonprofessionals are advised to clean from ground level and not from a ladder. Use accessories such as spray-arm extensions if necessary.

• Wear eye-protection goggles.

The nozzle of a pressure washer does the cleaning, and the angle of spray is sometimes adjustable. With adjustable nozzles, the zero-degree setting is the most powerful, while a setting as high as 40 degrees or more is usually all you need for simple washing.

Cold-water washers are less expensive, but not as effective as hot-water washers for cleaning extremely dirty or greasy spots. Hot-water washers, with inner coils or separate fuel pumps to heat water, are more complex machines that require more maintenance.

Most manufacturers have detergents and waxes approved for use in their equipment. Different formulas are available for cleaning houses and decks, degreasing, and car washing and waxing. But in many cases, you can get the job done with a solution of 20 parts water and one part dishwashing liquid, or with water alone.

Scrubbers

Plastic scrubbing pads come in a variety of strengths, color coded by manufacturers. White is for lightweight scrubbing, blue is all-purpose, green is heavy-duty, and black is heaviest duty (for barbecue grills, for example). Use a lightweight scrubbing pad whenever possible to avoid the risk of abrading a surface. While some manufacturers claim that their plastic scrubbing pads are safe for use on nonstick surfaces, it is best to use nylon scrubbers to clean nonstick pans.

Sponges

Small sponges can be used for, say, washing dishes and, in the absence of paper towels, for wiping spills and food off counters. Some sponges have two different textures: a soft side and, for hard-to-remove soil, a scrubbing side.

Unless they're kept scrupulously clean, sponges can become breeding grounds for germs. Wash sponges and dishcloths frequently, at least every few days and ideally every day, on the top rack of your dishwasher.

Steel wool

Made of long, fine steel shavings, steel wool is a useful cleaning tool. The grades of steel wool, from finest to coarsest, are 0000, 000, 00, 0, 1, 2, 3, and 4. Use a medium grade to clean pots and pans. A finer grade is appropriate for polishing a finished surface, while a coarser grade is good for jobs such as scraping paint. A soap pad combines steel wool with soap and detergent for added cleaning power.

Vacuum cleaners

You won't find any one vacuum cleaner that cleans all surfaces superbly, operates noiselessly, and maneuvers effortlessly. But if you're willing to live with a few shortcomings, you can find very good cleaning performance. In the continuing quest to make the perfect vacuum cleaner, manufacturers have loaded many of today's models with features. Unfortunately, some, such as dirt sensors and see-through, bagless dirt bins with "cyclonic action," may do little to improve utility.

Which type of vacuum cleaner to employ used to be a no-brainer. Uprights were clearly better for carpets, while canisters were the obvious choice for bare floors. That distinction has blurred. Today more uprights clean bare floors without spewing dust, and canisters do a very good job with carpeting. Attachments help you clean stairs as well as under furniture and other hard-to-reach spots. Stick vacs and hand vacs—lightweight cleaning machines that lack the power of a full-sized vacuum cleaner—do a decent job at removing loose dirt from hard surfaces.

What CONSUMER REPORTS tests have shown

The most common vacuum attachments are a dusting brush, a crevice tool, and an upholstery tool. Extension wands are a must for reaching high places, such as ceiling moldings. A long, flexible, sturdy hose can be helpful. Most canisters have a detachable power nozzle that cleans carpet more thoroughly than a simple suction nozzle.

Some vacs have a dirt sensor that triggers a light indicator based on the concentration of dirt particles in the machine's airstream. But the sensor signals only that the vacuum is no longer picking up dirt, not whether there's dirt left in your rug. It typically tells you to keep vacuuming longer than you would otherwise, meaning more work, with little gain in cleanliness.

Fine particles vacuumed up may pass through a vacuum's bag or filter and escape into the air through the exhaust. Many models claim to provide microfiltration capabilities, maybe by using a dirt bag with smaller pores or a second, electrostatic filter in addition to the standard motor filter. Some have a high-efficiency particulate-air (HEPA) filter, which may benefit someone with asthma. But many models without a HEPA filter performed as well in a CONSUMER REPORTS emissions test because the amount of dust emitted depends as much on the design of the whole machine as on its filter choices.

The internal design of a vacuum can make a difference in its durability. In some uprights, dirt sucked into the vac first passes through the blower fan and then enters the dirt bag. Most blower fans arc plastic and vulnerable to damage from a hard object. With canisters and many uprights, dirt is filtered through the dirt bag before it reaches the fan, so although hard objects can still lodge in the motorized brush, they're unlikely to break the fan.

A suction control, common with canisters, less so with uprights, is handy for vacuuming drapes or throw rugs. More uprights now have a self-propelled feature to make pushing easy, but that feature may make them even heavier, and harder to carry up or down the stairs.

Stick vacs and hand vacs can be corded or, using a nickel-cadmium battery pack, cordless. Instead of dirt bags, they typically have dirt-collection containers, which are messy to empty. Some have a revolving brush, which may help pick up surface debris from the carpet. Most stick vacs can hang on either a hook or, for cordless vacs, a wall-mounted charger.

A full-dirt-bag indicator may be a handy reminder to some people, since an overstuffed bag impairs a vacuum's ability to clean. Lately, many uprights have adopted a no-bag configuration with a see-through dirt-collection container: psychologically rewarding, perhaps, but CONSUMER REPORTS has found them to be messy to empty.

Virtually all of the uprights and canisters CONSUMER REPORTS tested did at least a good job overall. On the whole, bagless vacs filtered dust as well as bag-equipped models. But the process of emptying their bins released so much dust that it seemed advisable to wear a mask. Few stick vacs excel at all types of cleaning. Hand vacs overall do a better job of cleaning along wall edges than stick vacs do by coming closer to the moldings and angling into nooks and crannies.

Features such as dirt sensors and see-through bagless dirt bins with "cyclonic action" don't necessarily improve performance. And ignore claims about amps and suction. Amps are a measure of running current, not cleaning power. And suction alone doesn't decide a vacuum cleaner's ability to lift dirt from carpeting. Configuration of the bristles on the rotating brush counts, too. Suction power and air flow, however, do have a major bearing on attachment performance.

Base your vacuum-cleaner choice on personal preference for an upright or canister style. Unfortunately, you probably can't find all you need in one machine. You might end up with a vacuum-cleaner arsenal—for instance, an upright for carpets, a compact canister for the kitchen and laundry, and a hand vac or stick vac for quick touch-ups of floors.

Washing machines

Until recently, about the only place you would see a front-loading washing machine was in a coin laundry. But in the past few years, this type of washer, which you load the same way you load a clothes dryer, has gained in popularity. The vast majority of washers sold, however, are still top-loaders.

Full-sized machines range from 27 to 29 inches in width, while compact machines are slightly smaller, at 24 inches wide. Compact front-loaders and many full-sized front-loaders can be stacked with a matching dryer. Some compact washers can be stored in a closet and rolled out to be hooked up to the kitchen sink. With laundry centers, either full-sized or compact, the washer and dryer are located in one unit.

What CONSUMER REPORTS tests have found

Most top-loaders get clothes clean by agitating them. Front-loaders tumble clothes into water and are gentler on them. Front-loaders use less water, including hot water, and thus less energy than most top-loaders do. Two top-loading designs—one from Sears and Whirlpool, the other from Fisher & Paykel—work kind of like front-loaders. They fill partially with water and spray clothes with a concentrated detergent solution.

High-end washers typically have touch-pad controls; others have traditional dials. Controls should be legible, easy to push or turn, and logically arranged. A plus: lights or signals that indicate cycle. On some top-loaders, an automatic lock during the spin cycle keeps children from opening the lid. Front-loaders lock at the beginning of a cycle but usually can be opened by interrupting it, although some doors remain shut briefly after the machine stops.

Front-loaders automatically set wash speed according to the fabric cycle selected, and some also automatically set the spin speed. Top-loaders typically provide wash/spin speed combinations such as Regular, Permanent Press, and Delicate (or Gentle). A few models allow an extra rinse or extended spin. Some machines offer a hand-washing cycle.

Front-loaders and some top-loaders also set water levels automatically, ensuring efficient water use. Some top-loading models can be set for four or more levels; three or four are probably as many as you'd ever need.

....
Helpful Hint

Be aware that front-loading washers require front-loader detergent, which produces fewer suds than detergent for top-loaders. For more, see **Laundry detergents,** page 176.

Most machines establish wash and rinse temperatures by mixing hot and cold water in pre-set proportions. If your incoming cold water is especially cold, an automatic temperature control adjusts the flow to the correct temperature. A time-delay feature lets you program the washer to start at a later time of day—when your utility rates might be low, for example. Detergent and fabric softener dispensers automatically release powder or liquid. Bleach dispensers can prevent spattering.

A porcelain-coated steel inner tub can rust if the porcelain is chipped. Stainless-steel or increasingly common plastic tubs won't rust. A porcelain top or lid resists scratching better than a painted one.

All washers get clothes clean. In CONSUMER REPORTS tests, differences in washing ability tended to be slight. Differences in water and energy efficiency and in noisiness were greater. Front-loaders are generally quieter than top-loaders except when draining or spinning. Features such as extra wash or spin options or an automatic detergent dispenser are convenient but don't significantly improve performance.

The water efficiency of any washing machine rises with larger loads, but overall front-loaders use far less water per pound of laundry and excel in energy effi-ciency. Using electricity to heat water for six loads of laundry per week, the most efficient front-loaders typically save about 3,000 gallons of water and about $20 worth of electrical energy a year compared with the least efficient top-loader.

While front-loaders can cost less to operate, they are more expensive to buy, so this saving is not likely to make up the price difference over a washer's typical life span of 10 to 15 years.

Water filters

Many water filters are good at eliminating pollutants such as lead, parasites, or chlorine byproducts as well as removing unwanted tastes and odors. There are several types of filters, with some less expensive to maintain than others.

What CONSUMER REPORTS tests have found

Generally made of plastic, carafes are simple to use and typically come in a half-gallon or larger size. Many carafe models can fit on a shelf in the door of a fridge. You usually have to change the filter every month or so. Faucet-mounted filters are compact and easy to install. The filter should generally be changed quarterly.

Many carafe and faucet-mounted filters have a flashing light, color indicator, or some other signal to let you know it's time for a new cartridge. CONSUMER REPORTS has found that most of these signals aren't particularly accurate, but slower-than-usual performance alone may tell you that it's time to replace the cartridge. (As impurities collected from the water build up in the filter, the flow of water slows or even stops.) Faucet-mounted filters allow you to choose unfiltered water for cleaning or washing.

Some faucets are sold with filters built into them. This is a relatively expensive option if you don't need a new faucet.

There are two types of refrigerator filters: built-in, sold as a step-up feature with some refrigerators, and add-on, which must be installed (often by a plumber) in the tubing that supplies water to a refrigerator's ice maker or water dispenser. With either, you typically have to change the filter twice a year.

Countertop filters often rely on a single filter cartridge. Under-the-sink filters use one to three filter cartridges. Whole-house systems can be as simple as an in-line single-stage filter or as elaborate as a large carbon cylinder.

Some contaminants require special filters to remove them. You may need a plumber to install a reverse-osmosis system, typically under the kitchen sink. This water-filtration system combines conventional filters with a special cellophane-like membrane that removes many contaminants including industrial chemicals, lead, nitrates, and such toxic metals as barium and chromium.

Helpful Hint

CONSUMER REPORTS tests have shown that many faucet-mounted filters and one carafe reduce parasite contamination. NSF International and Underwriters Laboratories certify models.

In CONSUMER REPORTS tests, most carafes and faucet-mounted filters did an excellent or very good job of removing lead, chlorine byproducts (such as chloroform), and unwanted tastes and odors. Neither carafes nor faucet-mounted filters removed fluoride—an additive that reduces tooth decay. Reverse-osmosis filters removed some fluoride.

Faucets with a built-in filter didn't perform as well in tests as the faucet-mounted filters or most of the carafes did. Refrigerator filters fell short of the faucet-mounted units and the carafes, with most claiming only taste and odor removal. Under-the-sink filters didn't necessarily filter more effectively than countertop units. The best reverse-osmosis systems earned top scores across the board, but most people don't need that degree of filtration.

Consider your daily water use to help determine the filtering equipment that is appropriate. A carafe filter or a faucet-mounted filter might be fine if you need to filter only a relatively small amount of water daily. Determine how often you will have to change filters, which affects annual costs. Because bacteria can thrive inside a filter, it's a good idea to follow the manufacturer's recommended replacement schedule.

See also **Water**, page 144.

Wet/dry vacuums

These machines, used to pick up sawdust, wood chips, and spilled liquid, are to regular vacuum cleaners what pickup trucks are to sedans. Their place is typically in the basement workshop or garage, where their multigallon capabilities and appetite for rough stuff make them right at home.

Lately, manufacturers have been plugging their smallest portable models for kitchen duty: draining a clogged sink, sucking up soda spills, or picking up broken glass. Wet/dry vacs of any size make poor housemates, however. Even the quietest are as loud as the noisiest household version. And while their high-pitched whine is more annoying than dangerous, CONSUMER REPORTS tested one that was loud enough to make ear protection advisable.

Wet/dry vacs tend to spew fine dust into the air, which may be a problem if you have allergies. A high-efficiency cartridge filter is available with many units, usually at additional cost.

What CONSUMER REPORTS tests have found

Wet/dry vacs have claimed canister capacities ranging from 6 to 20 gallons for full-sized units and 1 gallon to 2 gallons for compacts. A medium-sized model with a claimed capacity of 10 to 15 gallons may be a good compromise. A smaller one is easier to store and maneuver but has to be emptied more often. With most units, about three-fourths of the canister can be filled with water before the float—an internal part designed to prevent overfilling and spilling—seals off the flow.

Claimed peak motor power varies, ranging from 1 hp for the smallest portables to more than 6 hp for the largest. Larger models with more powerful motors tend to be able to pick up debris or liquid faster, according to CONSUMER REPORTS tests. But some smaller units outperform larger ones. Claims of canister capacity and peak motor power should be used as a guide for comparing models within a brand or size group—not as an absolute.

The hose is usually one of two diameters: 1¼ inch or 2½ inches. We found that units with a wider hose pick up liquids and larger dry debris more quickly. A hose lock found in some models secures the hose to the canister better than a simple press-on fit, which can release as you pull the hose.

Most vacs come with accessories. A built-in caddie found on some units holds them conveniently. A squeegee nozzle, essentially a wide floor nozzle with a rubber insert, helps slurp up liquid spills more quickly and thoroughly. Other nozzles include a utility nozzle for solid objects and dirt and a crevice nozzle for corners. On some models, the nozzles include a brush insert for improved dry pickup

There are two basic types of filter: a cartridge filter and a two-piece paper/foam filter. CONSUMER REPORTS has found that a cartridge filter is easier to service. Moreover, it can stay in the unit for wet vacuuming; with a two-piece filter, you must remove the paper element for wet pickup. A high-efficiency cartridge filter, which typically costs $20 to $30, reduces the amount of fine dust that the unit spews into the air. Suction is reduced somewhat, but allergy sufferers should find the small sacrifice to be worthwhile.

Some wet/dry vacs have other capabilities you might find useful. Some models can be used as a handheld blower for outdoor debris or as a pump. Large carrying handles molded into the sides of the canister of some units let you move the vac securely over ledges and up stairs. An assist handle mounted at or near the top of the unit makes it easier to jock-ey the machine. A drain spout found in some models lets you simply open the drain rather than having to lift and tilt the unit. An adequately long extension wand makes for less stooping. Some units have power cords that are as short as 6 feet. But buy a unit with a cord at least 15 feet long; using an extension cord in standing water can be dangerous.

Performance roughly tracks with size. Compact models proved to be relatively wimpy in CONSUMER REPORTS tests, though they're fine for small areas and pint-sized spills. While virtually all units that were tested picked up small wood shav-ings, chips, and sawdust, those with the wider hose sucked up light dry and wet debris faster and, often, more thoroughly. Heavier dry waste is generally problematic for all sizes.

Maintenance of a wet/dry vac includes cleaning the filter—typically about a five-minute job that involves removing and brushing the filter clean (for paper elements) or washing it (for foam elements). An extra filter that you can pop in when one is dirty (about $15) can come in handy.

Special Cleaning Advice

Laundry

Guide to fabrics

The following is a general guide with basic information on how to launder a selection of fabrics. You should always look first at the care instructions and warnings on the fabric label of the garment that needs cleaning. A label that says "dry-clean only" means just that; a label that says "dry-clean" means that there is an unspecified alternative cleaning method. Of the fabrics listed, most are synthetic. Cotton, linen, silk, and wool are natural fibers.

Acetate. This material, which is used in inexpensive satin and the lining of clothing and draperies, usually requires dry cleaning. If the garment's label specifically permits washing, launder it in cold water with mild suds. Don't wring or twist the garment, and don't soak colored items. Once the garment is clean, do not dry it in a dryer. Instead, air-dry it by carefully spreading the garment out on terry-cloth bath towels on a horizontal surface or by draping it over a clothesline, avoiding direct sunlight. While it's still damp, press the garment inside out with a cool iron. If pressing right side out, use a pressing cloth.

Acrylic. Acrylic fabrics resemble wool and are often blended with wool. Modacrylic is an acrylic fiber that is flame retardant, lightweight, bulky, and warm. It is commonly used in fake fur, curtains, and wigs and for stuffing toys. Most acrylic garments are hand- or machine-washable, and they can also be dry-cleaned. Delicate items should be washed by hand in warm water. For machine-washable items, use warm water and your machine's gentle settings. Acrylic may pill, so turn your garments inside out before washing. Use fabric softener every third or fourth washing to reduce static electricity. After laundering, gently squeeze any water from the garment. Then smooth or shake it out. Acrylic sweaters should then be pulled into shape and left to dry flat on a horizontal surface. Dry other acrylic garments on nonrust hangers. If the care label permits machine drying, use a low temperature setting and remove the garment from the machine as soon as it is dry. Acrylic tends not to wrinkle, but if ironing is needed, set the iron to medium.

Cotton. A product of the cotton plant, cotton is absorbent and comfortable, and helps keep you cool when it's hot outside. The wide range of cotton fabrics includes canvas, chintz, corduroy, denim, gabardine, jersey, lace, muslin, organdy, percale, poplin, seersucker, ticking, and voile. Cotton wrinkles easily and can shrink, but it irons well and is not vulnerable to moths. Cotton-polyester fabric combines qualities of both cotton and polyester in different proportions according to purpose and manufacturer. It's more wrinkle-resistant than cotton and breathes better than polyester, so it's more comfortable. But it can pill and is more likely to stain than cotton or poly-

Special Fabric Cautions

Acetate	Do not use nail-polish remover or other cleaners that contain acetone, which will dissolve acetate.
Olefin	Do not iron—it can melt.
Silk	Never use chlorine bleach. Use color-safe bleach only. Do not use laundry detergent on nonwashable silk.
Spandex	Never use chlorine bleach. Use a color-safe bleach only.
Triacetate	Do not use nail-polish remover or other cleaners that contain acetone, which will dissolve triacetate.
Wool	Do not use laundry detergent on nonwashable wools.

ester alone. Cotton fabrics are usually washable and can be dry-cleaned, but read care instructions on labels carefully. Unless a garment or other item made from cotton is "pre-shrunk," it may emerge from the wash several sizes smaller if you use anything but cool water. Cotton-polyester should be washed on a permanent-press setting. Wash similar colors together, especially reds and other darks because cotton tends to lose its color in water. Chlorine bleach is safe for white cottons, but use color-safe bleach on dyed cottons.

To maintain shape, it's best to air-dry cotton on a line, but if you must use a clothes dryer, set the machine for air drying or very low heat. Use a permanent-press setting for cotton-polyester garments, turning them inside out to reduce pilling. Since 100 percent cotton is not easily scorched, you can press it with an iron set to high. Sometimes 100 percent cotton fabric is treated with a wrinkle-resistant finish.

Linen. Made from the stems of the flax plant, linen is similar in many ways to cotton. But it is not as strong or resilient and doesn't hold dyes as well. Still, it is pretty durable, and its appearance and "feel" improve with laundering. Linen-polyester is a blend often used in tablecloths, napkins, and place mats, which are often treated with permanent-press and soil-release finishes.

Some linens—most commonly drapery, upholstery, and decorative fabrics—may be dry-cleaned only. Linens that have been chemically treated for wrinkle resistance may withstand warm-water washing. Follow the instructions on the care label. Before washing colored linen, be sure to test for colorfastness. If possible, dry white linens in the sun to help them stay white. Iron linen while damp, although wrinkle-resistant linen may not need frequent ironing.

Lyocell. Lyocell is the generic fiber name for a form of rayon that is often marketed as the brand Tencel. In 1996, it became the first new generic fiber group in 30 years to be approved by the Federal Trade Commission. Lyocell is strong and easy to care for, and is used in woven and knitted fabrics (often blended with cotton), including jersey, sweaters, hosiery, denim, sueded fabrics, chinos, sheets, and towels. A few lyocell fabrics should be dry-cleaned only. But some lyocell fabrics should not be dry-cleaned. Check the care label; if it permits machine washing, wash warm, rinse cold, and dry on a permanent-press setting. Wrinkles may hang out. If your garment needs a slight touch-up, use an iron set on medium; don't iron fabric made from fine yarns or microfibers.

Nylon. This strong, lightweight fabric may yellow if dried in direct sunlight. It may fade, look gray, or attract dyes when washed with other garments. Hand-wash nylon stockings and other garments or machine-wash warm on a gentle setting with similarly colored items and fibers. Add a fabric softener to the final rinse cycle if you plan to air-dry. If you machine-dry, use a dryer sheet to reduce static electricity and remove garments as soon as they are dried. (Don't use softeners in washing or drying; they can build up.) Use a warm iron.

Polyester. Quick drying and resistant to wrinkling, shrinking, and fading, this synthetic material is nonetheless difficult to maintain. Polyester pills easily when laundered with other fabrics and attracts oil stains like a magnet. Dry cleaning is OK for most items. Hand-wash or gently machine-wash a polyester garment, turning it inside out to reduce the possibility of exte-

Understanding Care Labels

The Care Labeling Rule adopted in 1972 by the Federal Trade Commission requires permanent care labels on all textile products sold at retail in the United States. In 1984, amendments required care instructions to be more specific about washing, bleaching, drying, and ironing washable garments, and the dry-cleaning process. If specific care instructions are followed and an article does not hold up, the resulting damage is the responsibility of the manufacturer and the garment should be returned to the retailer.

rior pilling. Let the garment drip-dry or use a low temperature setting and remove the items as soon as the tumble cycle is complete. If ironing is needed, use a medium setting. If you want the convenience of polyester without its drawbacks, look for a garment made from a blend of polyester and natural fibers—it will be more durable and easier to care for than an all-polyester or all-natural-fiber garment.

This fabric attracts oil stains and soiling from other items in the wash. Wash oily stains as soon as you notice them by rubbing them with a wet bar of hand soap, then with a wet towel, and rinse.

Polyolefin (olefin). This fabric is often used in underwear, socks, sweaters, pantyhose, and swimwear. Items can be hand-washed or machine-washed in warm or cold water. Air-dry or tumble-dry on a gentle setting. Avoid ironing, but if it's necessary, use the lowest temperature settings.

Rayon. Also known as viscose, this fabric is lightweight and strong when dry but weak and flimsy when wet. It's prone to wrinkling and doesn't hold its shape particularly well. Dry cleaning is recommended for most rayon items. If the care label permits, hand-wash with mild suds in cool or lukewarm water, or machine-wash using a gentle setting. Do not twist or wring wet items. Lay sweaters flat to dry, but air-dry other items using nonrust hangers. Damp items can be ironed using a low or medium setting. Begin with the garment turned inside out; finish ironing right side out using a pressing cloth. Dry items should be pressed with a cool iron only.

Silk. Silk thread, secreted from the larva of a moth, is the strongest of all the natural fibers. It usually is wrinkle resistant and elastic, holds shape well, and is cool and light in hot weather. Sunlight can weaken the fabric and fade the color. When the natural gum is not cleaned from the fiber, it's called raw silk. Shantung, pongee, and tussah are all unevenly woven silks and are usually not dyed. A few special silk fabrics—such as crepe, chiffon, organza, voile, georgette, grosgrain, moiré, taffeta, and satin—are used for evening wear.

Most care labels recommend dry cleaning only since some silk dyes will dissolve in water, causing "bleeding" and color transfer. Some unlined silk items can be hand-washed in lukewarm water using dishwashing liquid or another mild soap, or machine-washed using a gentle cycle. If the care label recommends hand washing, test for colorfastness by washing a small, inconspicuous area first. Knead the garment gently in clear water to rinse, then hang and let air-dry. Store silk in a dark place because sunlight can weaken the fabric. Do not try to spot-clean stains, which can weaken the fabric and cause permanent marks. Never use bleach on silk.

Spandex. Also known as Lycra, spandex is used in swimwear, sportswear, underwear, and other garments, and provides shape and elasticity. Some fiber blends may be dry-cleaned, but usually hand or machine washing is preferable. To ensure that spandex maintains its elasticity, hand-wash items in lukewarm water, or machine-wash on a gentle setting, using a low temperature setting and a mild detergent. Never wash spandex with chlorine bleach or a detergent that contains it. Be sure to rinse well. Drip dry, or use your dryer's low temperature settings. It's usually not necessary to press an article of clothing made from spandex, but if you need to remove wrinkles, set the iron on a low temperature setting only and don't leave the iron on one spot for long. If wool blended with this fiber gets wet, air-dry away from heat or sunlight. Do not tumble dry.

....
Helpful Hint

Protect silk by storing it away from light and insects. Since perfume, strong deodorant, and perspiration can damage silk fibers, always clean your silk garments after wearing them.

Special Care for Wool

• Store knits folded on shelves.

• Hang other wool garments on shaped or padded hangers. In most cases, wrinkles will flatten out in 24 hours and garments will return to original shape. To hasten the process, hang the item in a steamy bathroom.

• Use a brush to remove soil from the surface of suits, and a damp sponge for knits and more delicate fabrics.

• If you are caught in the rain or snow, dry your wool garment at room temperature and away from a heat source.

• Dry-clean wool before storing it for the season.

Helpful Hint

Do not use nail-polish remover or other cleaners that contain acetone for stain removal. Acetone will dissolve triacetate. Triacetate may also be adversely affected by perfumes containing organic solvents.

Triacetate. Triacetate is used in sportswear and clothes in which pleat retention is important—such as robes, dresses, and skirts. It is shrink resistant, heat resistant, and easily washed. Pleated items should be hand-washed. Nonpleated items that are 100 percent triacetate can be machine-washed. Air- or machine-dry. Check the garment's care label before you iron—triacetate usually needs only touch-up ironing. Some garments or blends may be no-iron.

Wool. Made from the fleece of animals, wool retains color well. Most wool is water-repellent and wrinkle-, stain-, and soil-resistant. Types of wool include alpaca (from alpaca goats), angora (angora rabbits), camel hair (camels), cashmere (Asian goats), lamb's wool, llama, mohair (angora goats), and pashmina (Himalayan capra goat). Wool fabrics include jersey, gabardine, crepe, twills, and broadcloth.

Recycling wool is an old practice, and items made of recycled wool may be less expensive. "New" or "virgin" wool is made from wool that has not previously made up another product. It may be softer than other woolens. But a garment made from "100 percent new wool" is not necessarily superior because it may include some inferior grades of wool.

All wool garments can be dry-cleaned, but check your item's care label before hand- or machine-washing. "Dry-clean only" means just that—no wet washing. Some garments may be hand-washed carefully in cold water with a mild wool-washing product. Wools that can be machine-washed should be cleaned on a gentle cycle.

Turn a washable wool garment—one that does not contain mohair or angora—inside out before hand washing. Wash carefully in cold water with a mild wool-washing product. Do not wring wool items. Instead, lay hand-washed garments on a dry towel and then roll up the towel to remove excess moisture. Unroll the towel, remove the garment, and lay it flat to dry on a new towel so it will retain its shape.

Machine-washed garments should also be dried flat. They should be placed in a dryer only if the care label permits machine drying. However, you might want to forgo machine drying altogether. In CONSUMER REPORTS tests, machine drying damaged some sweaters made of machine-washable wool.

Don't press wool with a dry iron—use the wool/steam setting. To avoid an undesirable shine, iron the garment inside out or use a pressing cloth. (See **General rules for ironing,** page 235.)

Hand washing

Make sure that the bowl, bucket, or tub you're using is large enough to accommodate the clothing without having to jam it in. Fill it with water and make sure the washing product is completely dissolved. (To help you choose the right washing product, see **Detergents for Hand-Washables,** page 178.)

Lingerie, silk blouses, pantyhose. To gently agitate the items, bring the clothing to the surface, then drop it back into the water several times. Gently knead with your hands to help remove the dirt unless the care label advises against wringing or twisting. Rinse thoroughly until there is no sign of detergent. Add ¼ cup of white vinegar to the final rinse to remove any residue.

Drip-dry if possible or roll up in a clean, dry towel to remove

Seven Tips for Using Chlorine Bleach

1. Washable whites often can be bleached if they're made of acrylic, cotton, linen, ramie, or polyester. Never use chlorine bleach on cashmere, leather, mohair, nylon, rayon, silk, spandex, drip-dry cotton, or wool. Always follow the garment's care label. Even some whites made of the bleachable fabrics above will say "do not bleach."

2. Test the diluted bleach solution in an inconspicuous area of fabric to make sure it doesn't do more harm than good. Dab the fabric with a cotton swab dipped in a solution of one part bleach and two parts warm water. Let the tested area dry completely before proceeding. If the color comes out, do not bleach.

3. Never combine different types of bleaches.

4. Bleach should be diluted in water before pouring it into the wash tub—use about 1 cup of bleach to 1 quart of water.

5. Add the bleach-and-water solution about five minutes after the start of the wash cycle to allow the enzymes and whitening and brightening ingredients in the detergent to work.

6. The hotter the wash water, the more effective the bleaching action.

7. Soaking fabrics in the bleach-and-water solution for more than five minutes may remove stains, but it may severely weaken the fabric. Never soak a valuable old linen tablecloth in diluted chlorine bleach.

moisture, then lay flat on another towel or a rust-free window screen or other appropriate surface that will allow air to circulate. Or spin out in a washing machine to extract excess water. But do not agitate in the machine.

Wool. Woolen items should never be soaked for extended periods of time or agitated. To loosen dirt on items that are lightly or moderately soiled, soak them for 10 minutes or so. Badly soiled items may have to be soaked a bit longer.

Soaking and bleaching

Items that are heavily soiled will benefit from pre-soaking before being added to the regular wash. Soaking in ordinary washing detergent or in diluted bleach may have the same effect as using a commercial pre-soak product. Soaking helps to loosen soiling or dirt so that when the clothes are washed, the dirt will be removed more easily. Bleaching also takes the color out of stains, so the stain seems to have disappeared. Soaking in diluted chlorine bleach whitens whites; soaking in oxygen bleach brightens colors. (See **Bleach,** page 161.)

Before you pre-soak, scrape off any mud, dirt, or food debris. After checking the care label to make sure the fabric can be soaked, rub a little straight detergent on especially soiled spots such as collars, and then place the item in a tub with dissolved detergent and leave overnight or at least two hours. Or put it in your machine if it has a pre-soak cycle. Squeeze as much water as possible out of the item, then launder by machine or continue to hand-wash.

Should pre-soaking not remove the dirt, check the **Fabric and Carpet Stain-Removal Guide** on page 246 for alternative solutions or try using the appropriate type of bleach. Use all-fabric bleach (oxygen bleach) for colored items and white items whose labels say "do not bleach." A warm-water solution is better than a cool one. Hydrogen peroxide may be used as a mild bleach for silk and wool; to remove spots, use one part 3 percent hydrogen peroxide solution and two parts water.

Sorting and loading

As anyone who has ever turned their whites pink can tell you, the important work is done before the machine starts its wash cycle. Washing well is in large part determined by what you put in your washer and the way you put it in.

Sort and separate items. For best results, wash darks apart from lights and items that can be washed in hot water (generally cottons and whites) separate from items that need cooler temperatures (such as synthetics). Don't wash fabrics that shed lint, such as terry cloth and sweatshirts with fuzzy linings, together with fabrics that attract lint, such as corduroy, velour, and permanent press items. Turn lint-attracting pile fabrics like corduroy or velours inside out to reduce the chance of linting.

Test for colorfastness. If you suspect an item might not be colorfast, wet an inconspicuous area, such as a hem, with cold water.

Blot with a piece of white cloth, such as an old diaper or towel. If color transfers, wash the item separately or have it dry-cleaned.

If you are not sure the fabric can take chlorine bleach, see **Seven Tips for Using Chlorine Bleach** on page 232. If you are uncertain how fabric will respond to all-fabric bleach, mix 1 teaspoon of the product with 1 cup of hot water and put a drop on a hidden area. Check for any color change after about 15 minutes.

If you suspect that the dye in a fabric may run, try this old-fashioned remedy to "set" color. Rinse the item in 1 quart of water to which you have added 3 tablespoons of salt and 1 cup of vinegar. For dyes that have run, re-dye in a dye such as Rit, which will not run.

Pay attention to your clothes. Put delicate items, such as lingerie, in mesh bags or pillow slips. Trims, buttons, hooks and eyes, or any other items that could damage other garments should be fastened, turned to the inside, or removed. Empty pockets, close zippers, tie straps and strings, and buckle belts. Don't put torn items into the wash before you mend them; the rip is likely to get bigger.

For especially soiled areas, such as collars, cuffs, pocket edges, and seams, apply a paste of powdered detergent and water or a commercial pre-wash and remove with a brush or old toothbrush. (See **Pre-washers, boosters, and pre-spotters,** page 182. Some of these products may be applied several days before you do the laundry; check the product labels.)

Wash-load size matters. Washing machines have a maximum load guide. You can weigh the laundry in a bag on the bathroom scale or weigh yourself holding the laundry and subtract your weight. On the low end, top-loading machines hold about 6 to 8 pounds; a new large-capacity top-loading machine holds 12 pounds or more; front-loaders can hold as much as 18 pounds. For a better and more efficient wash, mix smaller items with larger items and make sure there's enough room for the load to agitate correctly.

Additions. Add soap or detergent as the washing machine is filling—ideally before adding the clothing. Follow instructions on the package about when to add bleach or water softener. Fabric softener or liquid starch should be added at the final rinse.

Drying

Machine drying. Check care-label advice regarding the correct temperature for machine drying. If you have added starch to the rinse water, dry the load separately in the machine on an air-only setting, and if they are dark-colored, turn them inside out.

Your clothes will be less likely to wrinkle if you keep the dryer load to less than half full. (An average washer load will fill about one-third of the dryer space.) Items of similar fabric weight will dry more evenly. Care labels will advise you regarding drying times and temperatures. Do not put rubber-backed bath mats in the machine; their backing can crumble. Remove dry items promptly to avoid wrinkling. Remove items that will be ironed while they are still damp.

Air drying and blocking. Hang washable garments on non-rust hangers and line-dry indoors or out. Easily stretched items should be hung on padded hangers or dried flat.

To ensure that the dried garment is sized properly, before washing it trace its shape using safety pins and a towel. After the item is washed, rinsed, and blotted, put the pattern on a clean, dry towel, then lay the garment on top. Gently pull and pat ("block") it to match the pattern and let it dry flat, away from direct heat as well as from the sun, which may bleach or discolor it. When it's dry on one side, turn it over.

General rules for ironing

Garments will be smoother if they are ironed when they are damp, so if possible remove them from the dryer or line before they are fully dry. Smooth out seams and pleats on garments and pull linens back into shape immediately upon removing them from the dryer or taking them down from the line; even if they still need ironing, the job will be easier.

If you can't get to the ironing immediately, let items dry fully. Dampen them when you're ready to iron, sprinkling them with water and rolling them in a towel to distribute the moisture; or use the spray on your steam iron as you go. You may be able to use local tap water in your iron instead of distilled water, depending on the manufacturer's instructions and how hard your water is.

When using starch or sizing, spray each item as you go, but allow a few moments for the starch or sizing to soak in so there's no buildup on the soleplate.

If you have a quantity of clothes to iron, deal with the garments that need ironing at the lowest temperatures first, such as synthetics and silk; as the iron heats up, work on the wools, then the cottons, and finally the linens.

Ironing Tips

Use these tips to put the snap back in your collar and restore the pleats in your favorite skirt.

Lace, silk, and wool: Press inside out. If that's not possible, use a dry pressing cloth. Lower and lift the iron; don't slide it back and forth. Prevent imprinting inside detail by placing a piece of brown paper or tissue paper under folds, seams, or darts.

Sequined, beaded, or metallic fabric: Place it face down on a soft surface—such as a thick towel or two—and press on low.

Restoring the nap to velvet: Hold the steam iron about an inch or two above the fabric and slowly move it around. Or hold the garment over a steaming kettle. Hang it in the bathroom and run a hot shower. Or use a fabric steamer—an appliance sold for this purpose.

Shirts and jackets:

1. Start at the point of the collar, working toward the middle.
2. Next, iron the yoke by arranging one shoulder over the narrow end of the ironing board, then do the same thing for the other shoulder.
3. Do the sleeves next, working down from the underarm. A sleeve board is a big help with ironing. Then open the cuffs and try to iron them flat.
4. Iron the back of the shirt next, slipping it over the wide end of the ironing board and shifting it as needed.
5. Iron the two halves of the front. Or if the shirt doesn't open, slip it over the ironing board and iron the front.

Dry cleaning

Professional dry cleaning. In both so-called dry cleaning and laundering, a dirty garment is put into a solution, agitated, then tumbled dry. Laundering, uses a solution of water and detergent. After the washing process, the solution is discarded and the garment is usually dried at a high temperature. Dry cleaning uses a special fluid, plus additives for brightening and sizing, detergent, and a bit of water. The drying temperature is much lower than it usually is with laundering.

During dry cleaning, soluble stains dissolve into the fluid, which is periodically purified by distillation. The cleaning fluid is also usually filtered throughout the cleaning cycle to carry away insoluble particles so they aren't redeposited. If

Pants:
1. If the pants have cuffs, unfold them and brush out any loose soil.
2. Turn the waistband inside out and pull out pockets to iron them flat.
3. Iron the zipper placket.
4. On the right side of the garment, iron the waistband and the rest of the top. Repeat on the left side.
5. Put leg seams together in the middle and fold the pants the long way. Lay them flat on the board, then fold back the top leg. Iron the inside of the lower leg, then turn and iron the outside.
6. Repeat with other leg.
7. Iron the two legs together (all four thicknesses at once).

Skirts: Iron from hem to waist in long strokes, but press (lift and lower) when continuing into the gathers.

Pleated skirts: Arrange pleats on the ironing board and hold them or pin them in place. Iron from top to bottom, but not over the pins.

Dresses:
1. Start with the lining.
2. Continue to the top of the dress as if you were ironing a blouse. A dress that doesn't open should be pulled over the end of a board; then iron the front and back.
3. Lift and press underneath any collar; then press the collar itself.

your dry-cleaned clothing appears dingy, it may be the work of a dry cleaner who has cut costs by doing less frequent distillation or by leaving out detergent.

Because dry-cleaning fluid can change color, avoid, say, dry-cleaning the skirt of a suit without dry-cleaning the jacket, too.

Remove and discard the plastic bags from dry-cleaned clothes; they trap odors and chemicals from cleaning that can't be released. If you want to cover the clothes, use a cloth garment bag.

Home dry cleaning. Home dry-cleaning products promise to clean and freshen dry-clean-only, dry-clean/hand-washable, and special-care garments in the comfort of your home laundry room. Home dry-cleaning kits usually contain a stain remover for pre-treating stains before cleaning and a cleaning product. After the pre-treatment, garments are run through a dryer with the cleaning product.

In CONSUMER REPORTS tests, home dry-cleaning products did a good job of removing smoke and cooking odors from a variety of garments. But stain-removal results were mixed. The products work well on some stains, including spaghetti sauce, but may not be as effective as professional dry cleaning on other stains. If you want to freshen up a lightly soiled garment or remove smoke or stale cooking odors, home dry-cleaning products can save you money and protect you from exposure to strong dry-cleaning solvents. As for convenience, while it may save you a trip to the dry cleaner, in some cases you have to spend time pre-treating stains or removing water spots afterward.

Carpeting

For information on removing carpet stains, see the **Fabric and Carpet Stain-Removal Guide**, pages 246–259.

Routine care and cleaning

For routine care, a vacuum cleaner is your most important tool. Vacuum at least weekly, more often where there is heavy traffic. Purists may advise you to go over a section of carpeting eight times to get it completely clean, but if you vacuum regularly you will probably find that a couple of swipes back and forth are sufficient. You can vacuum a new rug as soon as it is laid. It is normal for new carpeting to shed a lot of fluff.

Move and vacuum beneath furniture every six months or once a year if possible. More frequently, use special attachments to reach under furniture and to clean the edges of a carpeted room. Vacuum the backs of rugs occasionally.

Set the vacuum to the correct level of suction for your carpet. Deep-pile carpeting needs a different setting than a flat-

Carpet-Cleaning Challenges

The kind of carpeting you choose can affect how easy it is to clean. Here are some rules of thumb to keep in mind when you make your next carpet purchase:

Pile. The deeper and thicker the pile in your carpet, the more likely it is to retain dirt once the dirt sinks below the surface. Threads and lint, however, can stay on "top," where they can be very visible.

Level loop. Short, densely spaced loops, with both ends attached to the backing, create a surface that is fairly easy to vacuum because there aren't crevices for dirt to sink into.

Berber. This is a type of level-loop carpet made with a thick yarn, which creates harder-to-vacuum "hills and valleys."

Multilevel loop. The varying long and short loops of these carpets can make them difficult to clean. The low loops create pockets that break vacuum-cleaner suction and can make it harder to remove any dirt that has accumulated.

weave rug. Some vacuums adjust automatically. Some small, lightweight items—among them pine needles, threads, and pet hairs—are difficult to vacuum up. If your vacuum cleaner's attachments don't do the job, use a lint roller, or wrap your hand with packing tape with the sticky side out and "blot" up the elusive materials. To prevent the fringe on the edge of a rug from being sucked up into the vacuum cleaner, use an attachment with an old nylon stocking over the nozzle.

Change the vacuum cleaner bag when it becomes full. An overstuffed bag impairs a vacuum's ability to clean. Don't reuse bags because old ones don't trap dust, their pores can plug up with dirt and severely restrict air flow, and they eventually tear. Some newer-model upright vacuum cleaners have, instead of a bag, a dirt-collection container that lets you see when it is full. To minimize mess when emptying the container, place a plastic garbage bag over the opening before tilting the unit.

Removing ground-in dirt

Depending on the carpet manufacturer's advice and the amount of traffic across a carpet, it may be necessary to shampoo or deep-clean it once every year or two.

Carpet-Cleaning Cautions

Shampoos and even plain water can temporarily or permanently alter the size and color of carpeting. Take these simple steps to avoid problems:

• With any kind of cleaner, test the fastness of the dye by dampening an inconspicuous area and seeing whether loose dye comes off onto a white tissue. If so, rely on an expert to do the cleaning.

• Clean wall-to-wall carpeting in place to avoid shrinkage.

• When you use any water-based treatment, avoid overwetting. Never allow water to penetrate to the back of a rug. The backing may be damaged, and the color may bleed through to the floor.

• Remove as much furniture from the room as you can. You or the professionals you hire should put a small piece of aluminum foil under any furniture legs that are in contact with the cleaned carpet to prevent staining. Leave the foil in place for one or two days, or until the carpet is thoroughly dry.

For lightly soiled carpets, use just water and an absorbent cloth; a detergent may leave too much residue and make resoiling more likely.

Heavily soiled carpets require a thorough cleaning. This means renting or buying a deep-cleaning machine or shampooer and purchasing a special carpet-cleaning solution from the same rental outlet or retailer. Follow instructions for the machine and the cleaning solution; in particular, don't make the cleaning solution any stronger than recommended. Start by vacuuming thoroughly, going over each area several times. Then do the deep-cleaning or shampooing work in sections, blotting each section as you finish with an old white towel. Then brush the pile in the correct direction with a clean carpet brush and allow it to dry thoroughly.

Professional-cleaning tips. If your carpet has a significant amount of ground-in dirt or staining, you may want to hire a professional service. Ideally, personnel should visit your home to carefully evaluate the carpet's condition before providing an estimate, but often this does not happen. Some cleaning services provide a preliminary price pending closer inspection in the home. This is acceptable if the cleaners do a careful inspection and, if necessary, provide a new quote.

Before cleaning begins, know what to expect. The cleaning service should discuss its procedures in detail. Depending on a carpet's condition, it may not be possible to clean it completely. The company should inform the customer if its cleaners will not be able to remove a stain without damage, so there will be no surprises.

Ask the service what it will do if the carpet is damaged and how it will protect the furniture. Be sure to ask for and check references to see if the company adheres to such precautions. CONSUMER REPORTS suggests that area rugs, especially handmade ones, be removed and cleaned at a plant site rather than in your home. You usually can either take the rug in yourself or pay to have it picked up and dropped off.

Helpful Hint

If you're looking for a professional rug-cleaning service, ask friends for recommendations. Or consult one of these organizations:

- The Association of Specialists in Cleaning and Restoration (ASCR International); 800-272-7012 or *www.ascr.org.*

- Institute of Inspection, Cleaning and Restoration Certification; 360-693-5675 or *www.iicrc.org.*

Stain Removal

Restoring fabric and carpeting

Quick action is often the key to success with stain removal. Gather all the home remedies listed in the **Stain-Removal Kit** on pages 244 and 245, and keep them where they are easy to locate and out of the reach of children.

The wrong solution could permanently damage or destroy your garment or carpet. Always follow the care label on your garment or the instructions from your carpet's manufacturer. An inappropriate cleaning solution may not only set the stain, making it more difficult to remove, but also damage or discolor the garment or carpet. Always try stain-removal solutions in an inconspicuous area first.

If you're concerned that your attempt to remove a stain will cause damage, seek professional help. Be sure the professional you select—whether a dry cleaner or carpet cleaner—evaluates the stain and the stained material and informs you about any potential risks. Tell the professional about any remedies you may have already tried.

If you decide to do it yourself, locate the substance that caused the stain in the **Fabric and Carpet Stain-Removal Guide** on pages 246–259 and apply the recommended remedy. Use a white paper towel, napkin, or cloth. When working with paper, make sure it's strong enough to do the job. If the paper shreds or pills, don't use it.

When working, keep the following guidelines in mind:

Blot, don't scrub. Scrubbing can damage fabric or carpet. Instead, blot with a white paper towel or cloth until the area is completely dry. For semi-solids, gently scrape the residue up with the edge of a rounded spoon.

Do a colorfastness test. Pre-test each recommended cleaning agent on an inconspicuous area of the soiled item—the back of a tie or an inside seam; the area of a carpet where the sofa is placed; or, for upholstery, inside the flap that covers a zipper or under or in back of a couch cushion. On a multicolor fabric, conduct the test in a place where the different colors meet, or be sure to test each of the colors. Use the following pre-test procedure:

- Apply several drops of the cleaning agent to the testing area.
- Hold a wet white cloth on the area for 60 seconds. If you can get to it, do the same on the underside of the fabric.
- Examine the wet cloth for color transfer and the fabric or carpet for color change or damage. If any of these changes are evident, stop and seek professional help.

If no damage or color change is evident, you may begin the cleaning process.

Removing the stain. Work from the outer edge of the stain toward the center. Apply a small amount of the first recommended cleaning agent to a white paper towel or cloth and gently work it into the stained area. Problems can result from working with large amounts of cleaning materials, even water, so begin with a small amount and repeat the process as needed. Blot—do not rub or brush. Rubbing too harshly can cause unsightly distortion in your garment's fabric or carpet's fibers that may become permanent. For fabrics, place the front face on a white paper towel or cloth and work the cleaning agent into the fabric from the back (this is not always possible with upholstery).

Be patient. Repeat the procedure with additional clean white paper towels or cloths until you can't transfer any more stain to the towel or cloth. Do not proceed to the next recommended cleaning agent until this is done. Complete stain removal may require repeating the same step several times. In many cases it will not be necessary to use all of the recommended steps to remove the stain. When the stain is removed, flush with water to remove stain-removal products. Then blot.

Some cleaning agents may promote rapid resoiling. If the garment is washable, launder it as soon as possible after removing the stain. For carpets (and upholstery fabrics) that are water-safe, rinse or wash the area after the stain has been removed completely, but don't use excessive water. A mist-type sprayer prevents overwetting. If you are cleaning a non-washable fabric that will tolerate water, damp-sponge it with cool water to remove any residue from the stain-removal process. Blot dry.

Stain-Removal Kit for Fabric and Carpets

Product	Notes
Alcohol	Rubbing alcohol is available in drug and grocery stores.
Ammonia	Mix 1 tablespoon of household ammonia with $1/2$ cup of water. Apply in well-ventilated area. Never mix with bleach.
Amodex	This ink and stain remover worked well in Consumer Reports tests.
Baking soda	Can neutralize acids such as battery acid.
BenGay, extra strength	Can be used to remove chewing gum.
Bleach	Chlorine bleach breaks down color-producing particles and should not be used with colored fabrics; also, do not use with wool, silk, and other fine washables. Be sure to wear rubber gloves when using chlorine bleach, and always dilute it. Oxygen bleach is safe for virtually all fabrics but is mostly helpful in maintaining whiteness and restoring it.
Citrus-based solvent	Sold under such brand names as Citra-Solv and Goo Gone.
Cleaning solvent	Available at grocery, drug, specialty, and hardware stores. Use small amounts to prevent possible damage to backing materials or delamination. Use in a well-ventilated area away from open flames or sparks. Do not use on an olefin carpet. Most cleaning solvents are flammable.
Detergent solution	Mix 1 teaspoon of mild clear or white neutral detergent (a mild dishwashing liquid containing no alkalis or bleach) in 1 cup of warm water. Do not use laundry detergent, which contains optical brighteners that may discolor the fibers.

If the label of the garment you're cleaning says "dry-clean only," you may want to avoid using a water-based cleaning agent. Check the label of garments and upholstery fabrics for guidance; upholstery fabric labels are often found on the underside of a chair or sofa, or on the deck under the cushions. Once the stain is removed from upholstery fabric and the area has been rinsed, apply a thick pad of white paper towels or cloth and, as a final step, weight them down to absorb the excess water or cleaning material.

Product	Notes
Enzyme detergent	Mix a solution of enzyme laundry detergent by following the directions on the package. Allow the solution to remain on the stain for the length of time recommended by the manufacturer. Do not use on mohair, wool, or silk.
Fels-Naptha paste	Work one part grated Fels-Naptha soap and 10 parts water into a paste.
Hydrogen peroxide	Use the kind sold as an antiseptic—3% hydrogen peroxide solution.
Laundry booster	Can be effective when applied to stained fabric prior to washing with a high-performance laundry detergent. Use according to label instructions.
Laundry detergent	Mix 1 teaspoon with 1 cup of water.
Nail-polish remover	Acetone-based, non-oily.
POG (paint, oil, and grease remover)	Breaks down lipstick, shoe polish, and candle wax as well as paint, oil, and grease. Remove traces of POG with a cleaning solvent that you can buy at the hardware store.
Pet-odor remover	Enzyme-based. Available at pet specialty stores.
Petroleum jelly	Can be used to soften hardened paint, tar, and rubber cement on washable fabrics. Launder fabrics treated with petroleum jelly immediately after application.
Red-dye remover	Sold under such brand names as DiDiSeven and Stainerator.
Vinegar	Mix $1/3$ cup of white household vinegar and $2/3$ cup of water.

Fabric and Carpet Stain-Removal Guide

Before using any of these methods, test on an inconspicuous area and watch for possible damage or color transfer. Proceed to a second or third recommended cleaning agent only when you can no longer transfer any more stain to the cloth or towel you're using. With garments and, if possible, upholstery, turn the fabric inside out and work the cleaning agent in from the back. Blot—never rub or brush. Use water to rinse out the cleaning agents when the stain is gone, unless stated otherwise. See the **Stain-Removal Kit** on pages 244 and 245 for descriptions of the cleaning solutions.

Stain	Remedies	Notes
Acids	Don gloves—especially if the acid is strong. Blot immediately; apply dry baking soda to neutralize. Rinse with cold water.	—
Acne medication	Try a cleaning solvent. If that fails, have the item professionally cleaned. Do not use water.	Benzoyl peroxide is the active ingredient. Mixed with water, it bleaches out color and leaves a pink-orange spot.
Adhesives	If you have an adhesive solvent, apply it and scrape. If you don't, use nail-polish remover for clear adhesive and liquid grease solvent for latex adhesive. If you can't remove the stain from a pile carpet or if you have a pile carpet that has a built-in foam backing that could be dissolved by a stain remover or solvent, trim with sewing scissors.	You can often buy an adhesive solvent at the same time you buy the adhesive.
Airplane cement	Blot with a POG. If stain remains, try a cleaning solvent and then the detergent solution.	—
Alcoholic beverages	Blot with the detergent solution. If stain remains, try the vinegar solution. Rinse when the stain is gone.	Sugar residue will attract soil and caramelize over time, leaving a brown spot. Flush areas with warm water after initial stain removal. If a trace of stain remains, dab with 3 percent hydrogen peroxide.

Stain	Remedies	Notes
Ammonia	Blot immediately. Apply vinegar solution to neutralize. Rinse.	—
Animal stains	Blot with the detergent solution. If stain remains, try the ammonia solution and then the vinegar solution.	Consider applying an enzyme-based pet-odor remover.
Ballpoint pen	Apply rubbing alcohol to white toweling and blot. Move to clean area of towel, and apply more alcohol as needed. Blot with the detergent solution and then water. For upholstery, back with toweling and blot through.	Keep alcohol wipes in your desk if this is a frequent stain. Don't use hair spray—it has components that can make fabric, upholstery, and carpet sticky.
Battery acid	Neutralize area with dry baking soda. If that fails, have item professionally cleaned.	Applying water to a battery-acid stain on cotton or rayon will leave holes.
Beer	Blot with the detergent solution. If stain remains, try the vinegar solution and then the enzyme detergent solution.	Do not iron or heat until the stain is gone.
Blood	For fresh blood, flush fabric with cold water or 3 percent hydrogen peroxide. For dried blood, blot with peroxide, then try the enzyme detergent solution; rinse when blood is gone.	Blot—do not flush—carpet and upholstery. Cleaning agents should be used at room temperature (not warm or hot). Applying heat will cause the stain to set.
Burn marks	For small burn marks, vacuum area. Blot with the detergent solution. Rinse. Carefully trim beads (where burning started on synthetic carpets) and burn marks with sewing scissors.	For large areas, have a carpet installer or upholsterer patch the carpet by using a piece from a closet or a scrap.
Butter or cheese	Scrape off excess. Blot with a cleaning solvent. If stain remains, try, in this order, the detergent, ammonia, and vinegar solutions. Rinse when the stain is gone.	Old butter or cheese sauce stains are very difficult to remove. Do not iron or heat until the stain is gone.

Stain	Remedies	Notes
Candle wax	**For carpets:** Scrape off excess. Blot with a POG or a citrus solvent. If wax remains, try the detergent solution. With non-olefin carpets and upholstery, you can try layering paper towels or brown paper over wax and heating with a warm iron. Keep switching the paper to a clean spot. Continue until all the wax is absorbed. Don't heat an olefin carpet; it may melt. **For washable fabrics:** Pour boiling water through the fabric from a height of 12 inches. **For nonwashable fabrics:** Sandwich the fabric between paper towels and use a warm iron.	**For carpets:** Test the heat approach first in an inconspicuous spot to be sure that you won't flatten the pile. Also note that heat may drive the wax deeper into the carpet, requiring a professional to clean it.
Candy (hard)	Blot with the detergent solution. If stain remains, try, in this order, the ammonia and vinegar solutions. If the candy leaves a red stain, use a commercial red-dye remover.	Sugar residue will attract soil and caramelize over time, leaving a brown spot. Flush areas with warm water after initial stain removal.
Caulk, latex	Scrape residue. Blot with the detergent solution. Then try the ammonia solution. If stain remains, have the item professionally cleaned.	Blotting with methanol may also work.
Chocolate or cocoa	Scrape off excess material before cleaning. Blot with the detergent solution. If stain remains, try, in this order, the ammonia and vinegar solutions. If the spill has milk as a component, use the enzyme detergent solution. Rinse.	If a trace of the stain remains, dab with 3 percent hydrogen peroxide.
Coffee (black)	Blot with the detergent solution. If stain remains, try the vinegar solution. Rinse with warm water.	If a trace of the stain remains, dab with 3 percent hydrogen peroxide.

Stain	Remedies	Notes
Coffee (with cream and sugar)	Blot with a cleaning solvent. If stain remains, try, in this order, the detergent solution, the enzyme detergent solution (especially useful for removing cream), and the vinegar solution.	Sugar residue will attract soil and caramelize over time, leaving a brown spot. Flush areas with warm water after initial stain removal. If a trace of the stain remains, dab with 3 percent hydrogen peroxide.
Cola (regular)	Blot with the detergent solution. If stain remains, try the vinegar solution. Rinse with warm water to eliminate sugar residue, which attracts soils and will caramelize over time, leaving a brown spot.	If a trace of the stain remains, dab with 3 percent hydrogen peroxide.
Cola (diet)	Blot with the detergent solution. If stain remains, try the vinegar solution. Rinse with warm water.	If a trace of the stain remains, dab with 3 percent hydrogen peroxide.
Copier toner	Put an old nylon stocking over the vacuum nozzle and vacuum.	After vacuuming, call a professional; toner is a health hazard.
Correction fluid	Scrape off excess. If it's a solvent-based fluid, blot on a cleaning solvent or rubbing alcohol. If stain remains, try the detergent solution. If it's a water-based fluid, blot on the detergent solution.	Also contact the product's manufacturer for advice.
Crayon	Scrape excess crayon off with a dull-edged knife or metal spoon. Spray with WD-40 and let stand for a few minutes. With a small, stiff bristle brush, work into the stain and wipe with white paper towels. Respray with WD-40 and apply detergent solution to the sprayed area; work in with the brush, and blot. Then rinse.	For more tips, visit Crayola's web site (*www.crayola.com*).

Stain	Remedies	Notes
Cream sauce	Scrape off excess. Blot with a cleaning solvent. If stain remains, try the detergent solution and then the ammonia solution. Rinse.	The enzyme detergent solution may also help remove the stain.
Diaper stains	Blot with the detergent solution. If stain remains, try the ammonia solution and then the vinegar solution.	Bleach if possible.
Dirt	Brush off all dirt before proceeding, or vacuum with a nylon stocking over the attachment nozzle. Wash with the detergent solution, then rinse.	—
Driveway sealer	Try a cleaning solvent.	Professional cleaning may be needed.
Egg	Blot with the detergent solution. If stain remains, try the ammonia solution and then the vinegar solution. Rinse with cold water.	Enzyme detergent may help remove stain. Do not use warm or hot solutions. They will "cook" the egg.
Eggnog	Blot with the detergent solution and then water. If stain remains, try the vinegar solution, then a cleaning solvent.	Enzyme detergent may help remove stain.
Feces	Scrape up residue. Blot with the detergent solution. If stain remains, try the ammonia solution and then the vinegar solution. Rinse.	Apply an enzyme-based pet-odor product.
Fruit or vegetable juice	Blot with the detergent solution. If stain remains, try the ammonia solution and then the vinegar solution. Red-dye remover may help remove red coloration from fruit punch and cherry drinks.	Sugar residue will attract soil and caramelize over time, leaving a brown spot. Flush areas with warm water after initial stain removal.

Stain	Remedies	Notes
Furniture polish or stain	Blot with a cleaning solvent. If stain remains, try the detergent solution. Rinse.	You may need to call a professional.
Gasoline	Blot with a cleaning solvent. If stain remains, try the detergent solution and then the vinegar solution.	On colorfast textiles, a diluted bleach solution may remove gasoline odor. Pre-test before using this method.
Glue	Blot with water. If glue remains, try the detergent solution.	Soaking washables in warm water until the glue softens may help.
Grass	Blot with a cleaning solvent. If stain remains, try, in this order, the detergent, ammonia, vinegar, and laundry detergent solutions.	CONSUMER REPORTS tests have shown that Spray 'n Wash laundry booster may help remove grass stains from washable fabrics.
Gravy	Scrape off excess. Blot with a cleaning solvent. If stain remains, try the detergent solution and then the ammonia solution.	For washables, use Fels-Naptha paste. Do not put in the dryer until the stain is removed.
Grease	Scrape off excess. Blot with a cleaning solvent. If stain remains, try, in this order, the detergent, ammonia, and vinegar solutions.	For washables, use Fels-Naptha paste. Do not put in the dryer until the stain is removed.
Greasy foods	Blot with a cleaning solvent. If the stain remains, try the detergent solution.	For washables, use Fels-Naptha paste. Do not put in the dryer until the stain is removed.
Gum	Chill with an ice cube and scrape off what you can. Blot with citrus solvent. Or apply a teaspoon of extra-strength BenGay to gum, heat it with a hair dryer, and pick off residue with polyethylene (not PVC or Saran) food wrap. Then blot area with the detergent solution and rinse with warm water.	Don't use peanut butter to remove; it may compound the problem.

Stain	Remedies	Notes
Hair dye	Blot with the detergent solution, then try the ammonia solution.	Permanent dye may require professional cleaning.
Hair spray	Apply alcohol, then blot with the detergent solution. Rinse.	—
Hair tonic	First use a cleaning solvent. Then try, in this order, the detergent, ammonia, and vinegar solutions.	—
Ice cream	Blot with the detergent solution. If stain remains, try, in this order, the ammonia, vinegar, and laundry detergent solutions.	Do not put in the dryer until the stain is removed. Heat can set the sugar and the oil stains. For stubborn stains, try a cleaning agent.
Infant formula	Blot with the detergent solution. If stain remains, try a cleaning solvent.	For fresh stains on white washable cloth, try moistening with water and blotting with baking soda. Do not put in dryer until stain is removed.
Ink	For most types of ink, blot with rubbing alcohol or a cleaning solvent. If ink remains, try the detergent solution. Keep switching to a clean spot on towel, wiping as long as the spot continues to move. When ink is gone, rinse. Don't use hair spray for ink stains. It contains ingredients that can make carpets or fabric sticky.	An alternative is using Amodex ink and stain remover. It worked well in Consumer Reports tests. Don't use rubbing alcohol with fountain pen ink; use a cleaning solvent. For permanent ink, call a professional.
Iodine	Blot with the detergent solution. If the stain remains, try the ammonia and vinegar solutions. Rinse.	Photographer's "hypo" (5 percent sodium thiosulfate) is also effective.
Jam	Blot with detergent solution. If stain remains, try the ammonia solution and then the vinegar solution. If the jam leaves a red stain, use a red-dye remover.	Rinse with warm water to eliminate sugar residue, which attracts soils and caramelizes over time, leaving a brown spot.

Stain	Remedies	Notes
Ketchup	Blot with the detergent solution. If stain remains, try the vinegar solution. 3 percent hydrogen peroxide may help remove last traces of the stain.	Sugar residue will attract soil and caramelize over time, leaving a brown spot. Flush areas with warm water after initial stain removal.
Lacquer	Blot with denatured alcohol or a citrus solvent. If stain remains, try the detergent solution.	—
Lipstick and lip gloss	Blot with acetone-based nail-polish remover. It stain remains, try, in this order, a cleaning solvent and the detergent solution. Rinse.	—
Makeup (foundation cream or liquid)	Blot up excess and then blot with rubbing alcohol. If stain remains, try the detergent solution. Rinse with warm water.	—
Makeup (mascara, powdered shadow, or blush)	Blot with alcohol. If stain remains, try the detergent solution and then the ammonia solution. Rinse with warm water.	For powders, vacuum with an old nylon stocking placed over the attachment nozzle.
Margarine	Scrape off excess. Blot with a cleaning solvent. If stain remains, try, in this order, the detergent, ammonia, and vinegar solutions. Rinse when stain is gone.	Do not iron the garment until the stain is gone.
Mayonnaise	Scrape off as much as possible. Blot with a cleaning solvent. If stain remains, try the detergent solution. Rinse.	Laundering with an enzyme detergent may help.

Stain	Remedies	Notes
Mildew	Blot with 3 percent hydrogen peroxide (test in a hidden area first). With a 100 percent olefin or polyester carpet, you can also use a solution of 1 tablespoon of chlorine bleach and 1 cup of water. Dry thoroughly with a fan or heater. If there is residue, try the detergent solution.	Mildew may leave a permanent stain. Reduce humidity to prevent a reoccurrence.
Milk and milk products	Blot up excess and then blot with the detergent solution. If stain remains, try, in this order, the ammonia, vinegar, and enzyme detergent solutions, and then a cleaning solvent. Rinse with cold water.	Do not use any heat. It may "cook" the proteins.
Mud	Allow the mud to dry, then vacuum or brush away dirt. If stain remains, blot with the detergent solution. If that fails, have the item professionally cleaned.	—
Mustard	Mustard contains a dye that's extremely difficult to remove. Try successive applications of the detergent solution. When stain is gone, rinse. Dry in bright sunlight.	—
Nail polish	Use an acetone-based, non-oily nail-polish remover for most fabrics. For old stains, try a POG. If stain remains, try a cleaning solvent and then the detergent solution. Rinse.	Do not use acetone on acetate, triacetate, or modacrylic (which is very occasionally found in rugs). Acetone will dissolve those fibers.
Newsprint	Blot with a cleaning solvent. Then try the detergent solution. If that fails, have the item professionally cleaned.	Clean your hands of any newsprint before touching the stain. It might also help to first rub glycerin into the stain.

Stain	Remedies	Notes
Oil and grease	With most oil and grease stains, blot up excess and then blot with a cleaning solvent. If stain remains, try the detergent solution and then the ammonia solution. Rinse. For motor oil, use a POG. If stain remains, try a cleaning solvent and then the detergent and ammonia solutions. Particularly effective for nylon: a few drops of solvent, followed by Fels-Naptha paste if traces of he stain remain.	Spray 'n Wash and Shout aerosol laundry boosters help remove motor oil. Do not put in dryer until the stain is removed.
Paint (alkyd or oil)	For wet paint, blot with paint thinner. If stain remains, try a cleaning solvent and then the detergent solution. For dried paint, try a POG.	You may need to call a professional.
Paint (latex)	With wet paint, blot up excess. Blot with the detergent solution. If stain remains, try the ammonia solution. Rinse with warm water. For dried paint, use methanol to soften it.	You may need to call a professional.
Paint, finger	Blot with the detergent solution. Rinse with water.	For more tips, visit Crayola's web site (www.crayola.com).
Peanut butter	First apply a cleaning solvent, then blot with the detergent solution. Rinse. Launder if possible.	Do not put garment in dryer until the stain has been removed.
Pencil	Use a rubber or art gum eraser, then vacuum.	—
Perfume	Blot with the detergent solution. If the stain remains, try the ammonia and vinegar solutions.	—

Stain	Remedies	Notes
Perspiration	Blot with the ammonia solution. Then, if needed, try the vinegar solution and a cleaning solvent. Use the Fels-Naptha paste for washable items,	Do not put in dryer until the stain has been removed.
Play-Doh	Remove large clumps, taking care not to rub wet dough into the carpet. Allow dough to dry at least four hours, then slowly work it out of the carpet using soapy water and a stiff bristle brush. Blot away remaining stain; if it persists, use a commercial spot remover.	For more tips, visit the Crayola web site (*www.crayola.com*).
Pudding	Blot with the detergent solution. If stain remains, try, in this order, the ammonia, vinegar, and laundry detergent solutions	—
Rubber cement	Apply an adhesive remover. Or blot with a cleaning solvent. Try the detergent solution if needed. Rinse.	—
Rust	Apply a commercial rust remover, testing first in a hidden area. If you don't have a remover, apply a paste of white vinegar and table salt. Gently dab it into the mark. Let set for 30 minutes. Flush with warm water.	—
Salad dressing	Scrape off excess and then blot with a cleaning solvent. If stain remains, try the detergent solution. Rinse with warm water.	Do not put the garment in dryer until the stain has been removed.
Semen	Blot with the detergent solution. Then rinse.	—

Stain	Remedies	Notes
Shoe polish	Scrape and blot up excess and then blot with a cleaning solvent. If stain remains, try alcohol and then detergent solution. Rinse.	You may need to call a professional.
Shortening	Scrape up excess and then apply a cleaning solvent. If stain remains, try the detergent solution.	Do not put in dryer until the stain has been removed.
Soft drinks	Blot with the detergent solution. If stain remains, try the ammonia solution and then the vinegar solution.	Do not put in dryer until the stain has been removed.
Soot	Vacuum up small soot spots. If the rug or fabric is fragile, put an old nylon stocking over the nozzle. You can also use masking tape to lift soot particles. Then blot with the detergent solution. Rinse with warm water. If the soot is oily, use a cleaning solvent and then the detergent solution and warm water. For larger soot spots, clean entire area with a carpet shampooer or deep-cleaner. Apply deodorizer.	If there is a significant amount of soot, consider calling a professional with fire-restoration experience.
Soy sauce	Blot with the vinegar solution. If stain remains, use the enzyme detergent solution. Launder if possible.	Professional cleaning may be required for older stains.
Sunscreen	Blot up excess and then blot with a cleaning solvent. If stain remains, try detergent solution. Rinse with warm water.	For washables, a laundry booster and petroleum jelly (rubbed into loosen the stain) may help.
Syrup	Blot with the detergent solution. If stain remains, try, in this order, the ammonia, vinegar, and laundry detergent solutions.	Do not put in dryer until the stain has been removed.

Stain	Remedies	Notes
Tar, asphalt	Blot with a POG. If stain remains, try, in this order, a cleaning solvent and the detergent solution.	You may have to call a professional.
Tea (black)	Blot with the detergent solution. If stain remains, try the vinegar solution. Rinse.	If trace of stain remains, dab with 3 percent hydrogen peroxide.
Tea (with milk and sugar)	Blot with a cleaning solvent. If stain remains, try the detergent solution and then the enzyme detergent solution (especially useful for removing milk) and the vinegar solution.	Sugar residue will attract soil and caramelize over time, leaving a brown spot. Flush areas with warm water after initial stain removal. If a trace of the stain remains, dab with 3 percent hydrogen peroxide.
Tomato sauce	Blot with the detergent solution. If stain remains, try the vinegar solution. For an oil-based sauce, try dabbing with Fels-Naptha paste before laundering.	Sugar residue will attract soil and caramelize over time, leaving a brown spot. 3 percent hydrogen peroxide may help remove the last traces of the stain. Flush areas with warm water after initial stain removal.
Urine	If it's fresh, blot with the ammonia solution, and then the detergent solution. Rinse with warm water. If it's been on for more than 24 hours, blot with the vinegar solution and then the detergent solution.	Apply an enzyme-based pet-odor remover for either pet or human urine. Follow the directions carefully. Such a product needs time (12 to 48 hours) to work. If urine odor persists, call a professional. If urine is not completely removed, animals will keep returning to the same "spot."

Stain	Remedies	Notes
Vinegar	Blot with water and apply dry baking soda to neutralize. Rinse with cold water.	—
Vomit	Scrape up as much as possible. Blot with the detergent solution. If stain remains, try the ammonia solution. Rinse. If dog or cat food is a component of the vomit, you may need to apply a red-dye remover.	Consider applying an enzyme-based pet-odor remover.
Water colors	Blot with the detergent solution. If stain remains, apply the ammonia solution and then the vinegar solution.	—
Water stains	Apply the detergent solution and then, if stain remains, the vinegar solution. If that fails, have the item professionally cleaned.	3 percent hydrogen peroxide may help.
Wine (red)	Blot with water. If stain remains, try the detergent solution. 3 percent hydrogen peroxide is useful for removing the color from red wine. Trying to remove red wine with white wine leaves a nasty sugar stain.	Do not iron or heat until stain is gone. Trying to remove red wine with white wine leaves a nasty sugar stain.
Wine (white)	Blot with water. If stain remains, try the detergent solution.	Do not iron or heat until stain is gone.

Flooring

Floor coverings can represent a large investment, and they get more wear than most other surfaces in the home. When choosing flooring, remember that solid-colored floors show soil more quickly than patterned ones. Spills are more noticeable on very light and very dark floors.

Floors that are heavily trafficked require more frequent maintenance than those that get less use. Save elbow grease by placing mats at entrances to prevent dirt from being tracked into the house.

Wood floors. The most popular and readily available wood flooring is oak, but the choices also include maple, cherry, hickory, and other hardwoods, as well as pine, a lower-cost softwood. You can pay less for unfinished solid wood, which is what to buy if you decide to stain or varnish the floor yourself.

Remove dirt regularly with a broom, lightweight vacuum cleaner, or dust mop. Small particles can scratch the flooring. Surface-sealed floors have been finished with solvent-based or water-based varnish. If your wood floor looks as if it has been covered by a layer of clear plastic, it has probably been surface-sealed, making it stain- and water-resistant. Penetrating-sealed floors have been coated with an acrylic, oil, or wax that has penetrated the surface and soaked into the pores of the wood, hardening there. It usually has a satin or matte finish. Such a finish provides much less protection than surface-sealed finishes and requires more attention.

For routine care, clean a surface-sealed wood floor with a broom, dust mop, or vacuum cleaner, then damp-mop. Every once in a while, damp-mop with a scant amount of

Removing Stains from Wood Floors

When removing stains, work from the outside toward the middle. Before using any of these methods, test on an inconspicuous area. Surface-sealed floors have a finish of solvent-based polyurethane or water-based urethane. Penetrating-sealed finish floors have been coated with an acrylic, oil, or wax that has penetrated the surface. The latter usually require more attention.

Type of stain	Surface-sealed finish	Penetrating-sealed finish
Dried milk, food	Scrape with a plastic scraper, then rub with a damp cloth.	Scrape with a plastic scraper, then rub with a damp cloth. Refinish.
Standing water	Use a cleaner recommended by the manufacturer. Buff with a cloth.	Rub with No. 1 steel wool. Or try 90 to 120-grit sandpaper. Clean the spot and surrounding area with a wood-floor cleaner and let dry. Apply matching finish, and let dry.
Heel marks	Wipe off marks with an all-purpose cleaner.	Rub with fine steel wool and a wood-floor cleaner. Wipe dry and polish.
Mildew	Use an appropriate cleaner; if the mold is under the finish, you'll need to refinish. Bleach may discolor bare wood.	Use a wood-floor cleaning liquid with No. 1 steel wool. Bleach may discolor bare wood.
Gum, crayon, wax	Scrape with a plastic scraper Apply ice until the sticky spot is brittle and crumbles off. Try Ben-Gay, WD-40, Goo Gone, or Citra-Solv.	Same as for surface-sealed finish.
Cigarette burns	Scrape the affected area with a sharp knife and dab finish onto the spot.	Moisten a plastic scrub pad or sandpaper with soap and water. Refinish the spot.
Alcohol	Not generally affected.	Rub with a cloth dampened with ammonia.
Oil, grease	Wipe up with turpentine or TSP (trisodium phosphate). Buff with a clean towel.	Wipe up with a TSP solution.
Wax buildup	Not applicable.	Strip with wood-floor cleaner or turpentine. Use a cloth and fine steel wool to remove wax residue.

water and a mild detergent or a neutral pH wood cleaner recommended by the manufacturer. Wring out the mop before using it, and change the cleaning solution as often as possible.

For a penetrating-sealed floor, remove sticky marks with a damp (not wet) cloth. Do not mop. A penetrating-sealed floor that has become dull can be rebuffed. From time to time, apply a coating of wax with fine steel wool.

Do-It-Yourself Wood-Floor Refinishing

If you decide to refinish a surface-sealed wood floor yourself, follow these steps:

• Move the furniture out and sweep the floor. Seal off the area with drop cloths or old bed sheets to keep dust contained.

• To remove old varnish and smooth the wood's surface, pass the drum sander evenly over the old finish, moving in smooth, straight lines parallel to the floorboards. Work in several passes, starting with coarse-grit sandpaper and progressing to fine-grit until the old finish is removed and the surface is smooth and even. Follow each pass of the drum sander with the edge sander along baseboards and other tight spots, using the same progression of sandpaper. Keep the sanding machine moving while in use to prevent it from gouging the surface. Maintain even pressure and a steady pace. When starting or stopping, tilt the sanding portion upward. Sweep up after each sanding pass.

• Sweep up every trace of sawdust and grit, then follow up with a wet/dry vac or a household vacuum cleaner so debris doesn't become trapped in the varnish. Wipe up the last bits of dust with tack cloths. Be sure to dust walls, door frames, and other areas before applying varnish.

• Open all windows and doors to maximize ventilation. First brush varnish around the floor perimeter and other hard-to-reach areas. Then pour a thin line of varnish at the point that is farthest from the door, running parallel to the wood planks, and spread it in a continuous line with a lamb's wool pad. For smoother results, overlap each pass, angling the pad away from the area just covered to push excess varnish onto the new area.

• Prepare the fully dried surface for subsequent coats using a buffer or oscillating sander and a fine-grit screen. Make sure the surface is dry—use your thumbnail to check that the film is hard. Then vacuum and dust the surface again with tack cloths before applying the next coat.

• When the floors are dry, move the furniture back in. Let the varnish cure for a minimum of 12 hours to a day or two before walking on it a lot.

It's time to refinish a surface-sealed wood floor when the finish is worn through or the surface is badly nicked. (Deep gouges, split or warped boards, and other widespread damage are signs that the floor needs to be repaired or replaced.)

Start by deciding whether you'll hire a contractor to refinish the floor or do the job yourself. Consider hiring someone if the floor is especially uneven or needs repair. Whether you refinish the floor yourself or hire a pro, expect days of disruption, sanding, dust, and fumes.

Then choose which type of varnish to use. There are significant cost and convenience differences between water-based and solvent-based varnishes. Which one you choose rests largely on the look you want—and whether you're in a hurry. Water-based varnish provides faster drying time, easier cleanup, and excellent ultraviolet resistance. Solvent-based varnish leaves an amber finish, and drying time between coats is longer and cleanup messier. It also tends to darken under ultraviolet light. But CONSUMER REPORTS tests have found that dirt accumulation was less noticeable on samples finished with solvent-based varnish than with water-based varnish. Solvent-based varnishes tend to go further and cost less per square foot. But their longer drying time means more days to finish the job—and possibly more money you'll need to pay a pro if you hire the job out.

The major brands of floor varnish are Flecto Varathane, Minwax, and Pro Finisher (which is available only at Home Depot). Sheen levels range from satin to high gloss. Low-gloss finishes go on smoothest and with the fewest imperfections, and are less likely to raise the wood grain—a condition in which the wood fibers "stand up" and create a rough surface.

All varnishes require multiple coats, particularly in high-traffic areas. You'll need to wait an hour or two for each coat of water-based varnish to dry, compared with anywhere from five hours to overnight for most solvent-based products. Water-based varnishes require more coats for heavy traffic— typically four, compared with three for most solvent-based products. It's possible to get all of those coats down in one long day using a water-based varnish. However, you'll still have to wait anywhere from 12 hours to a day or two for any varnish to cure before it can handle heavy traffic.

Varnishing a floor is rigorous work. You may need three to four days to cover a moderate-sized area. Do the job in warm weather, since you'll need to open doors and windows for maximum ventilation. Try to work when humidity is low and rain isn't in the forecast since high humidity extends drying time. You'll need to buy a broomstick applicator, lamb's wool pads, and brushes (natural-bristle for solvent-based varnish, synthetic for water-based) for applying varnish to the floor's perimeter. In addition, you'll need tack cloths; plenty of sand-

Removing Stains from Non-Wood Floors

Stain	Removal Method
Alcoholic beverages	Rub with a clean cloth dampened with rubbing alcohol.
Blood	Before using any detergent, try clear, cold water. If the stain remains, cautiously apply a solution of ammonia and cold water, quickly rinsing to avoid discoloration. If the area is discolored, try 3 percent hydrogen peroxide.
Candle wax or chewing gum	Use ice cubes to make the material brittle. Then use a plastic spatula to carefully scrape the wax or gum from the floor.
Cigarette burn	Rub with a cloth dampened with a solution of lemon juice and water. For heavy stains, try scouring powder and a piece of fine steel wool or a plastic scouring pad dipped in water.
Coffee or fruit juice	Rub gently with scouring powder and a cloth dampened in hot water. If that doesn't work, try 3 percent hydrogen peroxide.
Dyes	After testing on an inconspicuous spot, rub with a damp cloth dampened with 3 percent hydrogen peroxide. If that doesn't work, try a solution of one part chlorine bleach and two parts water, and then scouring powder and a cloth dampened with hot water
Grease and oil	Remove as much as possible with newspaper, paper towels, or a plastic spatula. Or rub with a cloth dampened with liquid detergent and warm water or an all-purpose cleaner.
Ink	Try a commercial ink remover, carefully following instructions, or use rubbing alcohol.

paper in three grit levels, from coarse to fine; a sharp scraper for getting into corners; goggles; a dust mask; painters' gloves; and mineral spirits for solvent-based cleanup (use plain water for water-based varnish). Also count on renting a drum sander, an edge sander, a wet/dry vac, and a buffer.

Laminated floors. These floors are often referred to by brand names such as Pergo and Wilsonart. A top, or wear, layer protects against spills and stains and covers the pattern layer. A

Stain	Removal Method
Lipstick	First try taking the lipstick up with a paper towel. If that doesn't work, try fine steel wool wetted with all-purpose detergent and water. If the floor has a no-wax finish or is an embossed vinyl composition, use a plastic scouring pad instead of steel wool.
Mustard	Cover the stain with a cloth soaked in 3 percent hydrogen peroxide. Leave in place until the stain has faded, sponge with water, and wipe dry. Open your curtains for one to two days. The sunlight may fade residual mustard stains
Paint or varnish	Scrub with a concentrated solution of powdered detergent and water, or apply undiluted liquid laundry detergent.
Rust	Use a commercial rust remover intended for your type of floor. Be sure to follow precautions given on the label.
Shoe polish or nail polish	Try a concentrated detergent solution. If that doesn't work, try scouring powder or steel wool. Don't use nail polish remover.
Tar	Use ice cubes to chill the tar to brittleness, then scrape it carefully with a plastic spatula. To remove a tar stain, test kerosene, turpentine, or WD-40 in an inconspicuous area, then apply.
Urine	After testing on an inconspicuous spot, rub with a hot, damp cloth and scouring powder. Or try a commercial enzyme-based product (such as those found in pet supply stores).

fiberboard core supports the top layers. Plastic-laminate planks are interlocked with or without glue and held in place by their own weight in what is called a floating floor.

The wear layer can withstand a good deal of wear. Even so, surfaces are prone to scratches and water damage, so take the same precautions you would with a wood floor: Use glides under furniture legs, don't let copious amounts of water stand on the surface and joints, and never use abrasive cleaners. Vacuum regularly, using the bare-floor attachment rather than one that might scratch the surface. Damp-mop as needed, first with a solution of mild detergent and warm water, then with clear warm water, and buff with a dry cloth. You'll probably be able to remove most stains with a dry cloth to which you've applied a mild detergent. For stubborn stains, you can safely use a small amount of nail-polish remover on a soft cotton rag.

Once the wear layer becomes worn or damaged, it can't be sanded and refinished, as can a wood floor. You may be able to do minor touch-ups with kits sold by flooring manufacturers.

Linoleum floors. Never get linoleum really wet. Use a mop dampened in a weak solution of all-purpose cleaner. When you're finished mopping, rinse away all soap residue and wipe dry. Then apply a liquid, water-based emulsion polish (which will not water-mark) on kitchen and bathroom floors, and a wax polish on the floors of other rooms. Do not use ammonia or other alkalis; they will break down the linoleum and possibly cause it to crack. You can remove shoe scuff marks with paint thinner or a citrus-based cleaner. If wax builds up and starts to look dirty, first strip it off with a commercial stripping product, and then rewax.

Vinyl floors. Sweep a vinyl floor regularly to cut down on the need for washing, and occasionally use a mop lightly dampened with water only. To remove visible grime, add some mild detergent to the water, then rinse with clear water. Use a water-based polish, if desired. If the floor yellows, strip the polish and reapply. Remove shoe scuffs with baking soda on a damp cloth or sponge. To take care of a new or fairly new no-wax floor, use a plain damp mop or a little detergent followed by a rinse. When the floor really needs a polish, choose a no-wax-floor cleaning product or a combination cleaning and polishing product recommended for no-wax floors. Be sure to rinse off combination cleaners after use.

Other man-made flooring materials that are popular today include linoleum and rubber tile (a sound-absorbent flooring material). Natural flooring materials include wood, cork, marble, terrazzo, ceramic tile, quarry tile, terra-cotta, and concrete.

Ceramic tile floors. Mop floors with a solution of mild detergent and water. Buffing with a chamois cloth will restore shine to the tiles. Use a commercial tile cleanser for heavy-duty cleaning, but make sure it's safe to use on ceramic surfaces. Be careful when walking on wet ceramic tiles.

Fire and flood damage

Professional help is usually needed to repair damage after a fire or flood. After catastrophe strikes, one of the first things you should do is take photos of the damage and call your insurer. Much of the repair and rebuilding work may be covered.

You can't anticipate disaster, but there is action you can take on an ongoing basis to minimize damage to your home. Before winter comes, check roofs, chimneys, and gutters; clear drain gratings; and repair any leaks in walls.

Fire

After a fire, air out your home (or use a smoke-odor absorber). Remove undamaged items so they will not be damaged further. Close windows or holes with boards. Restore heat so pipes don't freeze; if that is not possible, drain water-heating appliances, pipes, and toilets (tanks and bowls). Bring in an electrician to check equipment. The water used to douse fire can cause extensive damage. For tips on flooding cleanup, see **Flooding,** on the opposite page.

Soot is very difficult to remove. Most fire-insurance policies cover soot cleanup.

Frozen and burst pipes

Many people think that frozen pipes burst because of pressure from the ice forming inside of them. In fact, leaks and ruptures are a result of the tremendous pressure ice puts on water trapped in the pipe. Ironically, burst pipes are a real problem in the South; building practices there may not adequately protect pipes from occasional subfreezing temperatures, according to the Building Research Council. The threshold is 20° F or below.

There are a number of things you can do to prevent your pipes from freezing or bursting. One temporary solution is to

---

allow the faucet to drip slowly. This may not prevent an ice blockage, but it can prevent the pressure from building up and possibly bursting your pipes. If the faucet stops dripping, don't close it—the open faucet may still be necessary to release the pressure.

If water isn't flowing to a faucet or appliance, a pipe somewhere in the house is probably frozen. Poorly insulated pipes that snake through attics, crawl spaces, or exterior walls are most likely to freeze. Where you can, cover water pipes with insulation. If freezes are common where you live, consider warming the problem pipes with electric heat tape.

To keep outside spigots from freezing, turn off the water to these lines and drain them.

If a pipe has frozen, open the spigot or faucet. Thaw the pipe applying a hair dryer or a towel soaked in very hot water along the pipe's length from the spigot or faucet toward the valve. Call in a plumber if you're not successful.

If a pipe bursts, turn off the zone valve or main stop valve and all water-heating appliances. Then call a plumber.

Flooding

If you have any advance warning of flooding in your area, move as many of your possessions as you can out of the basement and off the ground floor as soon as possible. Put sandbags along the bottoms of doors and basement windows. Do not use electricity or gas or draw off any tap water until the authorities say it is safe to do so.

If your home is flooded, have your insurance company assess the damage. Then remove any water from floors so they won't warp. Rent or buy equipment, such as a carpet deep-cleaner, a pump, or a wet/dry vac. Hang your rugs to dry, and wash walls and floors with a disinfectant to prevent mold and mildew. Leave your doors, windows, and built-in cupboards open. Remember that drying out can take months, so do not redecorate immediately. To avoid dry rot, allow at least six months to pass before relaying floor coverings.

Use a dehumidifier wherever carpets or furnishings have absorbed water. Since drying doesn't remove dead mold spores, carpeting is problematic; if mold is very bad, you may have to throw out your carpeting.

Don gloves when you work and bag and discard anything that has moldy residue (rags, paper, leaves or debris, wallboard, ceiling tiles, wood products). Also remove and discard all drywall up to at least two feet above the high water mark. Less porous materials, such as glass, plastic, or metal, can be retained, but they must be cleaned and disinfected.

To clean the contaminated areas, put on gloves, remove any food or mold, and use a non-ammonia soap, detergent, or commercial cleaner in hot water. Use a stiff brush to scrub the entire area, and rinse it clean. Then disinfect the area with a solution of one part household bleach and nine parts water. Apply it liberally with a sprayer or sponge, but not so much that you have runoff. Let the area dry overnight.

When handling or cleaning moldy materials, consider using a mask or respirator as protection from airborne spores, and wear clothing that covers you thoroughly and can be cleaned easily—or discarded. Do not allow anyone into an area while you are cleaning. Take frequent breaks in fresh air. Ventilate your house well during and after the work.

Follow-up cleanings may be necessary, particularly if mold persists. Keep drying and ventilating the area, and don't replace flooring or rebuild it until it is thoroughly dry.

Roof damage

If a storm or heavy snowfall damages your roof, use sheets of hardboard or plastic to keep out rain and snow. Shovel any snow off the roof, and remove any snow that may have fallen through a hole before it melts and drips through the ceilings below. Check gutters for blockages.

Homemade cleaning products

Most of these home remedies underperformed the best commercial products in CONSUMER REPORTS tests. An exception is the glass and window cleaner, which did as well as any commercial product. The other home remedies listed here, though, are often effective enough. All of the ingredients are available from supermarkets, hardware stores, pharmacies, or health-food or art-supply stores.

All-purpose cleaner

Soapy ammonia is a versatile cleaning agent. It can be used in place of a commercial all-purpose cleaner for everyday kitchen and bathroom cleaning. Dilute according to the instructions on the container.

Floor-wax stripper

½ cup of powdered floor cleaner
2 cups of ammonia
1 gallon of cold water
Apply this typical recipe for removing old floor wax with fine steel wool and a lot of elbow grease. Boost the formula with a little rubbing alcohol.

Furniture cleaner

Plain water and a little mild liquid detergent protect sealed wood furniture from common stains. Mix well and store in a water spray bottle. Spray onto furniture, then wipe over with a damp cloth and finish drying with a clean, lint-free cloth.

Glass and window cleaner

½ cup of soapy ammonia
1 pint of rubbing alcohol
Add enough water to the soapy ammonia and rubbing alcohol to make a gallon. Pour into spray bottles. This mixture should clean glass well and leave few or no streaks.

Silver cutlery cleaner

1 piece of aluminum foil
1–2 tablespoons of baking soda
2 quarts of very hot water
This technique removes the tarnish uniformly, so don't use it with antique or intricately patterned silver. Put a piece of aluminum foil into a plastic or glass container, lay the tarnished piece of silver on top, sprinkle it with baking soda, and cover with boiling water. Soak until bubbles stop, then rinse and polish with a soft cloth. What happens is that the silver sulfide (tarnish) breaks down and transfers to the aluminum foil, which you can throw out. The result: shiny silver. You can treat larger pieces in the sink this way.

Wall cleaner

1 part chlorine bleach
3 parts water
2 teaspoons of TSP (trisodium phosphate)
Make sure paint or wallpaper can be safely washed before attempting to clean it with this or any other liquid; do a test on an inconspicuous spot if you're unsure. Apply the cleaner with a sponge or soft brush, working from the bottom up—it's easier to clean streaks off of a clean surface. Rinse with a cloth dampened with clean, warm water.

Cleaning Caveat

Do not mix chlorine bleach with vinegar, toilet bowl cleaner, or ammonia. Handle these ingredients with care and store them safely.

Index

Modacrylic, 28, 100, 224
Mohair, 150, 230
Mold
on decks, 62
humidifier, 87
vaporizer, 87
Mops, 11, 208
dust, 203–204
Mother of pearl, 100
Mouse (computer), 100
Mustard, 254, 265

N

Nail polish, 254
Napkins, 95
Naugahyde, 101
Navajo rugs, 117
Neat's-foot oil, 179
Needlework, 101
Newsprint, 254
Nickel, 101
Nylon, 102, 227
upholstery, 138

O

Odors
cutting board, 51
futon, 82
garbage disposal, 83
mattresses, 99
oven, 99
skunk, 126
Oil
lamps, 103
paintings, 103
Olefin, 111, 225, 228
upholstery, 138
Onyx, 103
Opals, 89, 103
Oriental rugs, 103–104
Ormolu, 104
Ovens
cleaners, 180–181
continuous-cleaning, 105
microwave, 99
self-cleaning, 105, 180
shelves, 105
Oxalic acid, 62

P

Paint, 106, 265
Paintings
acrylic, 28

oil, 103
watercolor, 146
Paneling, wood, 148–149
Paper
acid-free, 108
contact, 45
towels, 209–210
wall covering, 143
Papier-mâché, 107
Pashmina, 150, 230
Pearls, 89, 90, 107
Percale, 57
Petroleum jelly, 182, 245
Pets
food bowls, 107
litter boxes, 96
stains, 247
Pewter, 107
tarnish, 107
Photocopiers, 107
Photographs, 108
Pianos, 108–109
Picture frames, 109
Pillows, 110. *See also Cushions*
Plastic
automobile, 34
curtain rods, 61
cutting boards, 51
furniture, 78, 110
laminated, 45
toys, 134
Platinum, 110–111
hardness, 89
Plungers, 68
Polyester, 111, 227–228
upholstery, 138
Polyolefin, 111, 228
Porcelain, 50
dolls, 67
Potassium bitartrate, 164
Pots
cooking, 101–102
earthenware, 72
nonstick, 101–102
terra-cotta, 132
Pressure washers, 210–211
Printers
inkjet, 88
laser, 93
printheads, 88
Prints, 111
Products and tools
all-purpose, 154–157
antibacterial, 51, 165–166, 174
automobile, 157–159
bathroom cleaners, 160–161
brass cleaners, 162–163
carpet cleaning, 164,197–198

copper cleaners, 162–163
daily shower cleaners, 161
deck-treatment, 62, 63
descaling cleaners, 165
dishwasher detergents, 166–167
dishwashing liquids, 167–168
disinfectants, 165–166
disposal, 24–25
drain cleaners, 69, 168–169
fabric softeners, 170
floor care, 170–172, 205, 208
furniture polishes, 78, 172–173
"green," 21
hand soap, 174
homemade, 271–272
ironing, 206–207
jewelry-cleaner, 90
laundry, 176–178, 182, 216–217
leather care, 77, 179, 184
metal cleaners, 179
mildew removers, 179
oven cleaners, 105, 180–181
painting cleaners, 103
scouring cleansers, 184–185
silver cleaners, 185–186
spot-removal, 86, 96
stone-cleaning, 132
stone sealer, 98
storage, 16, 21, 24
toilet cleaners, 187–188
upholstery cleaners, 137–140
vacuuming, 213–215, 219–221
water-repelling, 120
window cleaners, 189
wood sealing, 78
wood treatment, 79
Professional cleaning
carpet, 104, 241
pianos, 108–109
prints and drawings, 111
quilts, 112
slipcovers, 127
upholstery, 139
watercolor paintings, 146
PVC blinds, 40, 41

Q

Quarry tile floors, 112
Quilts, 112

278   **HOW TO CLEAN (AND CARE FOR) PRACTICALLY ANYTHING**

R

Radiators, 113
Rag rugs, 117
Ranges, 113–114
Rattan, 114–115
Rayon, 115, 138, 228–229
  Tencel, 97
  upholstery, 138
Redwood
  decks, 62
  furniture, 78
Refrigerators, 115–116
Reptile skin, 96
Rings
  on alabaster, 30
  on wood, 80
Rubies, 89, 117
Rugs, 117
  See also Carpet,
  Oriental rugs
Rush rugs, 125
Rust, 256
  automobile, 32, 34
  bakeware, 133
  chrome, 52
  on cookware, 55
  inhibitors, 183
  iron-frame beds, 39
  outdoor furniture, 151, 48
  removers, 183
  stains, 54, 77, 256, 265
  tin, 133
  toilet, 133–134

S

Saddle soap, 184
Salad bowls, wood, 149
Sapphires, 89, 118
Satin, 118, 124
Scanners, 118
Scotchgard, 139–140
Scouring cleansers, 184–185
Scratches, 80
Scrubbers, 212
Seashells, 118
Seersucker, 57, 118
Sewing machines, 119
Shag rugs, 119
Sheepskin, 119–120
Sheets, 120
Shelves
  book, 42
  lining, 45
  refrigerator, 115
Shoes, 120–121

Showers, 121–122
Shutters, 122
Siding, 122–123
Sieves, 123
Silk, 123–124, 225, 229
  curtains, 59
  raw, 124
  shantung, 124, 229
  upholstery, 138
Silver, 124–125
  cleaners, 185–186
  finishes, 84–85
  flatware, 66, 75
  hardness, 89
  jewelry, 125
  replating, 124
  tarnish, 76, 124–125, 175
Sinks
  bathroom, 37–38
  reglazing, 38
  stainless steel, 38
Sisal rugs, 125
Sizing, 186
Skunk odor, 126
Skylights, 126
Slate, 126–127
Slipcovers, 127–128
Smoke alarms, 128
Sneakers, 121
Soak and spin method, 112, 150
Soot, 50, 103, 257
  fireplace, 74
Spandex, 129, 225, 229
Split-cane rugs, 125
Sponges, 212
Stainless steel
  cookware, 55–56
  countertops, 129
  flatware, 66, 75
  refrigerators, 116
  sinks, 38
  tubs, 37
Stains
  acids, 246
  acne medication, 246
  adhesive, 80, 246
  advice on, 242–259
  alcohol, 80, 246, 264
  auto upholstery, 34
  bathroom, 38
  blood, 247, 264
  blue-green, 38
  carpet, 104
  caulk, 248
  on ceramic tile, 49
  chocolate, 248
  coffee, 248–249
  cookware, 101–102

  correction fluid, 57, 249
  countertop, 92
  crayon, 249
  deck, 62
  enamel, 72
  gasoline, 251
  glassware, 84
  glue, 251
  on granite, 85
  grass, 251, 264
  grease, 79, 104, 143, 247, 251, 257, 263
  gum, 251
  handbag, 86
  ink, 247, 252, 265
  iodine, 252
  jute, 90
  leather, 77
  lipstick, 253, 265
  makeup, 253
  marble, 98
  mattresses, 99
  milk products, 254
  nail polish, 254
  naugahyde, 101
  newsprint, 254
  oil-based, 77
  paint, 255, 265
  pet, 247
  removal, 242–259
  rust, 54, 77, 256, 265
  stainless steel, 55
  suede, 79
  tar, 258, 265
  on toys, 134
  urine, 99, 258, 265
  wallpaper, 143
  water, 48, 259
  wax, 248, 264
  wine, 259
  wood, 44, 80, 261
Starches, 186
Steel wool, 212
Stockings
  nylon, 102
  pantyhose, 231–232
  polyolefin, 111
Stone
  fireplaces, 75
  powdered, 75

Storage
  blankets, 40
  cleaning products, 16
  embroidered items, 101
  fur, 81
  lace, 92
  needlework, 101
  photographs, 108